Essential Computing Skills

Second Edition

Russel Stolins
Institute of American Indian Arts

LABYRINTH
LEARNING™

Berkeley, CA

Essential Computing Skills, Second Edition

Copyright © 2014 by Labyrinth Learning

Labyrinth Learning
2560 9th Street, Suite 320
Berkeley, California 94710
800.522.9746
On the web at lablearning.com

Product Manager:
Brian Favro

Development Manager:
Laura Popelka

Senior Editor:
Susan Scharf

Production Manager:
Rad Proctor

Senior Instructional Designer:
Arl S. Nadel

Editorial Assistant:
Alexandria Henderson

Production Assistant:
Andrew Kenower

Indexing:
Joanne Sprott

Cover Design:
Mick Koller, SuperLab Design

Interior Design:
Mark Ong, Side-by-Side Studio

ITEM: 1-59136-700-X
ISBN-13:   978-1-59136-700-0

Manufactured in the United States of America.

10 9 8 7 6 5 4 3 2

Table of Contents

Preface

In today's digital world, knowing how to use computers effectively is critical. Our goal is to teach new users how to take advantage of computer technology and use it to be successful in school and at work. We begin with brief concept discussions and quickly move to hands-on activities focused on skills development. Learners are led through exercises using visually appealing, interactive tools and then they are challenged to complete exercises on their own.

An online Student Resource Center accompanies this book. It contains Concepts Review quizzes, student exercise files, and other learning tools. The URL for the Student Resource Center is printed on the inside front cover of this textbook.

Supplemental Options

Video Tutorials: Many topics in this book are associated with a free, supplemental video tutorial that reinforces the concepts covered in this textbook. The videos are accessed on the Student Resource Center. Topics are clearly marked with a unique video number, which will help you locate the correct video online.

Guide Me Tutorials: All Develop Your Skills exercises in this textbook (and some other exercises) feature a free, interactive Guide Me tutorial to reinforce learning. Exercises are clearly identified, which will help you locate the correct tutorial on the Student Resource Center. You may be directed to complete certain exercises from within the Guide Me only.

eLab Course Management System: eLab is a web-based learning system that integrates seamlessly with this textbook. eLab is an option for students enrolled in instructor-led courses that have adopted eLab as part of their course curriculum.

Visual Conventions

This book uses visual and typographic cues to guide students through the lessons. Some of these cues are described below.

`Type this`	Text you type at the keyboard is printed in this typeface.
Action words	The important action words in exercise steps are presented in boldface.
Ribbon	Terms defined in the glossary at the back of the book are presented in a special typeface.
	Tips, notes, and warnings are called out with special icons.
Command→ Command→ Command→ Command	Commands to execute from the Ribbon are presented like this: Ribbon Tab→Command Group→Command→Subcommand.
Guide Me	Exercises featuring a Guide Me tutorial are marked with this icon.
Video	Topics featuring a supplemental video tutorial are marked with this icon.

Acknowledgements

This textbook has benefited greatly from the reviews and suggestions of the following instructors.

Anthony Adams, Savannah Technical College

Lori Allemand, Pearl River Community College

Richard Baugh Jr., Jefferson Adult School

Illaina Baylor-Johnson, College of Lake County

Marcia Bercot, SkillSource

Kim Bolden, EHOVE Career Center

Lawrence Bosek, Macomb Community College

Eric Bothur, Midlands Technical College

Odette Bradshaw-Sheeley, Mid-Del Technology

David Briggs, Upper Valley Career Center

Charlene Brooks, PGCC

Dawn Brown, Habersham Central High School

Marcus Brown, EnVision Communication Concepts

Pam Brunclik, Osceola High School

Melisa Bryant, Forsyth Technical Community College

Joy Bukowy, Robeson Community College

Dr. Pauline Camara, Bristol Community College

Ilda Casanova, Alamo College and Palo Alto College

Isabel Chan, Langara College

Laura Cinquini, Napa Valley Adult Education

Susan Clancy-Kelly, College of Lake County

Hyekyung Clark, Central New Mexico Community College

Dr. Frank T. Clements, Jr., State College of Florida

Stephanie Clymens, Crook County Open Campus

Lisa Cogley, Rhodes State College

Catherine Combs, Tennessee Technology Center at Morristown

Ioana Constantin, Globe Education Network

Rushia Cooper, Lanier Technical College

Lorie Costello, Saint Paul College

Becky Curtin, William Rainey Harper College

Roberta Czaplewski, Riverland Community College

Elaine Davis, Carroll Community College

Rhonda Davis, Isothermal Community College

Mike Deese, University of New Mexico

Candace Dejmal, Decatur Community Jr./Sr. High School

Anthony Dillon, SC Department of Education

Robert Doyle, Doña Ana Community College

Debbie Drake, Southwest Applied Technology College

Cindy Durkee, Wahconah Regional High School

Susan Fell-Johnson, Alexandria Technical and Community College

Jean Finley, ABTCC

Joseph Fischer, JTF Training

Suzette Fletcher, Billings Adult Education

Miriam Foronda, University of New Mexico-Taos

Brian Fox, Santa Fe College

Roger Fulk, Wright State University – Lake Campus

Marie Gabbard, Volunteer State Community College and Nashville State Community College

Alan Gandy, Lone Star College, University Park

Kay Gerken, College of DuPage

Debby Godwin, Lake Sumter Community College

Bryna Gonzalez, Norwalk Adult School

Elizabeth Gonzales-Hughes, Central New Mexico Community College

Stephanie Gordon, Washtenaw Community College

Barbara Grane, Orange Coast College

Ara Greeny, Visalia Adult School

Betty Haar, Kirkwood Community College

Norma Hall, Manor College

Robyn Hart, Fresno City College

Amanda Hayman, TCL

Mary Jo Heiberger, Visitation Catholic School

Michael Held, Portage Lakes Career Center

Donna Hendricks, South Arkansas Community College

Laura Henige, Macomb Community College

Anita Herndon, Tarrant County College

Sandi Highfill, High Plains Technology Center

Taheshia Hobbs, James Sprunt Community College

Ira Hogan, Ivy Tech Community College – Indianapolis

Ron Houle, Central Lakes College

Lisa Hubbard, Anoka Technical College

Lisa Hunke, Northeast Community College

Laura Hunt, Tulsa Community College

Stephen Hustedde, South Mountain Community College

John Hutson, Aims Community College

Dale Jaedike, Madison Area Technical College

Christie Jahn Hovey, Lincoln Land Community College

Loretta Jarrell, CATC Baton Rouge

Ylming Ji, University of South Caroline Beaufort

Guadalupe Jimenez, Coachella Valley Adult School

Kathy Johnson, Glenn Hills High School

Kerrie Johnson, McHenry County Shah Center

Marisa Johnson, NCKTC

Wendy Kauffman, Sandhills Community College

Vardeep Kaur, Calmat

Vickie Keitz, Grayson College

Donna Kilburn, Tennessee Technology Center at Ripley – Bells Campus

Jill Knight, Plemons-Stinnett-Phillips CISD

Ruby Kowaney, West Los Angeles College

Karon Kraft, Moraine Park Technical College

Cheryl Krider, Wattsburg Area School District – Seneca High School

Lisa Kropp, Miami Dade College

Ida Lambert, North Tech High School

Katharine Langille, Red River College

Gayle Larson, Highline Community College and Green River Community College

Sherry Lockman, Kilgore High School, Kilgore Independent School District

Teresa Loftis, San Bernardino Adult School

Sandi Lyman, Rocky Mountain Business Academy

Eileen Malin, Nassau Boces

Leslie Martin, Gaston College

John Martinez, Clovis Adult Education

Cheryl Martucci, Diablo Valley College

Alex Matthews, Austin Community College

Cindie Mayfield, Ozarks Technical Community College

Joe McCreery, Elizabethtown Community and Technical College

Donna McGill-Cameron, Woodland Community College

Joshua McMillan, Muskogee High School

Pam Meeks, Northeast MS Community College

Blanca Michaels, Career College Consultants, Inc.

Corena Miller, Computer Services Plus Online

Mary Miranda, Clovis Adult Education

Louis Mitchell, Edgecombe Community College

Susan Morrow, AIB College of Business

Janet Moulton, Nova Scotia Community College

Sheila Mullaney, Lincoln Technical Institute

Stephen Munsinger, Wyoming State Penitentiary

Michael Murphy, Meriden Adult Education

Diane Murray, Highlands College of Montana Tech

Christine Naylor, Kent State University – Ashtabula

Kay Nelson, The Lifelong Learning Center

Linda Nestor, Carroll Community College

Cora Newcomb, Technical College of the Lowcountry

Jean Newman, Charles A. Jones Career and Education Center

Tami Norris, Northwest State Community College

Stephanie Novak, Wisconsin Indianhead Technical College

Sandy O'Neil, Chase County Schools

Monika Olsen, Acalanes Adult Education

Arleen Orland, Santa Clarita Technology & Career Dev. Center

Guillermo Ortiz-Caceres, Bossier Parish Community College

Larry Overstreet, College Of DuPage

Morena Pacheco, Riverside Adult School

Christine Parrish, Southwest Georgia Technical College

Rex Parr, Aims Community College

Deloris Patterson, Chattahoochee Technical College

Betty Pearman, Los Medanos College

Rebecca Pein, Western Technical College

Mary Ester Perez, Palo Alto College

Joseph Perret, LA Pierce College

Felicia Peters, Delta College

Jason Peterson, College of Redwoods

Nancy Peterson, Central Catholic High School

Kari Phillips, Davis Applied Technology College

Gildga Pollard, LAUSD-Harbor Occupational Center

Jack Porter, El Centro College

Edna Prigmore, Palomar College

Marsha Ragen, Southwestern Illinois College

Tommie Redwine, Clatsop Community College

Brenda Rhodes-Martinez, Northeastern Jr. College

Sarah Rhoton, Savannah Early College High School/Savannah Technical College

Melinda Ricci, Sandusky Career Center

Patricia Richey, Jacksonville College

Carol Ricke, Pratt Community College

Sandra Roberts, Snead State Community College

Marsha Robison, Simi Valley Adult School

Valerie Romanczyk, Macomb Community College

Stephen Ross, Mississippi Delta Community College

David Rudnick, Lane Community College

Sonya Sample, Greenville Technical College

Joann Santillo, Mahoning County Career and Technical Center

Kellie Sartor, Lee College

Anita M. Schaffer, Tacoma Community College

Tina Schank, EHOVE Career Center

Don Schoesler, North Idaho College

Julie Sharrow, Kent State University at Trumbull

Susanne Silk, Western Technology Center

Sherri Silvian, Macomb Community College

Mary Sina, Fox Valley Technical College

Amy Sirott, Pierce College

Kathy Smith, Kaskaskia College

LaToya Smith, Piedmont Community College

Monica Smith, Irwin County High School

Randy Smith, Monterey Peninsula College

Sabrina Snider, Forsyth Technical Community College

Sheila Sokolinsky, Isaac Bear Early College

Debra Stafford-Gray, Kansas City Kansas Community College, University of Phoenix, and Colorado Technical University

Diane Stark, Phoenix College

Raymond Steinbart, Maranatha Baptist Bible College

Sheryl Stroud-Jones, Savannah Technical College

Cathy Struntz, ATN

Gary Sullivan, Weatherford College

Cynthia Sweeney, J. M. Alexander Middle School

Barbara Tietsort, University of Cincinnati Blue Ash College

Catherine Thomas, J. Sargeant Reynolds Community College

Pamela Toliver, Soft-Spec

Diana Tourney, Delta-Montrose Tech College

Tricia Troyer, Waubonsee Community College

Karen Ann Tuecke, Tuecke Consulting

Mona Valore, Kingsborough Community College

Garrett Wadkins, Duval County Schools

Jacqueline Wall, Chaffey College

Craig Watson, Bristol Community College

Miranda Watson, Colorado Mountain College

Laura Way, Fortis College – Ravenna

Sandra Webb, Central Louisiana Technical Community College – Alexandria Campus

Melinda White, Seminole State College

Amy Williams, Abraham Baldwin Agricultural College

Deborah Willwerth, Crittenton Women's Union

MaryLou Wilson, Piedmont Technical College

Leza Wood, SUNY Adirondack

Wanda Woods, Jireh Mobile Computer Training

Toni Wright, OUSD

Kevin Wyzkiewicz, Delta College

Peter Young, San Jose State University

Matt Zdybel, Macomb County College

Violet Zhang, George Brown College

Windows

1 Computer Concepts

in this lesson

A personal computer is a complex machine with millions of circuits and lines of software code working in perfect harmony. Fortunately, we don't have to understand these components to use or buy a computer or tablet. But by knowing some basic facts, you'll make better purchase decisions. In this lesson, you will learn what you need to know to compare computer models, interpret ads, and understand what different computer performance features mean.

Comparing Computers

Your notebook computer is four years old, which is about twenty-eight dog years (a good way to measure the "true" age of a computer). It's running your favorite programs more slowly now, which is frustrating. You tire of waiting even a few seconds. When you bought it, the computer was a bargain-priced model from a discount store. It was your first computer, and you were thrilled to have it, but it no longer meets your needs.

Looking online, you find all sorts of ads for new computers. They describe things like a processor, RAM, and screen size. But is a bigger number always better or important? There's definitely a price difference for some features. You want a computer that will meet your needs for the next few years, but you don't want to buy more computer than you need.

Lenovo Thinkpad Twist 12.5" Touch Screen Laptop

Item: 985048   Model: 33474HU

 Read 27 Reviews

- 3rd Gen Intel® Core™ i5 - 3317U 1.7 GHz 3MB L3 Cache Processor; Enjoy an automatic burst of speed when...

- 4GB 1333Mhz DDR3

- 500GB 7200RPM SATA Hard Drive plus 24GB SSD Cache

See more details

A web page gives basic details about a new laptop computer.

Categorizing Computer Systems

A computer system is a tightly integrated set of hardware and software. While they come in all shapes and sizes, two basic components are common to all computer systems.

- *Hardware*: The physical component. If you can pick it up and hold it, it's hardware. This includes storage devices, such as *USB (Universal Serial Bus) flash drive*s.
- *Software*: The logical component. You can't see software, but you can see its workings on the screen.

Computer systems come in several basic categories. Each is optimized for particular types of activities and levels of mobility.

Computer System Categories		
Category	**Description**	**Optimized For**
Laptop	A highly portable computer with a built-in monitor, keyboard, and touchpad; range from basic performance to the power of a desktop computer; smaller, less powerful laptops are called *netbooks*.	Mobile computing with the same programs run on desktop computers.
Smartphone	A mobile phone that can run custom apps	Mobile computing with specialized apps.
Tablet	A slim touchscreen computer that may also have cellular Internet access built in.	Mobile computing with specialized apps.
All-in-One	A variation of the desktop computer; all components, including the screen, come in a single package.	General computing in a compact space.
Desktop	The traditional computer used in office and academic settings; most can be customized with additional hardware.	General and professional computing, running sophisticated programs on one or more large screens.

Units of Measure

Units of measure indicate the performance and capacity of a computer system. When you shop for a computer, you'll see certain terms in advertisements. These terms break down into three categories:

- Volume/Capacity
- Resolution/Sharpness
- Speed

Measures of Volume/Capacity

These terms help you determine the size of a file and the capacity of a disk drive or flash drive to hold those files.

Term	Meaning	Examples
Bit	A single on-off switch (transistor) in a byte	0, 1
Byte	Eight bits strung together in a specific order to represent a single character of data	A, B, C, &, @
Kilobyte (KB)	One thousand bytes (characters) of data	Approximately two paragraphs of single-spaced text
Megabyte (MB)	One million bytes of data	About 900 pages of single-spaced text or three medium-length novels
Gigabyte (GB)	One billion bytes of data	Approximately 200 typical 5 MB digital photos or 250 four-minute songs in high-quality MP3 format
Terabyte (TB)	One trillion bytes of data	About 250,000 four-minute songs in MP3 format, 380 hours of DVD-quality video, or about 120 hours of HD-quality video

Measures of Resolution/Sharpness

These terms indicate the size and sharpness of the computer screen.

Term	Meaning	Examples
Resolution	The number of pixels (dots of light) arrayed horizontally and vertically on the screen	1366 x 768 (14" laptop screen) 1920 x 1200 (24" monitor) 1920 x 1080 (HDTV monitor)
Screen Size	A diagonal measurement of the screen's physical dimensions	24" monitor 15" screen (laptop)

Measures of Speed

These terms indicate the speed of a computer's processor or of an Internet connection.

Term	Meaning	Examples
GHz (gigahertz)	One billion cycles per second	1.8 GHz 3.2 GHz
Mbps (millions of bits per second)	The number of bits (not bytes) that a network connection can transmit or receive	3 Mbps (DSL service) 12 Mbps (cable modem)

Computer Hardware Categories

Computer hardware comprises the physical components of the computer system. Regardless of the basic type of computer you are using, all computers have common hardware components.

Hardware Components		
Hardware Category	Role	Examples
Processing	Processes data and interprets your commands	Processor, random access memory (RAM)
Storage	Stores programs you run and your own user data files	Solid state drive (SSD), hard drive, USB flash drive, cloud drive
Output	Displays and prints your work	Monitor, printer, video adapter
Networking	Connects you to the Internet and to other computers	Modem, router, wireless connection, hub, switch
Input	Used to issue commands, type, and interact with the computer system	Mouse, touchpad, keyboard, touchscreen, pen tablet

Processing Hardware

The logical hardware of the computer contains its processing capabilities. This hardware receives and interprets commands, runs software, and supports the most basic controls over other system hardware. The processing hardware components most critical to computer performance are:

- *Processor*: The "brain" of the computer
- *RAM (Random Access Memory)*: The "workbench" that passes code back and forth with the processor

Processor

This is the most important single component of a computer system. It contains all the basic circuitry of a computer with millions of transistors etched onto chips of silicon via incredibly precise microscopic techniques. Better processors are introduced every few months.

The processor's thin wafer of silicon sits on its mount, with a heat-spreading plate on top.

Multicore Processors

Most new processors contain the circuitry for two to six computers inside a single chip. These are called multicore processors, and their advantage is that different processors can simultaneously control or process different programs and hardware. For example, one processor might control storing *files* on the hard drive while another sends a print request to a printer. Since different processor cores can focus on each task, processing is faster and more efficient.

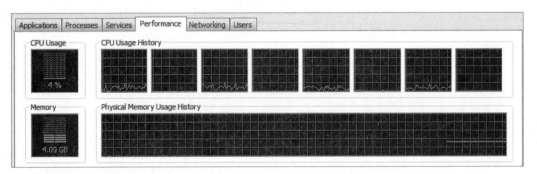

An Intel Core i7 processor appears to Windows as if it were eight individual processors, although they all reside in the single multicore chip.

Processor Performance

Features other than the number of cores have an impact on processor performance. For example, processors are designed to run at specific speeds measured in *gigahertz (GHz)*. Higher-speed processors can often perform tasks more rapidly than slower processors, though this is not a strict rule. Many details of the computer system as a whole bear on its performance.

Random Access Memory (RAM)

Random access memory (RAM) is best thought of as the computer's "workbench." RAM is installed on the computer's motherboard in the form of slim modules. It is temporary storage because it holds software code and user files temporarily while the processor is working with them. Everything you see on the computer screen happens in RAM.

Photo courtesy of Micron Technology, Inc.

RAM comes in snap-in modules of varying capacities.

One of the best ways to improve the performance of an older computer is to install more RAM. Another way is to install a solid-state drive (SSD).

RAM as a Workbench

RAM is where the work you see on the screen actually resides. The work isn't on any storage drive until you save it. RAM allows the processor to work as quickly as possible; it shuttles data back and forth for processing much faster than any storage drive.

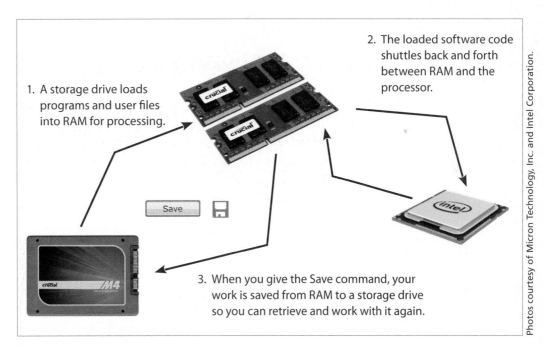

1. A storage drive loads programs and user files into RAM for processing.

2. The loaded software code shuttles back and forth between RAM and the processor.

Save

3. When you give the Save command, your work is saved from RAM to a storage drive so you can retrieve and work with it again.

Photos courtesy of Micron Technology, Inc. and Intel Corporation.

Don't confuse RAM with the storage memory provided by disk drives. While both are often called memory, their functions are quite different.

RAM and Performance

The RAM available to the computer makes a significant difference in its performance. Most computers allow you to add more RAM. In particular, having plenty of RAM helps a computer run more efficiently in two situations:

- **Running sophisticated programs:** A very powerful program, such as one used to edit photographs or produce video, requires plenty of RAM to hold all of its software components.

- **Running more than one program (multitasking):** Every program you run requires some space in RAM. When you run more programs than your available RAM can handle, the whole computer system slows down.

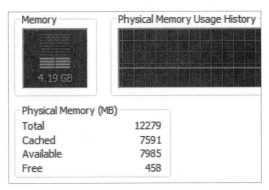

Windows displays current RAM usage.

Surge Protection

All of the delicate circuitry of the processor and other computer hardware require protection from electrical power surges. Always power the computer and other components via a good surge protector. Even the cable wiring for a cable or DSL modem should have surge protection.

Storage Hardware

Computer systems always have at least one permanent storage drive. The capacity of these drives is usually measured in terabytes (TB) of data. Increasingly, computers also make use of cloud-based storage, which can be virtually unlimited.

Permanent Storage Drives

Permanent storage devices are typically referred to as just storage devices (the "permanent" is implied). There are several primary types of storage drives that you should know about.

Storage Drive Types		
Drive Type	**Relative Speed**	**Relative Cost**
Solid-State Drive (SSD)	Very fast	Very expensive
Mechanical Hard Drive	Fast	Inexpensive
Fusion Drive	Very fast	Expensive
Cloud Drive	Slow	Expensive
USB Flash Drive	Fast	Inexpensive
Optical Drive	Slow	Inexpensive

- **Solid-State Drive (SSD):** This storage drive uses the same technology as USB flash drives but with much greater capacities. SSDs have no moving parts and are very fast compared to mechanical hard drives. They also use less electricity, which extends battery life on laptop computers and tablets. SSDs cost far more for a given amount of storage capacity compared to mechanical hard drives. Their storage capacity is typically measured in *gigabytes*.

Photo courtesy of Micron Technology, Inc.

This solid-state drive (SSD) stores large amounts of data with no moving parts.

- **Mechanical Hard Drive:** This complex device stores software on rapidly spinning platters. Read/write heads sweep back and forth across the platters to store and read data. The speed at which the platters spin varies from 5,400 to 10,000 revolutions per minute (rpm). Their storage capacity is typically measured in *terabytes*.

- **Fusion Drive:** This new storage technology combines an SSD with a mechanical hard drive to get the best of both. The drive stores the files you use the most on the fast SSD component; files used less often reside on the slower mechanical hard drive. Fusion drives are fast and economical. Their storage capacity is typically measured in terabytes.

- **Cloud Drive:** This drive essentially stores your files somewhere on the Internet. The files are available whenever you have an *Internet* connection. The physical location of the files doesn't really matter. In reality, cloud drives exist in huge warehouse-sized facilities around the world. Examples of cloud drives include Dropbox, Google Drive, and Microsoft OneDrive. One benefit of a cloud drive is that you can access your files from any computer, not just your personal computer, notebook, smartphone, or tablet. Many cloud drive services synchronize your files among your various devices.

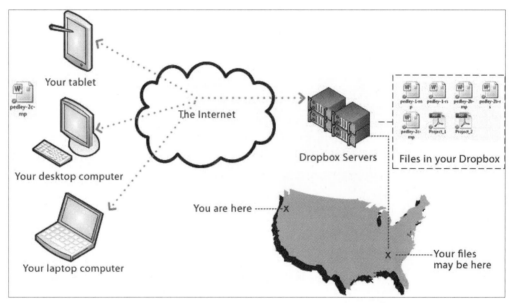

A cloud drive service such as Dropbox can offer access to your files on a variety of devices from any location with an Internet connection.

- **USB Flash Drive:** This small, solid-state storage device is often called a "thumb" or "pen" drive. It can store two or more gigabytes of data. You plug this drive into any USB *port* on the computer. Their storage capacity is typically measured in gigabytes.

Photo courtesy of SanDisk Corporation.

USB flash drives are a highly mobile storage device for everyday files.

- **Optical Disc Drive:** These drives read and write data to optical discs such as CDs, DVDs, and Blu-ray Discs. Few new computers have optical drives. Their storage capacity is typically measured in gigabytes.

External Drives

You can purchase and connect external drives to supplement any drives built into your computer. For example, you can connect and use an external hard drive to create backup copies of data on your internal hard disk drive. Or, use one for long-term storage of photos and videos. USB flash drives are another example of external (or "removable") storage hardware.

Card Readers

Many computers have a device called a card reader. You use a card reader to conveniently plug in storage cards used with smartphones and digital cameras.

Output Hardware

Output hardware allows users to receive processed information from a computer. Information can be made available visually on a computer screen, physically from a printer, or audibly through speakers.

Computer Screens

Computers come with a built-in screen or a separate display called a *monitor*. The screen's liquid crystal display (LCD) creates images out of small dots of light (*pixels*). A backlight displays pixel colors brightly. Screens differ in physical size (measured diagonally from corner to corner) and *resolution* (number of pixels in the display). The higher the resolution, the sharper the image. Most screens have a widescreen proportion (aspect ratio) of 16:9 or 16:10. This aspect ratio is the same used for high-definition televisions (HDTVs). (Previously, most computer screens used a 4:3 aspect ratio.)

Measuring Resolution
Screen resolution is expressed in the pixels it can display horizontally and vertically. For example, most 15" laptop screens have a native resolution of 1,600 pixels across by 900 pixels up and down, written 1600 x 900. A typical 13" notebook screen might have a resolution of 1360 x 768. Higher resolution screens display sharper images and text. For comparison, HDTV resolution is 1920 x 1080.

Photo courtesy of Lenovo.

This 14" laptop screen has a native resolution of 1600 x 900 pixels.

Native Resolution

All screens have a native resolution setting. This is the highest resolution the screen can display. You can reduce the resolution on most computers, but the resulting display is less sharp or the screen area used is reduced. Therefore, a screen's native resolution setting always provides the best results for viewing.

Printers

A printer is a common feature of most personal computer setups. In most office settings, one printer may serve several computers via a wired or wireless network.

There are two types of printers that are most popular today.

- **All-in-one:** These printers create images by spraying microscopic drops of ink on the page. They're affordable and can print beautiful color prints from digital photos. The printing cost per page can be high due to the cost of ink-jet cartridges. All-in-one printers have a built-in *scanner*, which allows you to use them as a copier and to create digital files from physical photos and pages.

- **Laser:** These printers are excellent for busy offices that need to print many pages rapidly. Color laser printers are available, but they generally cannot print colors as vividly as all-in-one printers. Laser printers generally have a lower printing cost per page compared to all-in-one ink-jet printers.

Input Hardware

Input devices help you control the computer or pass data to it: giving commands, starting programs, and typing text. There are a wide variety of input devices available. Most input (and many other) devices connect to the computer via a USB port.

Common Input Devices

Twenty-five years ago, personal computers primarily had just one input device available, the keyboard. Now a variety of specialized devices allow you to control the computer.

- **Mouse:** First invented in the late 1960s, the mouse got its name from the tail-like wire connecting it to the computer. An optical mouse uses a light or laser to track its movement across a flat surface. In addition to buttons, most mice now feature a scroll wheel. Wireless mice don't need a cord to connect them to the computer.
- **Touchpad:** This is the small pad at the base of the keyboard on notebook computers. Anything you can do with a mouse you can also do on a touchpad. Most touchpads let you tap the pad to click. You can also purchase touchpads for use with a desktop or all-in-one computer.
- **Keyboard:** Most keyboards have a conventional rectangular shape. Curved *ergonomics* keyboards allow typing with a more natural alignment of your forearms and hands. Like mice, many keyboards are available with a wireless connection to the computer, eliminating the clutter of cables.
- **Touchscreen:** Many new computers have touchscreen functionality, similar to a tablet or smartphone. You gesture via taps, swipes, pinching, etc., to give various commands, such as starting programs and zooming the view.
- **Pen tablet:** This device lets you write and draw on a pad with a pen-like stylus. Pen tablets are especially useful for fine graphic arts work such as photo editing.
- **Trackball:** A trackball works like a stationary mouse. You move the *mouse pointer* by rolling a small ball.

USB Ports

Most input devices connect to the computer via a rectangular connection called a *USB (Universal Serial Bus) port*. USB ports allow you to connect all manner of hardware to the computer. Most computers have two to six USB ports, and you can add more with a USB hub. Another advantage to USB is the ability to supply electrical power to many USB devices. This frees up space on your surge protector.

This typical notebook computer has USB ports along its side.

USB Versions

Over the years, USB ports have evolved into three versions capable of ever-increasing data transfer speeds. The most recent USB ports are always compatible with previous versions.

- **USB 1.0:** This is the earliest version of USB port, which became available in 1996.
- **USB 2.0:** First available in 2000, this version can theoretically support data transfer speeds up to 400 times faster than USB 1.0.
- **USB 3.0:** The first computers to support USB 3.0 went on sale in early 2010. This version can theoretically attain speeds up to twenty times faster than USB 2.0. USB 3.0 can also provide more electrical power to USB devices as necessary.

Thunderbolt

Thunderbolt is a relatively new high-speed connection that works similar to USB. Thunderbolt ports allow you to connect multiple devices, such as an external hard drive, optical drive, or even a second monitor. Thunderbolt can theoretically attain speeds up to four times faster than USB 3.0.

Webcams

A webcam is a small video camera and built-in microphone that allow you to capture and transmit video and photos from your computer. Webcams are standard equipment on most computers sold today. Webcams allow you to make video telephone calls via services such as Skype, create videos, and snap photos.

Computer Software

The logical, nonphysical component of a computer system is its software. Software allows computers to perform a variety of tasks with the same hardware. There are two basic categories of software you should be aware of:

- Operating system
- Application programs

Software comes in the form of files. So let's define this term before looking at these two categories in detail.

Software Files

Files are a group of data with a common purpose. No matter which type of drive it's stored on, all software consists of files. Sophisticated programs may be installed as dozens or even hundreds of individual files on your computer's internal drive. All software files have a file format (or file type).

Software Versions

Aside from files you create and store yourself (user data), all software programs (including the operating system) typically come in specific versions. Version identifications may include numbers (1.0, 2.0, etc.) or years (for example, Office 2013). Recent versions of Windows® use numbers, such as Windows 7 and Windows 8.1. The two latest versions of Microsoft® Office are Office 2010 and Office 2013.

The Operating System

An operating system (OS) is the most basic software your computer needs to function. When you first turn on the computer, it does a check of its hardware. Next, it searches for and loads an OS into RAM so it can begin doing work for you. Until the OS loads, a computer can recognize only the most rudimentary keyboard commands. After the operating system loads, the computer can interact with you normally.

Examples of Operating Systems

There are many operating systems available to run personal computers. This book is based on Microsoft Windows, the world's most widely used OS. Other computers run different operating systems. For example, Apple® Macintosh® computers run Mac OS X. Linux is an open source OS. The source code is widely available, and any programmer can contribute improvements to it. This book supports two versions of Windows:

- **Windows 7** (released 2009)
- **Windows 8.1** (released 2013)

Roles of an Operating System

An operating system performs many roles.

- **Interpreting commands:** The OS is the interface between you and all of the computer's hardware and software. When you point and click with the mouse or type on the keyboard, the OS receives the input and decides what to do with it.

- **Controlling hardware:** The OS controls all hardware in the computer system. When you need to load a program or a user data file from a hard drive, the OS locates it and sends it to RAM for processing. When you give a print command, the OS tells the printer how to print the desired document.

- **Keeping track of files:** All computer software resides on one (or more) storage drives as files. The OS sets the rules for naming and storing these files. A hard drive can only think in terms of bits and bytes stored on various tracks and sectors of its storage system. Fortunately, the OS allows you to give files easy-to-recall names and keeps track of how and where each file is stored. When you need a file or program, you tell the OS what you want, and it then tells the hard drive how to get it.

- **Running application programs:** Application programs are software that let you get work done. Most software is written and coded to run on a specific OS. The OS controls loading software into RAM and switching from one application program to another.

32- and 64-bit Versions

The Windows OS is available in 32- and 64-bit versions. As an end user, you need to know only three things about these two versions.

- **3 GB RAM limit:** The 32-bit version of Windows only supports up to three gigabytes (3 GB) of RAM. Any RAM beyond this limit is not recognized or used.

- **Application programs:** Many application programs come in 32- and 64-bit versions. A 32-bit program can run on a 64-bit version of Windows, but a 64-bit program can only run on 64-bit versions of Windows.

- **Hardware drivers:** A driver is software that tells the operating system how to interact with and control hardware attached to the computer. With rare exceptions, a driver written for the 32-bit version of Windows will not work in the 64-bit version. Unless your hardware is quite old, however, you will be able to find a 64-bit driver for it via the Internet. Many 64-bit drivers also come preinstalled on the 64-bit version of Windows.

Application Programs

An *application program* (application) is software designed to help you get work done. Anything useful you can do with a computer depends on its installed applications. Windows 8.1 introduced a new class of application called an app. These only run from the Start Screen and Tablet Desktop (never the traditional Desktop) on Windows 8.1, and can only be installed via the online Microsoft Store.

Most applications can be grouped into one of four categories.

Application Categories		
Category	**Description**	**Examples**
Proprietary (Commercial)	Applications for which you must purchase a license in order to use legally; some vendors let you use commercial software on a trial basis first	Office 2013 Photoshop
Shareware	Applications you are allowed to install and use without paying for initially; if you continue to use the software, you are required or expected to pay a license fee after the trial period ends	WinZip PDFCreator
Freeware	Free applications you do not have to pay for no matter how much you use them; these applications are copyrighted, which means others can't sell the freeware program themselves	Jing Firefox Star Office
Malware	Often called *viruses*, these are applications designed to harm your computer; they may erase files, transmit your passwords, or simply pop up ads and other nuisances	MyDoom Code Red Blaster

Types of Applications

The variety of applications available for computers is almost infinite. In this course, you will learn about some of the most popular types of applications.

- Word processor (Word)
- Spreadsheet (Excel)
- Database (Access)
- Presentation (PowerPoint)
- Email/personal information (Outlook)
- Web browsing (Internet Explorer)

Antimalware Software

A special type of application designed to counter malicious *malware* attacks is called antimalware, or sometimes *antivirus program* or Internet security. Antimalware software can counter a variety of programs such as spyware, Trojan horses, worms, email-borne viruses, and many others. Internet security suites add additional protections with features such as firewalls, antispyware, identity theft protection, and many others.

If your computer is connected to the Internet, you need an antimalware program to protect it.

User Files

User files are the saved products you create when you use an application program. A user file can be a letter, flyer, budget spreadsheet, presentation slide show, digital photo, video, song, or any of the other numerous creations possible.

File Formats

A file format is basically a technique for storing file data. There are numerous file formats and each is optimized to store a particular data type. For example, the JPEG file format is well suited for storing digital photos; most digital cameras use this file format by default. *MP3 (Moving Picture Experts Group Layer-3 Audio)* is another popular file format; it's optimized for storing music in compact files that take up less space than most other formats.

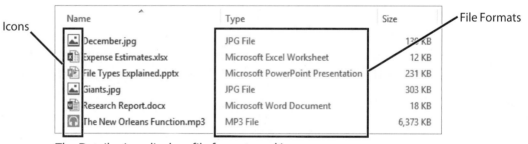

Icons ────────────── File Formats

Name	Type	Size
December.jpg	JPG File	139 KB
Expense Estimates.xlsx	Microsoft Excel Worksheet	12 KB
File Types Explained.pptx	Microsoft PowerPoint Presentation	231 KB
Giants.jpg	JPG File	303 KB
Research Report.docx	Microsoft Word Document	18 KB
The New Orleans Function.mp3	MP3 File	6,373 KB

The Details view displays file formats and icons.

Native File Formats

Every application has a native file format to store your work in the form of a file. File formats are usually identified by the hidden extension stored at the end of the filename. For example, Microsoft Office Word 2013 uses the .docx format introduced with Word 2007. Word 2003 uses the older .doc format introduced with Word 97. Windows normally hides filename extensions, which work in the background to link your user files to specific applications. Windows also uses a different file icon (picture) to indicate the two formats.

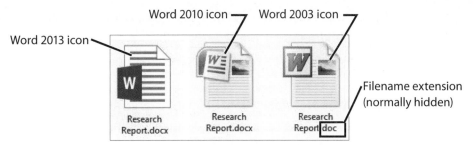

This is how Word files display when their hidden extensions are made visible. The letters after the period in each filename identify the file format.

In addition to their native file formats, many programs can save and open files in other popular file formats. When you install a program, Windows learns about its native file format and installs icons for file types the program creates. These icons also help you identify the files visually.

Links to Applications

Windows makes a link between any new file type an application needs and that application. This link tells Windows which application to start when you double-click a file. When you install a program that uses a file type that's already in use, sometimes you will be asked to choose which program you prefer to open that type of file.

Never change the extension of a filename if it happens to be visible.

Networking

A network is a system of hardware and software that actively connects computers. It allows computers to interact in a variety of ways, such as browsing the web, transmitting email, sharing files, participating in online conferences, etc. Computers on the same network can also share resources such as printers, drives, and internal messaging systems.

Types of Networks

Networks can be as small as two or as large as millions of computers. The Internet is a network of over five billion devices worldwide. Networks are often named for their size.

- **Local Area Network (LAN):** Spans a small physical location, such as a home or office building
- **Wireless LAN (WLAN):** A LAN where computers connect wirelessly (no physical cables)
- **Wide Area Network (WAN):** Spans a large area and often consists of several connected LANs; for example, a multibuilding business complex may be served by its own WAN; a WAN can extend to LANs based in several different cities
- **Campus Area Network (CAN):** Connects computers and other hardware across a college campus

Networks can rarely be categorized as a single type of network. For example, a midsize college campus that offers wireless connectivity and access to the Internet might be considered a LAN, WLAN, CAN, and WAN.

Networking Hardware

Network connections give you access to the Internet. In a business environment, networks also give access to printers and servers holding critical data. Virtually all computers now offer some way to connect to a network. Three critical components of network hardware are modems, routers, and wireless access points.

Modems

A *modem* (*m*odulator-*dem*odulator) takes digital data from the computer (bits and bytes) and converts it to sound (waves) that can travel along wires and cables. A modem and the receiving end of the transmission then converts the sound waves back into digital data bytes. All modems require a subscription with an Internet service provider (ISP) that provides the actual Internet connection.

There are three types of modems in common residential use today.

- **Cable modem:** This allows you to receive an Internet connection via a television cable system. Compared to other types of modems, *cable modem*s permit the fastest Internet connection speeds.
- **DSL (digital subscriber line) modem:** This allows you to make an Internet connection via the wiring of a common telephone jack. For DSL to work, your telephone company must install special hardware within a limited range of your home (often not available in rural areas).
- **Dial-up modem:** This older technology allows you to connect to the Internet via almost any telephone jack (no special hardware required). The speeds possible via a dial-up modem are *very slow* compared to cable or DSL.

Network Connection Hardware

A router lets you connect two networks, such as connecting your home network to the Internet. Cable and DSL modems perform the function of a router. Most routers for home use contain four network cable ports to connect multiple computers.

Most home routers are also a wireless access point. They send data wirelessly to compatible wireless adapters on any computers within range. This network connection includes any available Internet connection active on the router/wireless access point.

Types of Wireless Access

As with many other computing standards, wireless access standards continue to evolve, allowing ever-faster connections over an ever-increasing range. Most wireless access points can connect via multiple wireless connection standards.

- **Wireless-b:** This is the oldest standard still in use. It is also the slowest and shortest-ranged of the three most popular standards.
- **Wireless-g:** This standard emerged in 2003 and is still used in some locations. Compared to wireless-b, -g has similar range and can attain higher transfer speeds.
- **Wireless-n:** This standard came into common use around 2007. It theoretically has twice the range and greater speeds compared to the wireless-g standard.
- **Wireless-ac:** This, the latest standard, began coming into use in 2013. It can transmit data about twice as fast as Wireless-n (under real-world conditions).

Security/Encryption

Most private wireless access points require a login password for access. This prevents others from tapping into your wireless bandwidth (data transfer capacity) without your permission. Encryption prevents someone nearby from monitoring your wireless transmissions and stealing private data (such as credit card numbers and online banking login information). All wireless access points support one or more encryption types.

Network Protocols

For computers, routers, hubs, switches, and wireless access points to communicate on a network, they must speak the same language and follow the same set of rules (a protocol). While there are several different networking protocols, Ethernet is the most widely used. It is a standard used for both wired and wireless networking, and most network switches installed in homes and businesses are based upon Ethernet technology.

concepts review

To check your knowledge of the key concepts introduced in this lesson, complete the Concepts Review quiz by choosing the appropriate access option below.

If you are...	Then access the quiz by...
Using eLab	Logging in, choosing Content, and navigating to the Concepts Review quiz for this lesson
Not using eLab	Going to the Student Resource Center (see the inside front cover)

reinforce your skills | ecs-0101a

Check Your Computer's Basic Specs (Windows 7)

Windows 8.1 Users: Skip to the next exercise.

In this exercise, you will display the basic specifications of your computer.

1   Click the **Start** 🔘 button.

Windows displays the Start menu.

2   Click **Computer** with the right (not the left) mouse button.

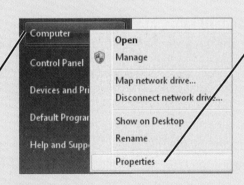

3   Choose **Properties** with the left (not the right) mouse button.

A new window appears to display the basic details of your computer.

4 Review your computer's details:

A Notice the Windows version.

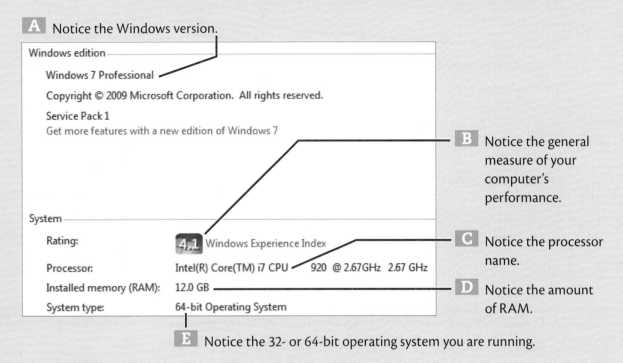

Windows edition

Windows 7 Professional

Copyright © 2009 Microsoft Corporation. All rights reserved.

Service Pack 1
Get more features with a new edition of Windows 7

B Notice the general measure of your computer's performance.

System

Rating: **4.1** Windows Experience Index

Processor: Intel(R) Core(TM) i7 CPU   920 @ 2.67GHz 2.67 GHz

Installed memory (RAM): 12.0 GB

System type: 64-bit Operating System

C Notice the processor name.

D Notice the amount of RAM.

E Notice the 32- or 64-bit operating system you are running.

5 **Close** [X] the window.

---

reinforce your skills | ecs-0101b

Check Your Computer's Basic Specs (Windows 8.1)

Windows 7 Users: Skip to the next exercise.

In this exercise, you will display the basic specifications of your computer.

1 Point at the **bottom-left** corner of the screen until the **Start** button appears, then click the **right** (not the left) mouse button.

Event Viewer
System
Device Manager
Disk Management
Computer Management
Command Prompt
Command Prompt (Admin)

Task Manager
Control Panel
File Explorer
Search
Run

Desktop

2 Choose **System**.
A new window appears to display the basic details of your computer.

3   Review your computer's details:

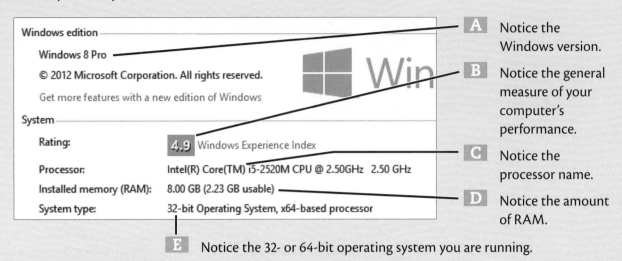

A   Notice the Windows version.

B   Notice the general measure of your computer's performance.

C   Notice the processor name.

D   Notice the amount of RAM.

E   Notice the 32- or 64-bit operating system you are running.

4   **Close** ⊠ the window.

---

reinforce your skills | ecs-0102a

Check Your Screen Resolution (Windows 7)

Windows 8.1 Users: Skip to the next exercise.

In this exercise, you will display the resolution of your screen (monitor).

1   Point at any clear area of the screen, then click the right (not left) mouse button to display a pop-up menu.

Pop-up menus are often referred to as *context menus*.

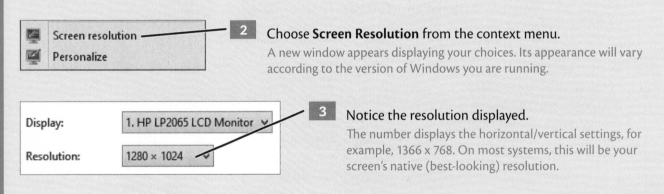

2   Choose **Screen Resolution** from the context menu.

A new window appears displaying your choices. Its appearance will vary according to the version of Windows you are running.

3   Notice the resolution displayed.

The number displays the horizontal/vertical settings, for example, 1366 x 768. On most systems, this will be your screen's native (best-looking) resolution.

4   Click **Cancel** to close the window. (Don't change the screen resolution.)

reinforce your skills | ecs-0102b

Check Your Screen Resolution (Windows 8.1)

Windows 7 Users: Skip to the next exercise.

In this exercise, you will display the resolution of your screen (monitor).

1 Click the Desktop tile. (This may not be in the same location as the figure at left.)
Windows displays the Desktop.

2 Point at any clear area of the screen, then click the **right** mouse button to display a pop-up menu.
Pop-up menus are often referred to as context menus.

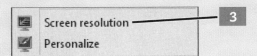

3 Choose **Screen Resolution** from the context menu.
A new window appears to display your choices. Its appearance will vary according to the version of Windows you are running.

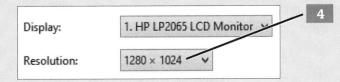

4 Notice the resolution that displays.
The number displays the horizontal/vertical settings, for example, 1366 x 768. On most systems, this will be your screen's native (best-looking) resolution.

5 Click **Cancel** to close the window. (Don't change the screen resolution.)

What Matters Most

You are going to purchase a new computer for personal use. In this exercise, you will consider the features that matter most to you and whether these features are supported primarily via hardware or software.

- List the four features of the computer you use that matter most to you. For example, portability, storage space, battery life, and a large screen (or perhaps a touchscreen). Other features you might list include multitasking, processor power, weight, shared applications, syncing music and documents between devices, etc.

- Choose the type of computer that would give you most of what you want, such as a small (or large) laptop, desktop, or all-in-one computer, or a tablet. Briefly explain the reason for your choice in terms of the features that matter most. Would you have to give up a feature you really like to get the other features in your list above? Or would one category of computer provide all those features?

- Assume that the category of computer you chose above was not available or affordable. Indicate your second choice and briefly describe your reason.

Submit your work based on the guidelines provided by your instructor.

New Job, New Computer

You've just started a new job and have been asked to define your computer needs. In this exercise, you will use a combination of online and other sources to create a realistic estimate of the type of computer, as well as the software and accessories, you'll need.

- Your instructor will state the job for this assignment, or leave you free to state a job on your own.

- Your instructor will give you a budget for this assignment, or give you a range to formulate your own budget. Your lists of hardware, software, and peripherals must fit within your budget.

- Specify the cost and other details of hardware that will be necessary for your new computer. For example, the capabilities of the processor or the screen size.

- Specify any software that would be critical to your new job. If you know the name of a program, include it; if you don't, describe what the software would do. Include the cost for specific programs you'd want to use, or estimate the cost for programs that would help you get specific tasks done.

- List any additional pieces of hardware, such as a printer, monitor, and accessories (such as a carrying case). Keep in mind that these additional items must be within your budget.

Submit your list of items and costs based on the guidelines provided by your instructor.

Set Yourself Up with a New Computer

In this exercise, you will spec out the sort of notebook, tablet, or desktop computer you'd like to purchase new.

- Your instructor will give you a budget for your new computer and any peripherals (e.g., a printer) needed.

- First, consider the software needed. Make a list of software applications you would like to run and/or tasks you'd want perform on the computer. Then, find the hardware that runs the software effectively. Make sure the new computer has enough processor power and RAM to run the applications.

- Make a list of the computer (laptop, desktop, or tablet) you want to purchase, plus any peripherals that fit within your budget. Justify your choice of processor and RAM. (The most expensive computer with the most RAM might be more than you really need.)

Submit your work based on the guidelines provided by your instructor.

The Right Computer for Each Job

In this exercise, you will help your supervisor determine the best computers for use by your coworkers. Consider the tasks each person performs and then recommend a computer that has the power and/or mobility the staff person needs to accomplish those tasks efficiently. Give two or three reasons for each recommendation.

- **Receptionist:** This person staffs the front desk at the lobby each day. He or she must often look up appointment calendars and telephone numbers for other employees.

- **Salesperson:** This person makes sales calls at customer locations throughout the state. He or she presents videos and slide shows via a video projector.

- **Stockroom Clerk:** This person inventories and frequently must locate items in a large warehouse/stockroom.

- **Graphic Artist:** This person designs brochures, catalogs, flyers, and other printed media. He or she also works a great deal with digital photos of various persons and products.

Submit your work based on the guidelines provided by your instructor.

Windows

2 Controlling Programs

Skills YOU Will Learn

- Log on and off of Windows
- Identify significant features of the Windows Desktop
- Start any installed Windows program
- Place program windows where you want them on the screen
- Switch among programs

in this lesson

Every program runs in a program window. You can make program windows fill the screen, disappear, or change shape to fill just part of the screen. You can also run more than one program at the same time and quickly switch from one running program to another. This can be useful when you look up information in one window and use it with a different program in another window. There are also easy methods to locate and start the programs you use most often. In this lesson, you will open, position, and switch among program windows.

ecs02.1

Using the Best Program

Sometimes, the best program is three of them. You are working on a report late at night. Part of the report requires calculations. You work out the math in Excel, since this is what Excel does best. You write your report using Word, and you create a slide show presentation in PowerPoint using details created in Word and Excel. As you work, you switch from program to program, copying items from one and pasting them into another. When one program clutters the Desktop, you minimize it. The finished report leverages the strengths of all three programs.

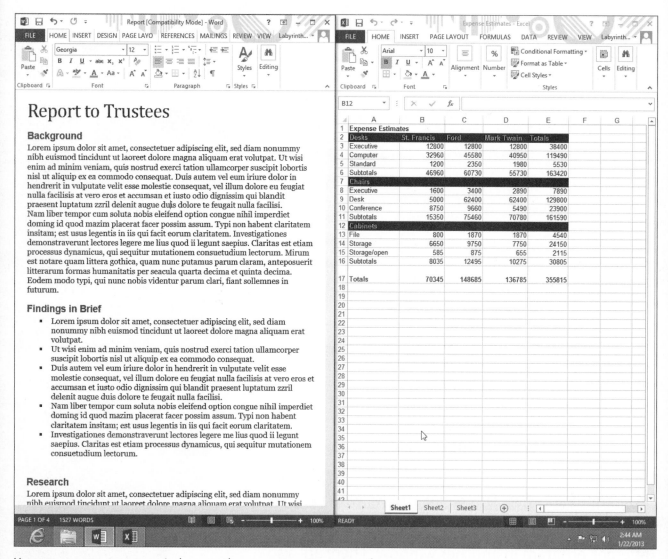

You can arrange program windows on the screen to suit your needs.

Starting Windows

 Video
The first thing your computer does when it "wakes up" is locate and load an *operating system*, such as Windows, into its RAM. This book covers the two versions of Windows that can run Office 2013: Windows 7 and Windows 8.1.

Starting a Session

Once Windows loads, it indicates that it's ready for you to start working. Depending on how the computer is configured, you will see one of the following:

- A Welcome screen displaying all of the usernames that can log on
- A network login screen in which a username and password must be typed

develop your skills | ecs-0201a

Log On to Windows (Windows 7)

 Guide Me
Windows 8.1 Users: Skip to the next topic.

In this exercise, you will log on to Windows 7 and view the Desktop.

1 If necessary, switch on the power to the computer and monitor.
The computer goes through its start-up routine, ending with a Windows logon screen.

2 Write your logon information below. Your instructor will give you this.

Username: _____

Password: _____

3 Follow the steps under the applicable heading below, depending on the login screen that you see:

Network Logon Prompt

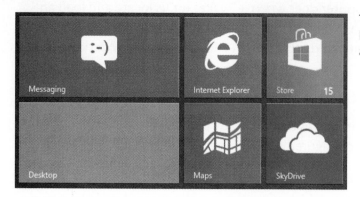

This is one example of a network logon screen. If you encounter others, have your instructor assist you.

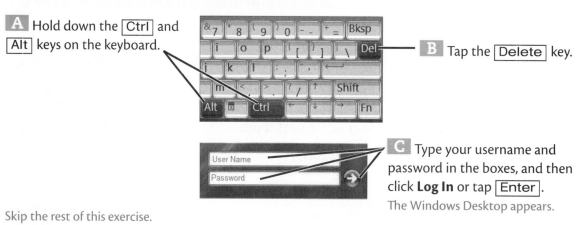

A Hold down the [Ctrl] and [Alt] keys on the keyboard.

B Tap the [Delete] key.

C Type your username and password in the boxes, and then click **Log In** or tap [Enter].
The Windows Desktop appears.

Skip the rest of this exercise.

Welcome Screen with Account Names Displayed

A Click the username for the account you will use.

B Type the password, and then tap [Enter] or click the **Log In** button.
The Windows Desktop appears.

labstudent11

Signing On (Windows 8.1)

 Video

Windows 8.1 renames the "log on" command to "sign on." It's similar to the Windows 7 command, with one exception: Signing on with a *Microsoft account* sends data from your work sessions to Microsoft. Microsoft uses this data to perform tasks such as syncing your personal settings between devices. It may also use such data to target personal ads in some programs or web browsing sessions. Signing on with a *local* (non-Microsoft) account does not send out data.

develop your skills | ecs-0201b

Sign On to Windows (Windows 8.1)

Guide Me   **Windows 7 Users:** Skip to the next topic.

In this exercise, you will sign on to Windows 8.1 and view the Desktop.

1 If necessary, switch on the power to the computer and monitor.

The computer goes through its start-up routine, ending with a Windows Welcome screen.

2 Write your sign on information below. Your instructor will give you this.

Username: _____

Password: _____

3 Click once anywhere on the **Welcome** screen.

A sign on screen appears, displaying the available usernames.

4 Click the username you've been assigned for the course.

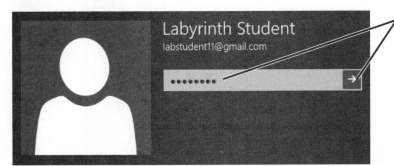

5 Type your password, and then tap ⎡Enter⎤ or click the **Submit** button.

The Start screen appears, displaying tiles for various activities and programs.

6 Click the **Desktop** tile (location and picture may vary).

The Windows Desktop appears, similar to the one you may be used to from previous versions of Windows.

Windows displays the Desktop.

The Windows Desktop

 Video

The Windows *Desktop* is where all computing activity takes place in Windows 7. It's also where you run traditional Desktop application programs in Windows 8.1.

The Windows 7 Desktop

The Desktop appears after you first log on to Windows 7. This figure displays significant features of a typical Windows 7 Desktop.

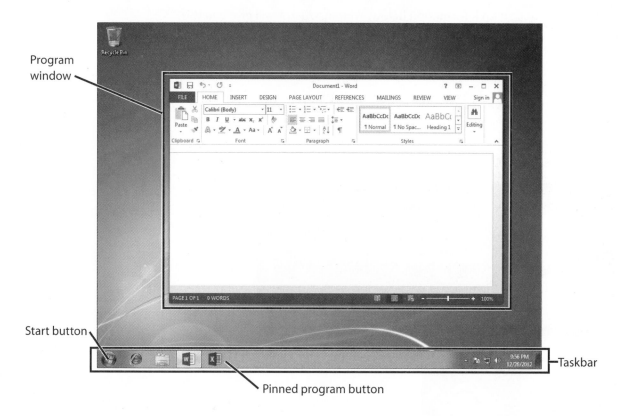

Program window

Start button

Taskbar

Pinned program button

Windows 8.1 Has Two Desktops

Windows 8.1 has two Desktops. One is similar to that used in previous versions of Windows; it runs traditional Windows applications. The *Tablet Desktop* runs only the new apps designed for Windows 8.1 and Windows Phone. These apps always fill the screen completely. You can run programs on both Desktops simultaneously and switch between them.

The following figure displays features typical of the Windows 8.1 Desktop.

Pinned applications on the Taskbar

Start screen button

Windows 8.1 Terminology

The following terms will be used in regard to Windows 8.1.

- **Application:** A traditional Windows Desktop application program, such as Word, Excel, and PowerPoint.

- **App:** A program that only runs from the Windows 8.1 Start screen and Tablet Desktop, such as Mail, Photos, and Messaging.

- **Tile:** A rectangular button on the Windows 8.1 Start screen. A tile can start either an app or an application.

develop your skills | ecs-0202

Try a Windows 8.1 App

 Guide Me **Windows 7 Users:** Skip to the next topic.

In this exercise, you will start an app from the Start screen.

1 Tap the **Windows** key on the lower-left corner of the keyboard.
The Start screen appears.

2 Click the **Internet Explorer** app tile.
The Internet Explorer app appears. Notice that it fills the entire screen automatically and that there are no window sizing buttons at the top-right corner of the screen.

3 Tap the **Windows** ⊞ key to display the Start screen again.

Starting Applications

 Video

Windows offers a variety of methods to start application programs (applications). As you work with various applications, you'll find or create favorite ways to start them.

The Start Menu (Windows 7)

When you install a new application, a folder for that application is usually created in the Start menu. If you don't recall where an application was installed, you can search for it. Applications you use frequently can be "pinned" to the Start menu and Windows taskbar for easier access.

Application program folder ——

Applications pinned to taskbar ——

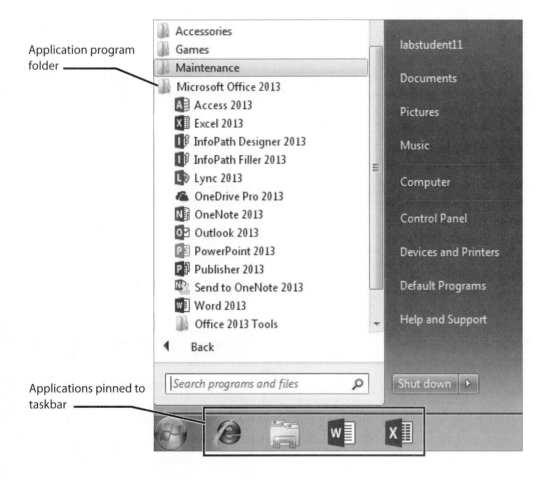

The Start Screen (Windows 8.1)

The Windows 8.1 Start screen performs functions similar to the Start menu on Windows 7. This figure displays features typical of the Windows 8.1 Start screen.

Tiled app buttons

Desktop application buttons "pinned" to the Start screen

 Depending on your Windows sign-on ID and activities, tile locations can change. The image displayed on some tiles may also change.

Basic Mouse Motions

There are five basic motions you can perform with the mouse. If your computer has a touchscreen, there are additional motions (gestures) you can use.

Mouse Motions	
Command Name	**Description**
Point	Point at a spot on the screen without clicking
Click	Tap and release the main (left) mouse button
Double-click	Quickly tap and release the main mouse button twice
Right-click	Tap and release the secondary (right) mouse button
Drag	Hold down the main mouse button as you move the mouse

 This book covers the use of the mouse only. It does not include touchscreen gestures.

Start an Application (Windows 7)

Guide Me   **Windows 8.1 Users:** Skip to the next exercise.

In this exercise, you will start Word 2013.

1 Click **Start**.

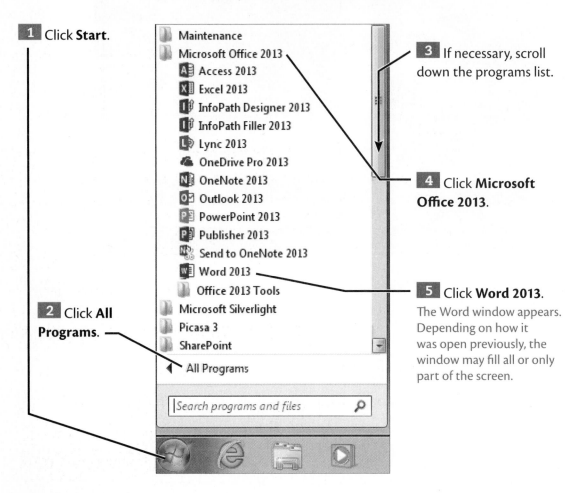

2 Click **All Programs**.

3 If necessary, scroll down the programs list.

4 Click **Microsoft Office 2013**.

5 Click **Word 2013**.
The Word window appears. Depending on how it was open previously, the window may fill all or only part of the screen.

6 Choose **Blank Document**.
Word displays a new, blank document.

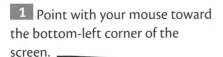

develop your skills | ecs-0203b

Start an Application (Windows 8.1)

 Guide Me **Windows 7 Users:** Skip to the next topic.

In this exercise, you will start Word 2013.

1 Point with your mouse toward the bottom-left corner of the screen.

2 Click the **Apps** button.

3 Scroll over to the **Microsoft Office 2013** group. (Try using the scroll wheel on the top of your mouse.)

Microsoft Office 2013

A▤ Access 2013

X▤ Excel 2013

P▤ Publisher 2013

N▤ Send to OneNote 2013

W▤ Word 2013

4 Click **Word 2013** (location may vary).

Windows 8.1 displays the Desktop and opens the Word program window.

5 Click **Blank Document.**

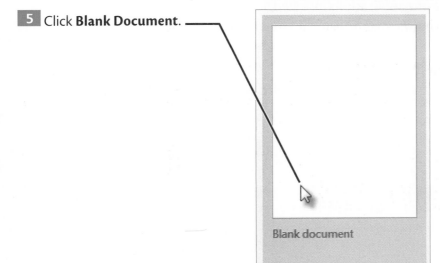

Blank document

The Windows Taskbar

 Video

The Windows *taskbar* along the bottom of the screen displays buttons for each active application. Use them to switch among applications and to minimize application windows.

Pinning Programs to the Taskbar

You can "*pin*" frequently used programs directly to a spot on the taskbar. This keeps these application buttons in a stable location that's easy to access. Not only can you start applications from the taskbar buttons, you can also quickly view and select open application windows.

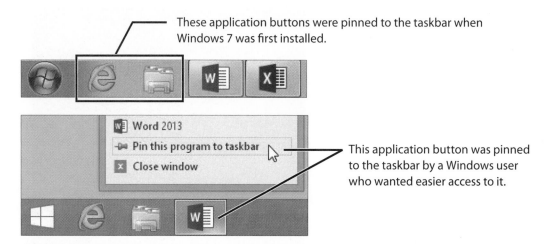

These application buttons were pinned to the taskbar when Windows 7 was first installed.

This application button was pinned to the taskbar by a Windows user who wanted easier access to it.

Searching for Programs

If you have numerous applications installed, it may be difficult to find one you don't use very often. Windows has a Search feature to help you locate applications.

Start Menu Search (Windows 7)
The Windows 7 Start menu contains a Search box. This box can search for programs and files.

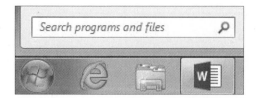

Search Charm (Windows 8.1)

Charms are a set of basic commands available via the Charms bar. You can access charms from both Windows 8.1 Desktops.

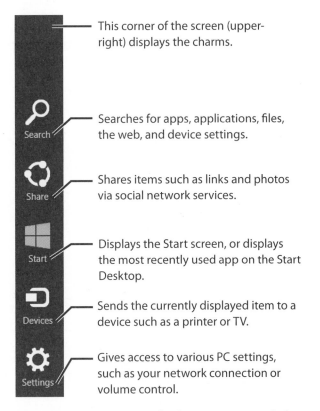

This corner of the screen (upper-right) displays the charms.

Searches for apps, applications, files, the web, and device settings.

Shares items such as links and photos via social network services.

Displays the Start screen, or displays the most recently used app on the Start Desktop.

Sends the currently displayed item to a device such as a printer or TV.

Gives access to various PC settings, such as your network connection or volume control.

The Windows 8.1 Search charm can search for programs, files, and perform web searches. If the Everywhere setting finds too many items, you can limit the search.

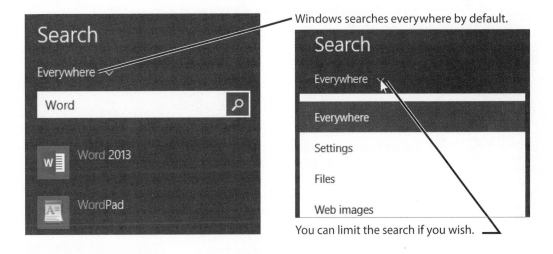

Windows searches everywhere by default.

You can limit the search if you wish.

develop your skills | ecs-0204a

Search for an Application (Windows 7)

 Guide Me **Windows 8.1 Users:** Skip to the next exercise.

In this exercise, you will search for and start one application and pin another to the taskbar.

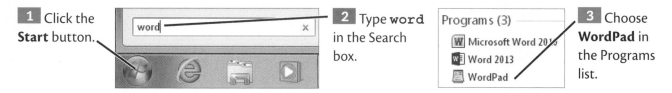

1 Click the **Start** button.

2 Type **word** in the Search box.

3 Choose **WordPad** in the Programs list.

Windows opens WordPad, a basic word processor built into Windows.

4 **Close** ✕ the WordPad window.

The Word window remains open, as does its taskbar button.

5 To pin Word to the taskbar, right-click (don't left-click) **Word 2013**.

6 Choose this option.

Windows pins the Word 2013 button to the taskbar, which means you can start the application without using the Start menu.

develop your skills | ecs-0204b

Search for an Application (Windows 8.1)

 Guide Me **Windows 7 Users:** Skip to the next topic.

In this exercise, you will search for and start one application and pin another to the taskbar.

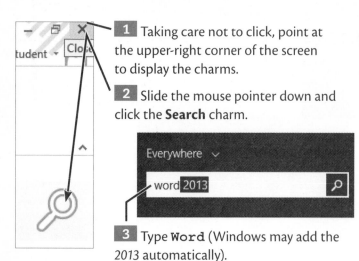

1 Taking care not to click, point at the upper-right corner of the screen to display the charms.

2 Slide the mouse pointer down and click the **Search** charm.

3 Type **Word** (Windows may add the 2013 automatically).

4 Click **Wordpad.**

Windows opens Wordpad, a basic, built-in word processor.

5 **Close** ✕ the new WordPad program window.

The Word window remains open, as does its taskbar button.

6 To pin Word to the taskbar, right-click (don't left-click) **Word 2013**.

7 Choose this option.

Windows pins the Word 2013 button to the taskbar, which means you can start the application without using the Start menu.

Controlling Desktop Windows

 Video

Every application running on the Desktop has one or more program windows, which you can position as you see fit. Many beginning Windows users forget that they can instantly size a window to fill the entire screen, which reduces scrolling to view your work. Program windows open with quick sizing buttons that help you change the placement of Desktop windows.

NOTE

Windows 8.1 apps always fill the Tablet Desktop and have limited resizing capabilities.

Program Window Features

Several features are common to virtually all program windows.

Ribbon (or menu bar in other programs)   Title bar (shows filename and program name)   Quick sizing buttons

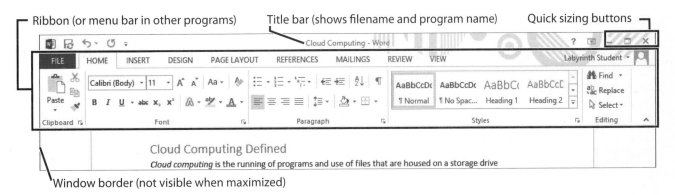

Window border (not visible when maximized)

Quick Sizing Buttons

Most program windows have three quick sizing buttons for issuing common window commands. The center button changes depending on how the window is sized.

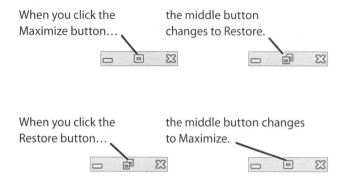

When you click the Maximize button… the middle button changes to Restore.

When you click the Restore button… the middle button changes to Maximize.

Quick Sizing Buttons		
Command Name	**Icon**	**Description**
Close	☒	Closes the program window and exits the program
Maximize	◻	Makes the program window fill the entire screen
Restore	▣	Restores a maximized program window back to filling only part of the screen
Minimize	–	Removes the program window from the screen but leaves it running in the background
Ribbon Display Options	⬆	Controls options for displaying the Ribbon in Office 2013 programs

develop your skills | ecs-0205

Use Quick Sizing Buttons

 Guide Me   In this exercise, you will use the quick sizing buttons to change the appearance of an application window.

1 Click the **Maximize** quick sizing button if it's visible.

The Word program window now fills the entire screen.

Go to the next step if the window is already maximized.

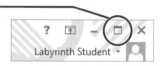

2 Click the **Restore** button so the window fills only a portion of the screen. ——————————

3 Click the **Minimize** button. ——————

The program window disappears, but Word is still running. Any work being done in the program is still there.

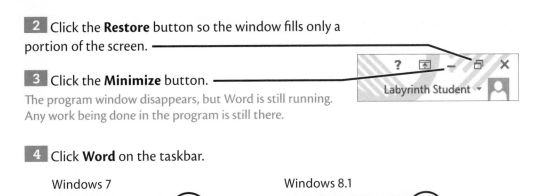

4 Click **Word** on the taskbar.

Windows 7   Windows 8.1

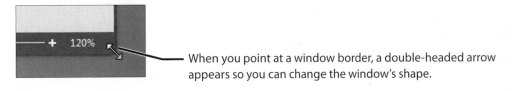

The Word window reappears in whichever shape it was when minimized. Leave Word open.

Positioning and Shaping Program Windows

 Video

You can adjust the position and shape of restored (not maximized) program windows. There are two methods:

- **Drag the title bar:** Drag the title bar of a restored window to place it anywhere on the Desktop.

The mouse pointer over a typical title bar.

- **Drag window borders:** Drag the borders of a restored window to change its dimensions.

When you point at a window border, a double-headed arrow appears so you can change the window's shape.

Neither of these methods works on a *maximized* window.

Shape a Program Window

Guide Me   In this exercise, you will control the size and shape of a program window.

Make sure that the Word window is *not maximized* (doesn't fill the entire screen). You can't change the shape of a maximized window.

1 Point at the **title bar**.

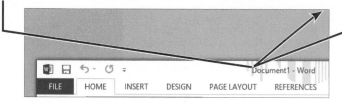

2 Hold down the left mouse button and drag up and to the right 1–2 inches.

3 Release the mouse button near the top-right corner of the screen.

4 Drag the **Word** window by its title bar until it is near the top-left corner of the screen.

Now you will change the window's shape from the corner.

5 Point near the corner until you see a double-headed arrow.

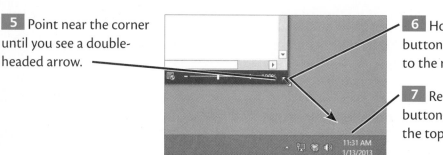

6 Hold down the mouse button and drag down and to the right.

7 Release the mouse button once you're near the top of the taskbar.

8 Point at the right-side border of the window until you see a double-headed arrow, and then hold down the mouse button and drag until the window becomes narrower.

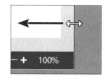

9 Practice changing the window's position (drag the title bar) and shape (drag borders) until you can reliably move and size a window.

Multitasking

 Video

Running more than one program at the same time is called *multitasking*. It can definitely enhance your productivity. For example, you can view a web page in one window while writing about a related topic in Word. Or, you might enter data in an Excel spreadsheet while preparing a PowerPoint presentation. Although only one window at a time is active, you can view any inactive windows. You can switch the active window instantly as you change tasks.

a closer look

Multitasking and RAM

Everything you see on the screen takes place in RAM (Random Access Memory). The more programs you multitask, the more RAM you need to run all those programs efficiently. (Windows can run more programs than it has RAM to support, but everything will slow down.) Fortunately, you can install more RAM on most computers.

Below are two views of RAM usage from the Windows Task Manager. As more programs run, Windows allocates RAM for them. When it runs out of physical RAM, Windows uses a storage drive to temporarily mimic additional RAM. But this RAM isn't as fast as physical RAM, so the system runs more slowly.

RAM use running a single program

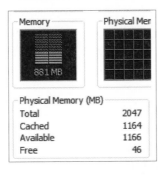

RAM use running five programs

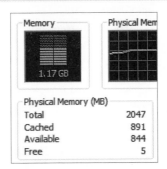

Multitask with Three Programs

 Guide Me   In this exercise, you will run three programs at once.

 NOTE   **The Word program should be running.**

1 Following the steps for your Windows version, start Excel:

Windows 7

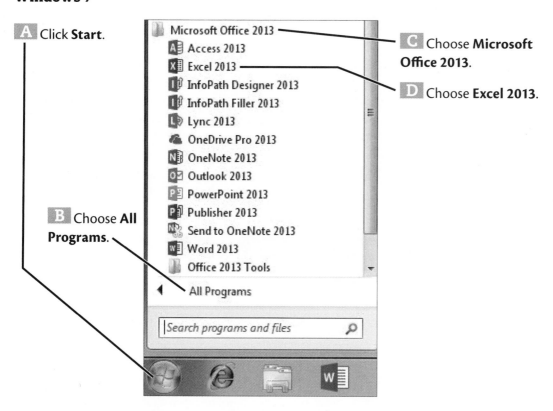

A Click **Start**.

B Choose **All Programs**.

C Choose **Microsoft Office 2013**.

D Choose **Excel 2013**.

Windows 8.1

A Tap the **Windows** key.

B Click **Excel** on the right side of the screen (scroll the screen to the right if necessary). —

The Excel program window appears. It may be maximized, depending on its state when the program was previously closed.

Excel is now the active program. Now you will create a blank workbook.

2 Choose **Blank Workbook**.

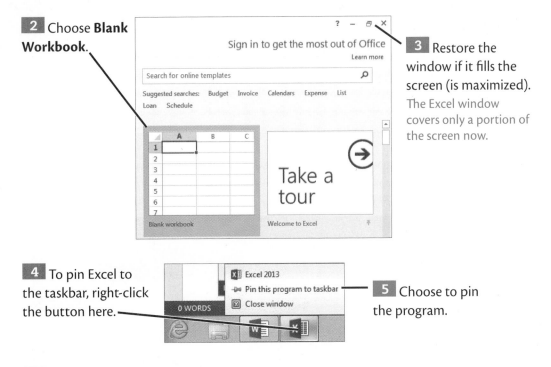

3 Restore the window if it fills the screen (is maximized). The Excel window covers only a portion of the screen now.

4 To pin Excel to the taskbar, right-click the button here.

5 Choose to pin the program.

6 Start **Internet Explorer**.

Windows 7

Windows 8.1

A web browser window appears and becomes the active program. Depending on its state when the program was closed, Internet Explorer may fill the screen.

7 Restore **Internet Explorer** if its window currently fills the screen (is maximized).

Windows 7

Windows 8.1

8 Click the **Word** button.
Word becomes the active program.

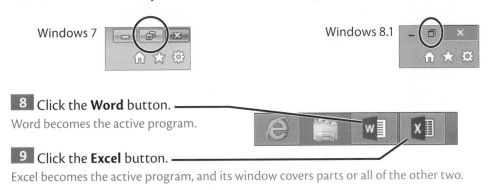

9 Click the **Excel** button.
Excel becomes the active program, and its window covers parts or all of the other two.

10 **Minimize** ▬ Excel.
Since it was the active program just before Excel, Word becomes active again.

11 Click its taskbar button to make **Internet Explorer** active.

12 **Minimize** ▬ / ▬ Internet Explorer.
Only the Word window remains visible on the Desktop, though Excel and Internet Explorer can be made visible again from the taskbar.

Switching Programs

 Video

When you run multiple programs, Windows offers keyboard shortcuts for switching among them. You can also clear the Desktop with a single command (minimizing all visible program windows).

Aero Flip 3D (Windows 7)

The Aero Flip 3D command displays a miniature of each program window's contents as you cycle through them.

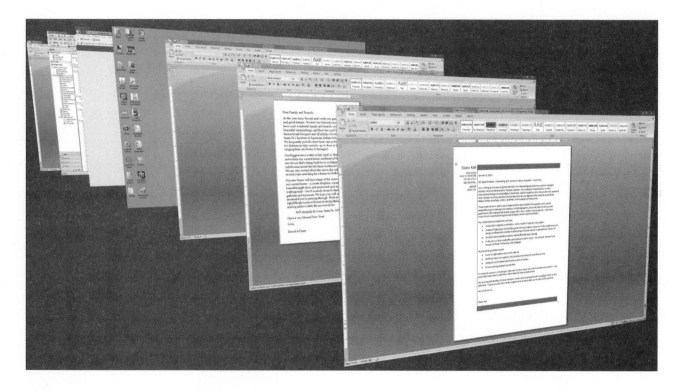

Flip Among Program Windows (Windows 7)

Guide Me   **Windows 8.1 Users:** Skip to the next exercise.

In this exercise, you will flip among programs using the keyboard.

Word, Excel, and Internet Explorer should be running.

1 Hold down the Alt key on the keyboard and keep it held down.

2 Tap the Tab key.

A window displaying icons for currently running programs appears in the middle of the screen.

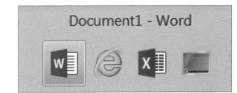

3 With the Alt key still held down, tap Tab again.

The highlight in the program icon display moves to the next program.

4 Still holding down Alt, tap Tab until the highlight returns to **Excel**; release Alt.

Excel becomes the active program.

5 Use Alt + Tab to switch back to **Word**.

6 To use Aero Flip 3D, hold down the **Windows** 🪟 key and tap Tab.

Windows displays miniatures of each open program window.

7 With the **Windows** key still held down, tap Tab until **Internet Explorer** comes to the front of the display; release the **Windows** key.

Internet Explorer becomes active.

8 Hold down the **Windows** key and tap Tab until **Word** becomes the active program; release the **Windows** key.

Word becomes active again.

develop your skills | ecs-0208b

Flip Among Program Windows (Windows 8.1)

 Guide Me   **Windows 7 Users:** Skip to the next topic.

In this exercise, you will flip among programs using the keyboard.

Word, Excel, and Internet Explorer should be running.

1 Hold down the Alt key on the keyboard and keep it held down.

2 Tap the Tab key.

A window displaying icons for currently running programs appears in the middle of the screen.

3 With the Alt key still held down, tap Tab again.

The highlight in the program icon display moves to the next program.

4 Still holding down Alt, tap Tab until the highlight returns to **Excel**; release Alt.

Excel becomes the active program.

5 Use Alt + Tab to switch back to **Word**.

6 To use Aero Flip, hold down the **Windows** ⊞ key and tap Tab.

Windows displays any apps running on the Tablet Desktop at the upper-left corner.

7 Release the **Windows** ⊞ key.

The Internet Explorer Tablet app (not the traditional Desktop application) becomes active.

8 Hold down **Windows** ⊞ and tap Tab.

The Desktop is chosen on the upper left.

9 Release **Windows** ⊞.

You return to the traditional Desktop and Word.

Aero Window Commands

 Video

Aero interface window commands make many common program window arrangements automatic. For example, with *Snap*, you can instantly make a program window fill just half the screen. The Aero window commands also make the Maximize and Restore commands even more intuitive.

Aero Window Commands	
Aero Command	**Description/Use**
Aero Snap	Snaps program windows to fill the right- or left-half of the screen, or maximizes them
Aero Peek	Briefly makes all program windows transparent so you can view the Desktop
Aero Shake	Causes all but one program window to minimize
Aero Flip 3D (Windows 7 Only)	Gives a 3D view of each program window as you flip

develop your skills | ecs-0209

Use Aero Desktop Features

 Guide Me   In this exercise, you will use Aero Desktop shortcuts to control program windows.

1 Make sure **Word** is the active program window and that it is not maximized.

2 Drag the **Word** window title bar to the top of the screen.
The Word window snaps to maximized.

3 Drag the **Word** title bar away from the top of the screen.
The Word window snaps back to its restored shape.

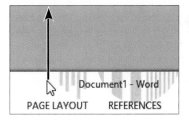

4 Drag the **Word** title bar to the left side of the screen.

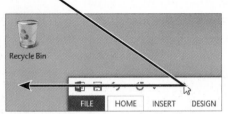

5 Release the mouse button when the mouse pointer touches the edge of the screen and an outline displays on half of the screen.
The Word window fills half the screen. This can be very useful on widescreen displays.

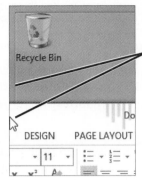

6 Make the **Excel** window active.

7 Use **Aero Snap** to make Excel fill the right half of the screen.

8 To restore Word, drag the **Word** window title bar down and to the right.

9 Release the mouse button.
Windows restores the Word window to its previous shape.

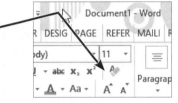

10 To use Aero Shake, point at the **Word** window title bar; then hold down the mouse button and shake the window back and forth for a couple of seconds.

The Excel window (and any other open windows) minimize, leaving Word the only window visible on the Desktop.

11 Click **Excel** on the taskbar to make it visible again.

12 Click the **Show Desktop** button (Windows 7) or corner (Windows 8.1).

Windows 7

Windows 8.1

All open windows are minimized simultaneously.

13 Click the **Show Desktop** button or corner again.
All open windows are restored. Internet Explorer was not restored because it was already minimized when you initially gave the Show Desktop command.

Sleep and Other Modes

 Video   Besides being active and logged on, you can put the computer into other modes of operation. The most useful mode is *Sleep*, which puts the computer into a low-power state until you "wake" it. Other modes of operation are described in the following table.

Windows Modes of Operation	
Mode	**Description/Use**
Sleep	Puts the computer into a low-power mode until a key is tapped or the mouse is moved
Lock	Blocks any view of the Desktop until you reenter your password
Switch User	Allows another user to logon while other users remain logged on; Windows 8.1 allows this mode when you sign on additional users from the Start screen
Log Off/ Sign Out	Closes your Windows session, which shuts down all running programs and Windows

Logging Off (Windows 7)

Logging off the computer in Windows 7 keeps the computer running and allows you and other users to log on later. Any programs you were running are closed.

Signing Out (Windows 8.1)

Signing out in Windows 8.1 is identical to logging off in previous versions of Windows. Your program windows close and Windows signs you out of any active services.

develop your skills | ecs-0210a

Change Modes (Windows 7)

 Guide Me   **Windows 8.1 Users:** Skip to the next exercise.

In this exercise, you will put Windows into various modes.

1 Click **Start**.   **2** Click the **Shut Down** menu button.

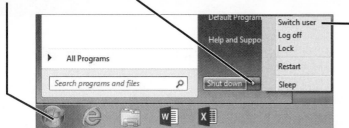

3 Choose **Switch User**.

The logon screen appears. Now someone else can log on, or you can return to your own Windows session. In this case, you will return to your Windows session.

NOTE   A command like this will often be written as follows:
Choose Start→Shut Down ▶ menu button→Switch User.

4 If prompted, use Ctrl + Alt + Delete to get to a logon screen.

5 Choose your logon name, type your password, and tap Enter.
You are back at your Windows session.

6 To lock the computer, choose **Start→Shut Down ▶ menu button→Lock**.
Windows locks the screen and displays your username for unlocking.

7 Type your password and tap Enter.
Windows displays your Desktop again.

8 To put the computer to "sleep," choose **Start→Shut Down ▶ menu button→Sleep**.
Windows turns off the screen and goes into a low-power state.

9 Tap any keyboard key or move the mouse to exit Sleep mode.
Windows "wakes up" the computer and (usually) prompts you for a password.

10 Type your password and tap Enter.
Windows displays your Desktop again.

Change Modes (Windows 8.1)

Guide Me   **Windows 7 Users:** Skip to the next topic.

In this exercise, you will view other users who could sign on to your computer, then put the computer into Lock and Sleep modes.

1 Tap **Windows** 🪟 to display the Start screen.

2 Click your username in the top-right corner.

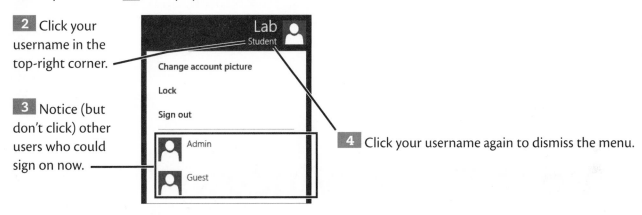

3 Notice (but don't click) other users who could sign on now.

4 Click your username again to dismiss the menu.

Now you will lock and unlock the computer.

5 Click your username.

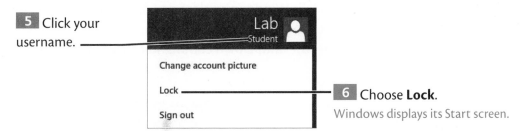

6 Choose **Lock**.
Windows displays its Start screen.

7 Click the **Start screen**.
Windows displays a password box.

8 Type your password and tap ⎙Enter⎙.

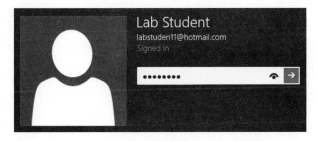

Now you will put the computer to "sleep."

In the next step, if you are studying with a tablet, display Charms and then choose Settings to display the power button.

9 Choose **Power.**

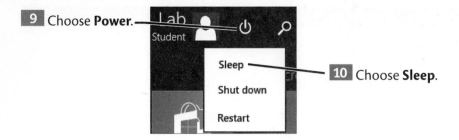

10 Choose **Sleep**.

11 Tap any keyboard key or move the mouse to exit Sleep mode.
Windows "wakes up" and the Start screen or a password prompt appears.

12 Click the **Start screen** if it appeared.

13 Type your password and tap Enter .
You are back at your Windows session. All previously running programs are in the same state they were in when you put the computer to sleep.

Shutting Down Windows

Video

Always shut down the computer properly; don't press or hold down the power button. The Shut Down command tells Windows to close any open application windows and then shut off power to the computer. If your computer needs to install some updates to its software, the Shut Down command can also perform this task.

This icon tells you that Windows needs to shut down to install software updates (Windows 7 only). ————— ⏻ Shut down ▶

Restarting Windows

Sometimes when you install or uninstall software, you need to restart the computer. The Restart command shuts down and then immediately restarts the computer.

If the computer seems especially sluggish, a restart will often clear unnecessary program code and help it run more efficiently.

develop your skills | ecs-0211

Shut Down and Restart

Guide Me   In this exercise, you will shut down and then restart the computer.

1 **Close** ☒ the Excel window. Choose **Don't Save** if asked to save any work.

If you had typed anything in Excel, the program asks if you want to save it. In this case, that's not necessary.

2 **Close** ☒ the Word window. Choose **Don't Save** if asked to save.

It's always a good idea to close open program windows before shutting down the computer. This gives you a chance to save changes to any work you've been doing. Since Internet Explorer doesn't really create anything, it's okay to leave it open.

3 Following the steps for your Windows version, restart the computer:

Windows 7

A Click **Start**.   **B** Click the **Shut Down ▶ menu button**.

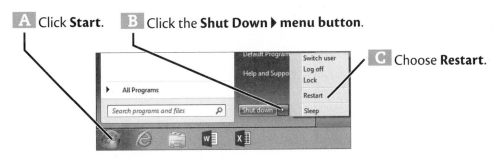

C Choose **Restart**.

Windows 8.1

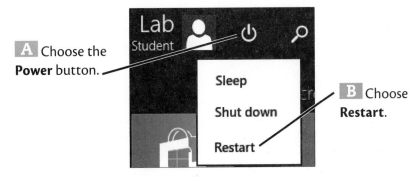

A Choose the **Power** button.

B Choose **Restart**.

Windows goes through its shutdown routine and then restarts the computer.

4 Log in or sign on, depending on your Windows version.

5 Following the steps for your Windows version, shut down the computer:

Windows 7

A Click **Start**.

B Choose **Shut Down**.

Windows goes through its shutdown routine and then powers off the computer.

Windows 8.1

A Click the **Power** button.

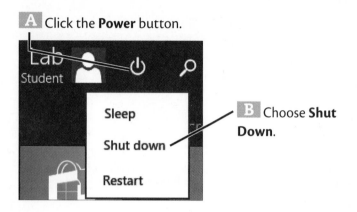

B Choose **Shut Down**.

concepts review

To check your knowledge of the key concepts introduced in this lesson, complete the Concepts Review quiz by choosing the appropriate access option below.

If you are...	Then access the quiz by...
Using eLab	Logging in, choosing Content, and navigating to the Concepts Review quiz for this lesson
Not using eLab	Going to the Student Resource Center (see the inside front cover)

reinforce your skills | ecs-0201

Sign On and Start Windows Programs

In this exercise, you will start programs, switch programs, and arrange program windows.

Start Windows

1 Power on the computer and log in or sign on, depending on your Windows version.

Explore the Windows 8.1 Tablet Desktop

Windows 7 Users: Skip to step 11.

2 Click **Weather**.

The app starts and fills the screen. All Windows 8.1 apps do this.

3 Choose **Allow** if the app asks if it can use your location.

If your location can't be detected, Weather will ask you to enter a location.

4 Right-click anywhere on the screen and click **Places** if you don't see a prompt to enter a location, and then click the **Plus**. Otherwise, go to the next step.

5 Type your city name and then choose your city from the list.

6 Right-click and choose **Places**.

7 Click the **Plus** and then type and choose another city.

Weather adds the city to Places.

8 Click the new city tile. Then right-click and choose **Home**.

9 Tap the **Windows** ⊞ key to display the Start screen.

10 Click the **Desktop** tile.

Start Applications

11 Start the Publisher application:

Windows 7

A Click **Start**.

B Choose **All Programs→Microsoft Office 2013→Publisher 2013**.

Windows 8.1

A Tap **Windows** ⊞.

B Scroll to the right and click the **Publisher 2013** tile if it's visible and then skip to step 12. (Continue with C–D if it isn't visible.)

C Click the Apps button ⊕.

D Find the Microsoft Office 2013 programs and click publisher 2013.

12 Click a publication type and then click **Create**.
Publisher loads a photo album template or creates a new publication.

13 If necessary, **Maximize** ☐ the Publisher window.

14 Search for the Character Map application:

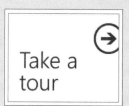

Windows 7

A Click **Start** and type **character** in the Search box.

B Choose **Character Map**.

Windows 8.1

A Display the charms (top-right corner) and choose **Search**.

B Type **character** in the Search box.

C Choose **Character Map**.
The application appears on the Desktop. It helps you find and insert special characters into documents.

15 Search for and start the **Notepad** application.
Notepad lets you type and edit unformatted documents.

Use the Windows Taskbar

16 Click **Notepad** on the taskbar.
Notepad minimizes.

17 **Minimize** ▬ the Character Map.

18 Click **Notepad** on the taskbar.
Notepad returns to the Desktop.

19 Click **Publisher** on the taskbar.
Publisher becomes the active program, covering Notepad.

20 Click **Publisher** on the taskbar again.
Publisher minimizes.

21 Right-click **Publisher** on the taskbar, and then pin it.

22 **Close** ☒ / ☒ Notepad.

23 Make **Publisher** active and then close it. Choose **Don't Save** if asked to save.

24 Activate **Character Map** and then close it.

reinforce your skills | ecs-0202

Multitask with Windows

In this exercise, you will start programs, switch programs, and arrange program windows on the Desktop. You will also switch modes and shut down Windows.

Start Applications

1 If necessary, power on the computer and log in/sign on.

2 Start applications:

Windows 7

A Choose **Start→All Programs→Microsoft Office 2013→PowerPoint 2013** and then click **Blank Presentation**.

B Start **Word 2013** and click **Blank Document**.

C Start **Excel 2013** and click **Blank Workbook**.

Windows 8.1

A If necessary, display the **Start screen** with **Windows** 🪟.

B Click the Apps button 🔽.

C Scroll to the **Microsoft Office 2013** group.

D Choose **PowerPoint 2013** and then click **Blank Presentation**.

E Choose **Start Screen→All Apps→Microsoft Office 2013→Word 2013** and then click **Blank Document**.

F Choose **Start Screen→All Apps→Microsoft Office 2013→Excel 2013** and then click **Blank Workbook**.

Control Desktop Windows

3   **Maximize**  Excel if it doesn't fill the screen.

4   Make the **PowerPoint** window active.

5   Use Alt + Tab to make **Excel** active again.

6   **Minimize** ▬ Excel and PowerPoint, and then **restore** ⯜ Word if it's maximized.

7   Make the **Word** window larger by dragging a corner of the window.

8   Move the **Word** window down by dragging its title bar.

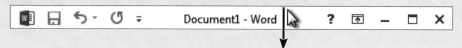

9   Move the **Word** window up by dragging its title bar.

10   Drag **Word's** title bar to the left side of the screen.

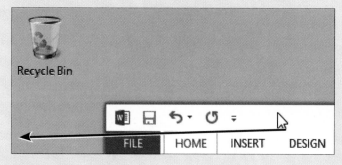

11   Make **PowerPoint** active.

12   **Restore** ⯜ PowerPoint if it's maximized.
You cannot adjust the size and shape of a maximized window.

13   Make **PowerPoint** fill the right half of the screen.

14 Make **Excel** active and then drag its title bar down from the top of the screen.

15 **Close** ☒ Excel. Choose **Don't Save** if asked to save.

Use Sleep Mode

16 Put Windows into Sleep mode:

- **Windows 7:** Choose **Start→Shut Down ▶ menu button→Sleep.**

- **Windows 8.1:** Point at the top-right corner and choose **Settings→Power→Sleep.**

17 Tap any key or move the mouse.
Windows restores power to the computer and monitor.

18 Type your password and tap ⎡Enter⎤.

Shut Down Windows

Before you shut down the computer, it's a good practice to close all program windows.

19 **Close** ☒ PowerPoint. Choose **Don't Save** if asked to save.

20 **Close** ☒ Word.

21 Shut down Windows:

- **Windows 7:** Choose **Start→Shut Down.**

- **Windows 8.1:** Click the **Power** button, then choose **Shut Down.**

Windows goes through its shutdown routine. Sometimes it installs system updates during the shutdown process and, if so, you may see a message.

apply your skills | ecs-0201

Sign On to Windows and Start Programs

You've just purchased a new computer! In this exercise, you will find various applications and set up the taskbar for easy access to those you'll use most often.

Start Windows

1   Log in or sign on, as applicable.

Explore the Windows Desktop

2   **Windows 8.1 Only:** Start **Internet Explorer** as a full-screen Tablet app (not on the traditional Desktop).

Start Applications

3   Start **Word 2013**, **Excel 2013**, and **Paint**.
It doesn't matter how the program windows are arranged on the screen, as long as all three programs are running.

4   Pin **Paint** to the taskbar.

5   Close **Paint**.
Paint's taskbar button remains, because you pinned it there.

6   Start the Snipping Tool:
The Snipping Tool, which comes standard with Windows, lets you create pictures of the screen.

■ **Windows 7:** Choose **Start→All Programs→Accessories→Snipping Tool**.

■ **Windows 8.1:** Display the **Start** screen and click the **Apps** button. Then click **Snipping Tool** in Windows Accessories.

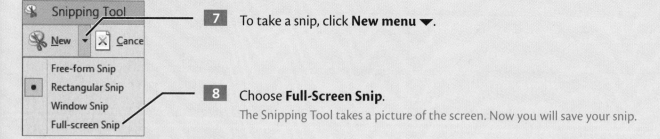

7   To take a snip, click **New menu** ▼.

8   Choose **Full-Screen Snip**.
The Snipping Tool takes a picture of the screen. Now you will save your snip.

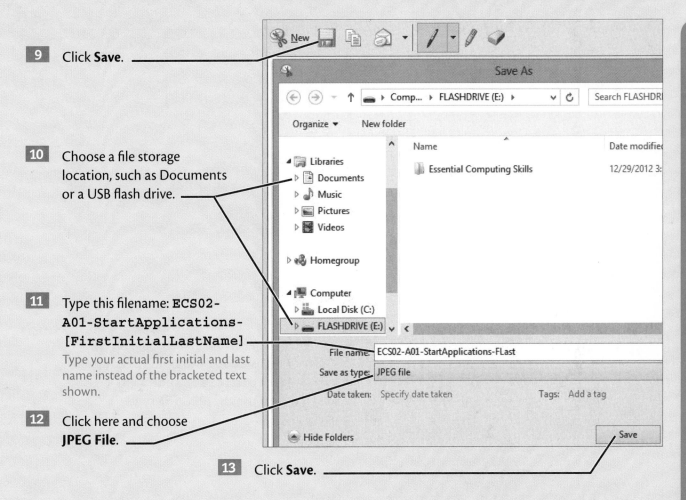

9 Click **Save**.

10 Choose a file storage location, such as Documents or a USB flash drive.

11 Type this filename: **ECS02-A01-StartApplications-[FirstInitialLastName]**
Type your actual first initial and last name instead of the bracketed text shown.

12 Click here and choose **JPEG File**.

13 Click **Save**.

14 Submit your snipped screen based on the guidelines provided by your instructor.

---

apply your skills | ecs-0202

Multitask with Windows

You are working on a project and need to multitask. In this exercise, you will start the applications you'll use and arrange them to suit your needs.

Get Started

1 Log in or sign on, as applicable.

2 Start **Word 2013**, **Excel 2013**, **PowerPoint 2013**, and **WordPad**. Create a blank file in each.

Control Desktop Windows

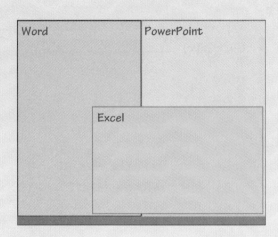

3   Arrange the program windows like this:

- **Word:** Left half of the screen

- **PowerPoint:** Right half of the screen

- **Excel:** Overlapping Word and PowerPoint

- **WordPad:** Minimized

4   Start the **Snipping Tool** and take a full-screen snip.

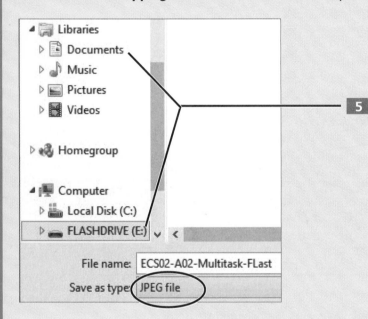

5   Save the snipped screen to a file storage location (such as the Documents folder or a USB flash drive) as **ECS02-A02-Multitask-[FirstInitialLastName]**. Be sure to use the **JPEG File** type.

Use Sleep and Other Modes

6   Put Windows into **Locked** mode. Then, unlock Windows.

7   Put Windows into **Sleep** mode. Then, bring Windows out of Sleep mode.

Shut Down Windows

8   Shut down **Windows**.

9   Submit your snipped screen based on the guidelines provided by your instructor.

Sign On, Start Programs, and Multitask

You just purchased a new computer! You start some programs you'll use often and practice arranging them on the screen in different ways.

Start Windows

1 Log in or sign on, as applicable.

Explore the Windows Desktop

2 **Windows 8.1 Only:** Start **Pictures** as a full-screen Tablet app (not on the traditional Desktop).

Start Applications

3 Start **Word 2013**, **Publisher 2013**, **Sticky Notes**, and **Calculator**. Create a blank file in the first two.
It doesn't matter how the program windows are arranged on the screen, as long as all three programs are running.

4 Pin **Sticky Notes** to the taskbar. Then, close **Sticky Notes**.
The Sticky Notes' taskbar button remains, because you pinned it there.

5 Start the Snipping Tool:
The Snipping Tool, which comes standard with Windows, lets you create pictures of the screen.

- **Windows 7:** Choose **Start→Accessories→Snipping Tool**.

- **Windows 8.1:** Display the **Start** screen and click the **Apps** button. Then click **Snipping Tool** in Windows Accessories.

6 To take a snip, click **New menu** ▼.

7 Choose **Full-Screen Snip.**
The Snipping Tool takes a picture of the screen. Now you will save your snip.

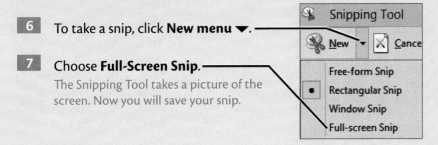

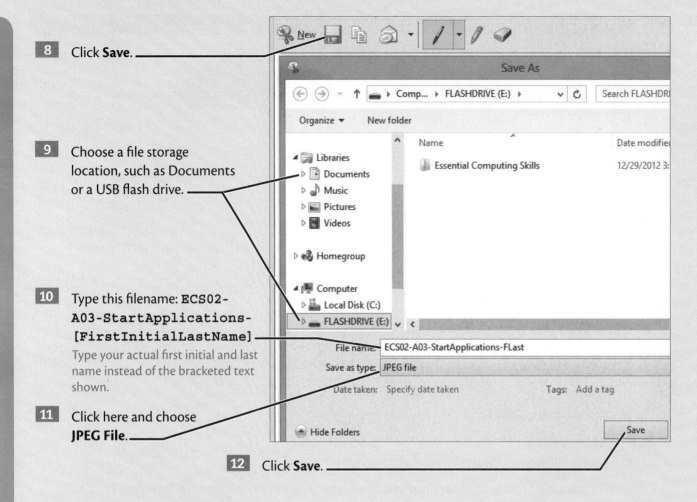

8 Click **Save**.

9 Choose a file storage location, such as Documents or a USB flash drive.

10 Type this filename: **ECS02-A03-StartApplications-[FirstInitialLastName]**
Type your actual first initial and last name instead of the bracketed text shown.

11 Click here and choose **JPEG File**.

12 Click **Save**.

Control Desktop Windows

13 Arrange the program windows like this:

- **Word:** Left half of the screen

- **Publisher:** Right half of the screen

- **Calculator:** Bottom-left corner of the screen, visible on top of the Word window

- **Sticky Notes:** Minimized (you will need to restart this program)

14 Start the **Snipping Tool** and take a full-screen snip.

15 Save your snip to the same location you used earlier. Name the file **ECS02-A04-Multitask-[FirstInitialLastName]** and use **JPEG File** as the type.

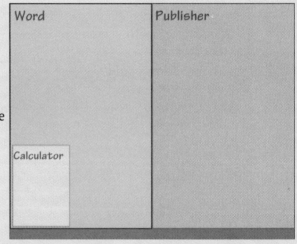

Using Sleep and Other Modes

16 Put Windows into **Locked** mode. Then, unlock Windows.

17 Put Windows into **Sleep** mode. Then, bring Windows out of Sleep mode.

Shutting Down Windows

18 Shut down **Windows**.

19 Submit your snipped screens according to the guidelines provided by your instructor.

learning projects | ecs-0201

Make the Desktop Work for You

In this exercise, you will arrange program windows and taskbar buttons to accomplish a task efficiently.

- Define some activity that will require multitasking to accomplish efficiently. Write down at least three applications you'd want to use regularly for this activity.
- Start the applications you'll need for the activity. Pin applications to the taskbar and/or Start menu/screen so you can start them easily.
- Arrange the application windows so it's easy to switch between them for the activity.
- Take a full-screen snip and save it as `ECS02-L01-Desktop-[FirstInitialLastName]`.

Submit your work based on the guidelines provided by your instructor.

learning projects | ecs-0202

Make the PC Easier to Use

In this exercise, you will help a coworker find and start Ease of Access tools.

- Open the Ease of Access Center. You may need to perform a search to find this. It explains and offers access to various accessibility features built into Windows. Make a snip of the Ease of Access Center and name it `ECS02-L02-EaseOfAccess-[FirstInitialLastName]`.
- Start the onscreen keyboard. Try typing on it using the mouse. Move it to a convenient place on the screen. Make a snip of the onscreen keyboard and name it `ECS02-L02-OnscreenKeyboard-[FirstInitialLastName]`.
- Start the Magnifier app. Try magnifying a portion of the screen and take a full screen snip of the entire screen. Save your snip as `ECS02-L02-Magnified-[FirstInitialLastName]`.

Submit your work based on the guidelines provided by your instructor.

Windows 7

3 Managing Files

Skills YOU Will Learn

- Browse files on the computer
- Open files from a folder window
- Create new folders
- Rename files and folders
- Copy and move files
- Delete and restore files with the Recycle Bin
- Back up files on a USB flash drive

in this lesson

When you begin working with a computer, you will have just a few files to keep track of. As your use of computers grows, so will the number of files you must manage. After several months, you may have more than one hundred files; after a year, hundreds more. Windows gives you a very effective tool for managing files: folders. With folders, you can group related files. You can even create folders inside of other folders. In this lesson, you will find files, organize them into folders, and move them from one location to another.

Creating Folders for a New Semester

Esmeralda is taking five courses at her community college, one of which will require her to submit a term paper. In preparation for the work, Esmeralda creates folders on her computer to organize files as she does her research. She also creates a folder for each of her classes—as well as folders inside the class folders to further organize her files. For example, she creates Project folders for the different word processor documents she will create. Esmeralda also creates a Term Paper folder to hold files, web pages, and notes related to her large research paper. She even creates an Old Stuff folder (not shown below) for everything she thinks she doesn't need but does not yet want to delete.

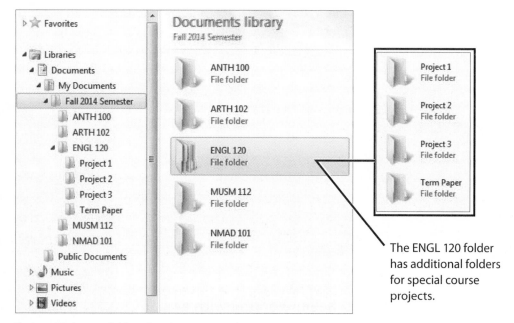

The ENGL 120 folder has additional folders for special course projects.

Esmerelda's new folders for the semester's courses.

What Is File Management?

File management is the organization of your work and entertainment data for easy access and security. The convenience of digital devices such as cameras, smartphones, and tablets makes the accumulation of large numbers of files inevitable. The consequences of lost files (or files you simply can't find) make file-management skills essential.

File-Management Tasks

To perform file management effectively, there are several tasks you will (or should) undertake regularly.

- **Finding files:** Look for files in various storage locations. Sometimes you'll need to find a file you don't recall the exact location of. For example, a paper or report you worked on six months ago.
- **Organizing files:** Organize files into logical groups. The primary tool for organizing files is folders. For example, organizing files for a college course or work project.
- **Moving and copying files:** Move/copy files to reorganize and share them. For example, copying files to a USB flash drive to share them with someone.
- **Backing up files:** Regularly back up important files. For example, digital photos, tax records, and ongoing coursework. Increasingly, these backups can be made automatically online, but sometimes you'll want a secure local backup copy as well.

Secure storage of digital photos is a good example of file management in action. Ten years from now, the program used to view or tag these photos may not exist, but a rational folder organization will.

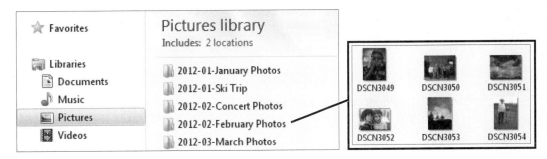

Folders organize photos for the ages.

Browsing Files

 Video

Browsing to locate files is a key skill. You can accumulate a lot of files as you use a computer. If you have a digital camera, for example, you can end up with thousands of photo files within a year. Being a student requires the creation of numerous files each semester. There will be times when you need to locate a file you haven't used in months. Windows Explorer is the primary tool to locate files on your computer, flash drives, and cloud storage.

File Explorer

The File Explorer lets you navigate to various parts of the computer system, for example, to a specific folder, USB flash drive, or other storage location. Take care not to confuse the *File Explorer* with *Internet Explorer*. Internet Explorer is a program for browsing web pages, not the computer system.

 In Windows 7 the *File Explorer* **was called** *Windows Explorer*. **In these lessons, the Windows 8.1** *File Explorer* **name will be used instead.**

Forward and Back buttons to navigate

A toolbar for file-management tasks

Links to frequently browsed locations

The address bar displays the current location you are browsing

A box to search for files

Windows 7 File Explorer.

develop your skills | ecs-0301

Open File Explorer

Guide Me In this exercise, you will open File Explorer and view the lesson folder.

Before You Begin: Download the student exercise files from the Student Resource Center. Instructions for downloading the files are included there.

1 If necessary, start the computer and log on to **Windows**.

2 Carefully insert your USB flash drive, if you're using one as your file storage location. Otherwise, skip to step 4.

3 **Close** ▬X▬ AutoPlay if it appears.

4 Open the File Explorer and display your file storage location:

USB Flash Drive

A Click the **File Explorer.**

B Click **Computer.**

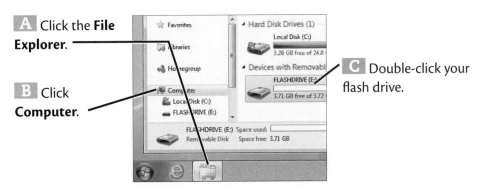

C Double-click your flash drive.

Documents Folder

A Click the **File Explorer.**

B Click **Libraries.**

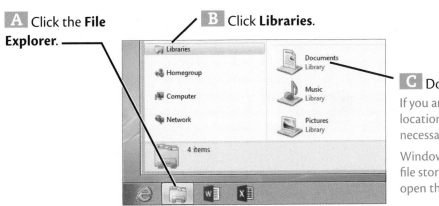

C Double-click **Documents.**
If you are using a different storage location, ask your instructor for help if necessary.

Windows displays the folders in your file storage location. Now you will open the ecs-L03 folder for this lesson.

5 Maximize the window, if necessary.

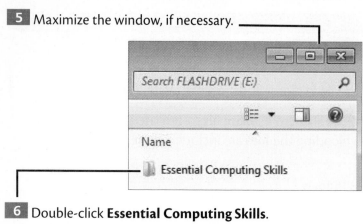

6 Double-click **Essential Computing Skills**.

A list of folders for course lessons appears.

7 Double-click **ecs-L03**.

Windows displays the contents of the ecs-L03 folder.

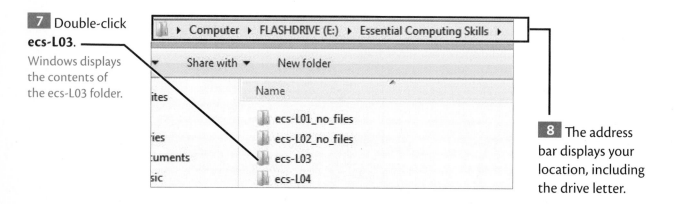

8 The address bar displays your location, including the drive letter.

Changing the View

You can change the way files and folders are displayed in the File Explorer window. For example, you can display files as large thumbnails or lists.

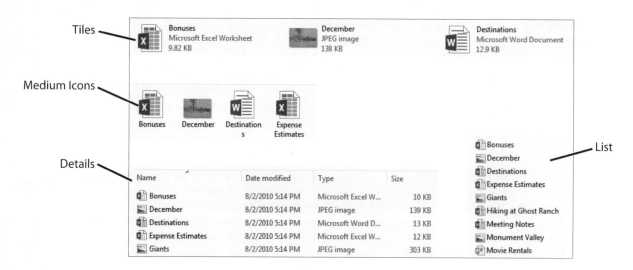

a closer look

The File Storage Hierarchy

 Video   Windows uses a flexible, four-level hierarchy to organize files and folders, as listed here.

File Storage Hierarchy

Level	Definition	Examples
Drive	A physical place in which you store files.	• Internal hard drive • USB flash drive • Cloud drive
Library	A collection of folders and files on a local or network drive. Libraries can contain items from more than one drive.	• Documents • Music • Pictures
Folder	An electronic location in which you store groups of related files and folders.	• Folder to store all files for an application program • Folder to store files you type for a project
File	A collection of computer data that has some common purpose.	• Letter you've typed • Photo you've taken

About Libraries

Libraries are collections of related groups of files and folders located on one or more storage locations, for example, files on the local hard drive and on cloud storage. Windows starts you with four basic libraries; you can also create new libraries.

Each library has a personal folder.

Files in Public folders are shared with everyone who uses this computer.

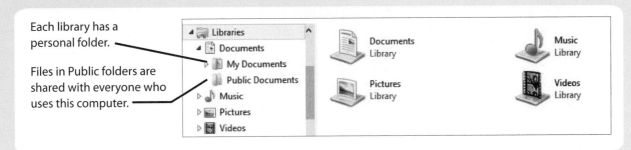

Windows sets up four basic libraries for each username. Each library can contain one or more folders.

Opening Files

 Video

When you double-click a file's icon, Windows launches the program used to create or edit that file and displays it in the program window. This is a convenient way to start working with a file after you find it.

Creating Favorites Locations

The *Favorites* section of the File Explorer window has links to frequently browsed locations. You can add your own links to this list.

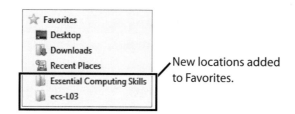

New locations added to Favorites.

develop your skills | ecs-0302

Open Document Files

 Guide Me

In this exercise, you will open a file in your lesson folder. You will also add new locations to Favorites.

1 Change the view of files:

A Click the **menu button**.

B Choose **Large Icons**.

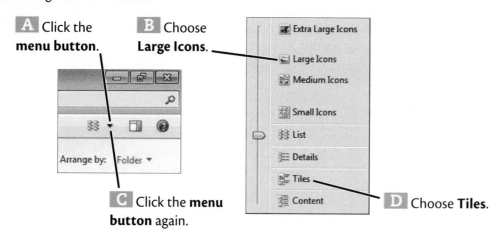

C Click the **menu button** again.

D Choose **Tiles**.

2 Examine the files in the File Explorer:

A Notice the different icons for specific file types (Word, Excel, etc.).

B This application will open the file.

C Pictures may show a thumbnail.

Bonuses
Microsoft Excel Worksheet
9.82 KB

Destinations
Microsoft Word Document
12.9 KB

December
JPEG image
138 KB

Expense Estimates
Microsoft Excel Worksheet
11.0 KB

3 To open the **Meeting Notes** file, double-click the icon.

Windows starts Word and displays the file. Windows knows to start Word because Word was used to create the file.

Giants
JPEG image
302 KB

Meeting Notes
Microsoft Word Document
18.0 KB

Movie Rentals
Microsoft PowerPoint Presentation
66.0 KB

4 Click **File** on the Ribbon.

FILE   HOME   INSERT

Export

Close

Account

Options

5 Choose **Close**. Choose **Don't Save** if prompted to save changes.

The Meeting Notes file closes, but Word remains open.

6 Close **Word**.

The ecs-L03 folder window is visible again. Now you will add the folder to Favorites.

?   🔼   —   🗗   ⊗

Sign in 👤

7 Click **Back**.

8 Click this triangle if items aren't displayed below Favorites.

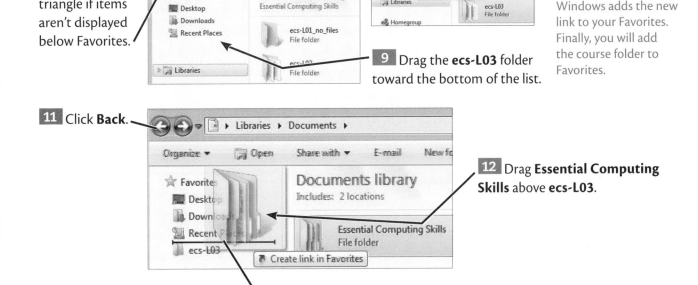

▶ Libraries ▶ Documents ▶ Essential Computin

Organize ▾   Share with ▾   New folder

▷ ☆ Favorites
   Desktop
   Downloads
   Recent Places

▷ Libraries

Documents library
Essential Computing Skills

ecs-L01_no_files
File folder

ecs-L03
File folder

9 Drag the **ecs-L03** folder toward the bottom of the list.

Documents library
Essential Computing Skill

ecs-L01_no_files
File folder

ecs-L03
File folder

Create link in Favorites

Libraries

Homegroup

10 Release the mouse button when a bar appears.

Windows adds the new link to your Favorites. Finally, you will add the course folder to Favorites.

11 Click **Back**.

▶ Libraries ▶ Documents ▶

Organize ▾   Open   Share with ▾   E-mail   New fo

☆ Favorites
   Desktop
   Downloads
   Recent Places
   ecs-L03

Documents library
Includes: 2 locations

Essential Computing Skills
File folder

Create link in Favorites

12 Drag **Essential Computing Skills** above **ecs-L03**.

13 Release the mouse button when the bar is here.

Opening Recently Used Files

 Video

Applications such as Word and Excel can display your most recently used files. If you recall the program you used to create it, this is often a more convenient way to locate a file you've worked on.

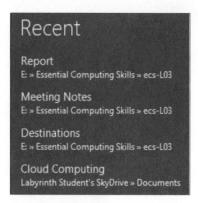

Word displays recently saved files.

Searching for Files

If you recall the name or part of the name of a file, Windows can search for it. You can limit a search to a specific folder, or search the entire computer system.

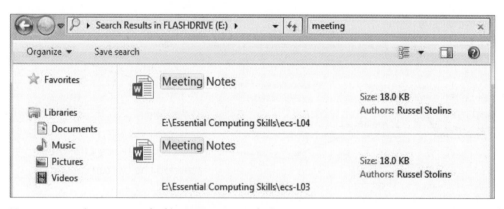

You can search on parts of a filename in specific locations.

About Drive Letters

Windows identifies each storage drive on the computer with a *drive letter*. When you attach a USB flash or external drive to the computer, Windows assigns it the next available drive letter. Thus, your USB flash drive may have a different drive letter on different computers. This makes no difference in terms of the files you store on the drive.

Cloud Storage

Depending on the computer's configuration, you may see a Dropbox, OneDrive, or some other sort of cloud-based storage drive in Favorites. Because they aren't physical locations, these drives do not receive drive letters.

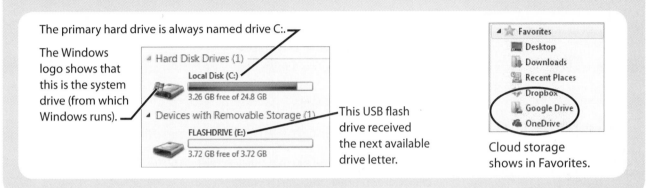

The primary hard drive is always named drive C:.

The Windows logo shows that this is the system drive (from which Windows runs).

This USB flash drive received the next available drive letter.

Cloud storage shows in Favorites.

---

develop your skills | ecs-0303

Find Files

 Guide Me   In this exercise, you will open a file in your lesson folder. You will also search for and open a file.

1 Display the **ecs-L03** folder using the link in Favorites.

2 Double-click the **Report** document.

Word displays the document.

3 Click the FILE tab.

4 To open another document, choose **Open**.

5 Choose **Recent Documents**.

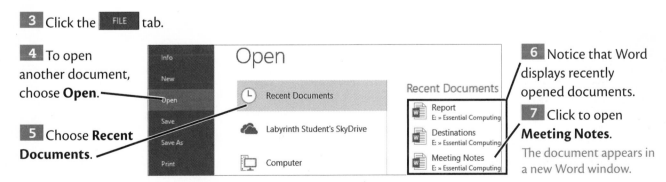

6 Notice that Word displays recently opened documents.

7 Click to open **Meeting Notes**.

The document appears in a new Word window.

8 **Close** ☒ Word. Choose **Don't Save** if asked to save.

9 **Close** ☒ Word again. Choose **Don't Save** if asked to save.
Word closes the Report document.

10 Use ⌐Alt⌐ + ⌐Tab⌐ to display the **ecs-L03** folder.

11 Search for a file:

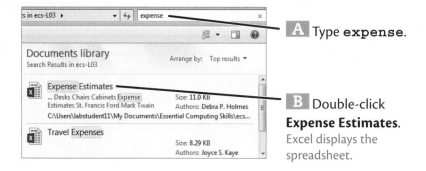

A Type **expense**.

B Double-click
Expense Estimates.
Excel displays the
spreadsheet.

12 **Close** ☒ Excel. Choose **Don't Save** if asked to save the file.

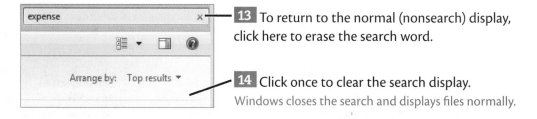

13 To return to the normal (nonsearch) display,
click here to erase the search word.

14 Click once to clear the search display.
Windows closes the search and displays files normally.

Creating Folders

 Video

A *folder* is an electronic location where you store groups of related files and folders. Folders are important tools for organizing files. Over time, you can accumulate hundreds and thousands of files. If you create new folders as you need them, you'll always feel well-organized.

Folders help you divide your files into easy-to-find groups. What if you could only view your files in a single, long list? This would be similar to finding a book in a library that had only one long bookshelf. You could find the book eventually, but it would no doubt take you a long time.

Folder Hierarchy

Folders form a hierarchy on a storage drive or Documents window. You can create new folders inside of other folders to add multiple layers to your file organization.

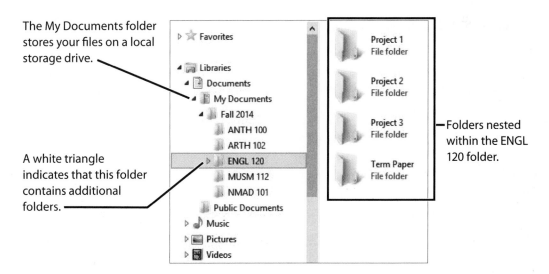

The My Documents folder stores your files on a local storage drive.

A white triangle indicates that this folder contains additional folders.

Folders nested within the ENGL 120 folder.

Create Folders

Guide Me   In this exercise, you will create six folders on your file storage location.

Before you begin, make sure the ecs-L03 folder is on the screen.

1 Return to the base level of your file storage location:

- **USB flash drive:** Click your flash drive.

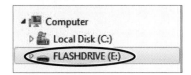

- **My Documents:** Click **My Documents**.

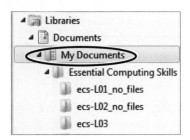

If you are using a different storage location, ask your instructor for help if necessary.

Now that the location where you wish to create a new folder is displayed, you can begin. The figures in the rest of this exercise show the My Documents location. Your screen may display some other location.

2 Create a new folder:

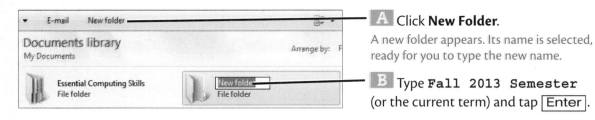

A Click **New Folder**.

A new folder appears. Its name is selected, ready for you to type the new name.

B Type **Fall 2013 Semester** (or the current term) and tap ⎡Enter⎤.

3 Double-click your new folder. It's empty now, but you will place files in it later.

4 Click the view menu ▼ button and choose **Tiles**.

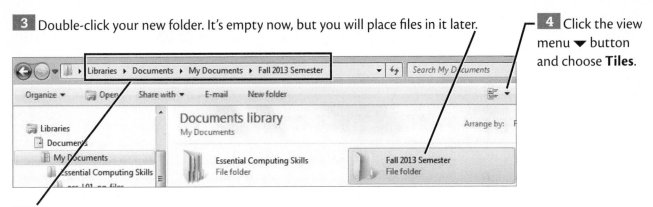

5 Notice that the address bar displays the folder you are viewing.

Now you will create more folders within the semester folder.

6 Click **New Folder**.

7 Name the folder **ANTH 100**.

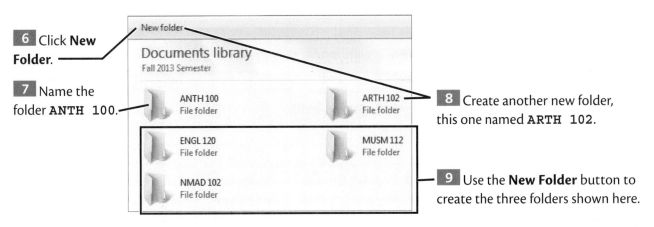

8 Create another new folder, this one named **ARTH 102**.

9 Use the **New Folder** button to create the three folders shown here.

10 Double-click the **ENGL 120** folder.

Notice the folder name in the address bar. The new project folders you create next will be placed within the ENGL 120 folder.

11 Click **New Folder**.

12 Name the folder **Project 1**.

13 Use **New Folder** to create three more new folders with these names.

14 Go **Back** to the semester folder.

Windows displays the course folders.

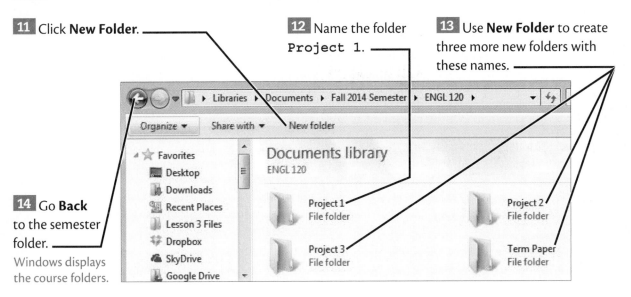

Moving and Copying Files

 Video

Windows lets you move and copy files from one drive to another and from one folder to another using several techniques. This lesson will teach two methods.

- **Copy and Paste:** Copies files into a new location
- **Cut and Paste:** Moves files to a new location

Selecting Multiple Files for Commands

You can move and copy a single file or dozens of files with the same command. Before you give the Cut or Copy command, select the file(s) you wish to be affected by the command. To select a single file, simply click it. The two easiest methods for selecting multiple files use the Ctrl and Shift keys. Combine these two techniques as you like.

You can select nonconsecutive files for Cut and Copy commands. In this example, only picture files are selected.

Selecting Files with Ctrl and Shift	
Method	**How It Works**
Ctrl+click	Adds a new item to your selection with each click, or deselects any already selected item
Shift+click	Selects all the items between two clicks

develop your skills | ecs-0305

Copy and Move Files

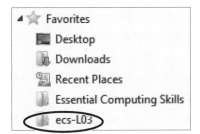 **Guide Me**   In this exercise, you will use the Cut, Copy, and Paste commands to move files.

1 Navigate to the **ecs-L03** folder from your Favorites list.

```
▲ ☆ Favorites
    🖥 Desktop
    📥 Downloads
    📋 Recent Places
    📁 Essential Computing Skills
    📁 ecs-L03
```

2 Select and copy all files in the ecs-L03 folder:

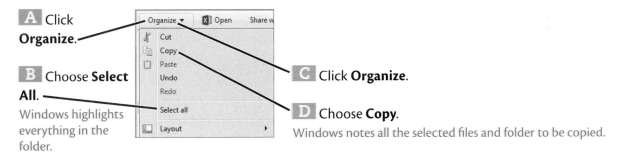

A Click **Organize**.

B Choose **Select All**. Windows highlights everything in the folder.

C Click **Organize**.

D Choose **Copy**. Windows notes all the selected files and folder to be copied.

3 Click the **Back** button.

4 Windows jumps you back to the previous (semester) folder.

5 Click **Organize** and then choose **Paste**.

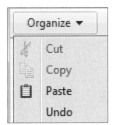

Windows pastes the files and folder you copied in step 2. Now you will cut a file for pasting.

6 Click once (do not double-click) **Bonuses**.

7 Choose **Organize→Cut**.

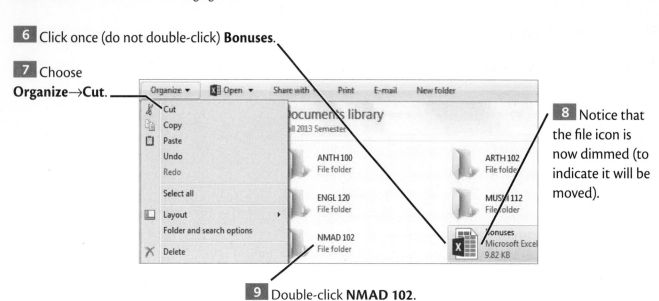

8 Notice that the file icon is now dimmed (to indicate it will be moved).

9 Double-click **NMAD 102**.

Now that you are viewing the destination, you can give the Paste command.

10 Choose **Organize→Paste**.

Windows pastes the file into the folder.

11 Click **Back** to confirm that the file was moved.

Notice that a different file shifted up to replace the moved Bonuses file. Also notice that a file icon now appears as part of the icon for NMAD 102.

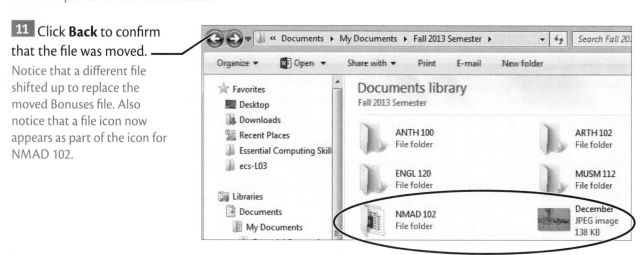

12 Select and cut multiple files:

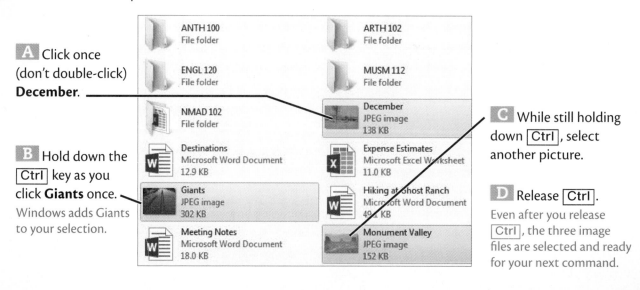

A Click once (don't double-click) **December**.

B Hold down the Ctrl key as you click **Giants** once.
Windows adds Giants to your selection.

C While still holding down Ctrl, select another picture.

D Release Ctrl.
Even after you release Ctrl, the three image files are selected and ready for your next command.

13 Choose **Organize→Cut** and notice that the file icons are dimmed.

14 Double-click **ARTH 102** and then choose **Organize→Paste**.

The moved files appear in the window.

15 Go **back** to the semester folder.

Notice that the three image files are no longer in the semester folder.

Renaming Files and Folders

Video

There may be times you'll want to rename a file or folder. You can rename files from the File Explorer window or from within a program. For example, if you save a file with a default name like Document1 or Workbook1, you'll want to rename it. Windows gives you plenty of flexibility for creating filenames.

File-Naming Rules

There are two important rules for naming Windows files.

- **Length:** Filenames can be a maximum of 260 characters.
- **Special characters:** Many special characters are permitted in filenames, such as ( ) **& + −** . These characters can't be used: **\ / ? : * " > < |**.

Changing a Filename from Within a Program

You may want to change the name of a file while you are working on it. For example, you can open a previously written letter, and then change its name to create a new version of the same letter to someone else.

Rename Files and a Folder

Guide Me   In this exercise, you will rename files and folders using three methods.

Before you begin, make sure the semester folder is on the screen.

1 Double-click the **NMAD 102** folder.

2 Right-click (don't left-click) **Bonuses**.

3 Choose **Rename**.
Windows highlights the filename, ready for you to rename it.

4 Type `Bonuses Jan-June` and tap Enter.
The new filename replaces the old. Now you'll use the click-pause method to rename a file.

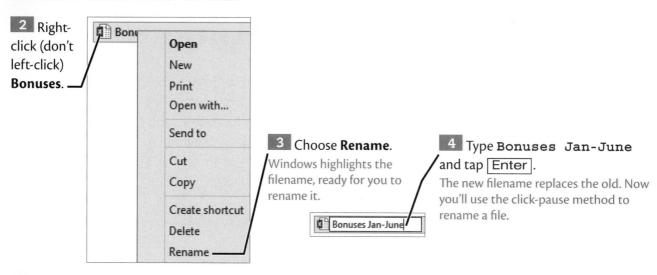

5 Click a clear area of the window to deselect the file.

6 Click once on the **Bonuses Jan-June** filename (not the icon).

7 Pause one second and click again.
The filename is highlighted for editing.

8 Tap the ← key until the *insertion point* is blinking to the left of the B in *Bonuses*.
Arrow keys move the insertion point without deleting any part of the filename.

9 Type `Company`, tap Spacebar, and tap Enter.

10 Go **back** to the semester folder.

11 Rename the **MUSM 112** folder to `MUSM 115`.

12 Double-click the **Meeting Notes** document.

13 Click  FILE .

14 Save the document with a new name:

A Choose **Save As**.

B Choose **Computer**.

C Choose the **Current Folder**.
Windows displays the Save As dialog box. Now you will change the filename and save the new document.

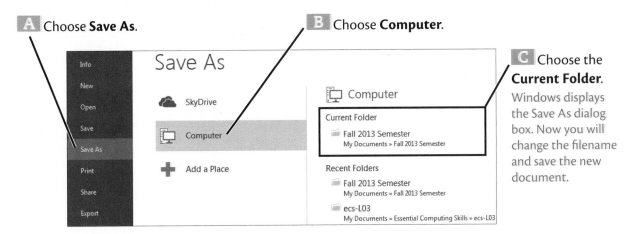

15 Click at the end of the filename, then type a dash (–) and add today's date, including a comma.

16 Click **Save**.
Word may display a prompt about the file format.

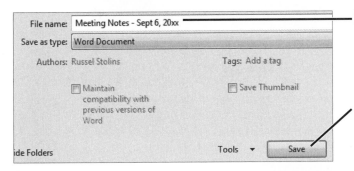

17 If the prompt appears, place a checkmark here and click **OK**.

18 Notice the new filename displayed in the title bar.

19 **Close** ✕ Meeting Notes. Choose **Don't Save** if prompted to save the file.

20 **Close** ✕ Report. Choose **Don't Save** if prompted to save the file.

Deleting Files and Folders

Video

You can delete unneeded files and folders to free up space on a storage drive. When you delete a folder, any other folders and files inside that folder are deleted as well. However, the Delete command doesn't necessarily mean erase. Windows takes steps to help avoid the loss of files you may not have meant to delete.

What Happens to Deleted Files and Folders?

Windows does not physically erase a deleted file from the hard drive. Instead, the file is placed in the Recycle Bin. (Exception: See the Warning below.) The Recycle Bin holds the deleted files until you give a command to empty it, or until it runs out of the space allotted to store deleted files.

Recently deleted files and folders reside in the Recycle Bin.

Files and folders deleted from *USB flash drives* or a network drive *are not* sent to the Recycle Bin! They are *immediately deleted* when you issue the Delete command.

Restoring Files and Folders

If you delete files or folders from a local storage drive, you can usually restore them to their previous locations from the Recycle Bin. For example, you might accidentally delete some photo files and realize your mistake. You could look for these files in the Recycle Bin and restore them.

Delete Files and a Folder

 Guide Me In this exercise, you will delete some files. Then you will delete a folder and view the contents of the Recycle Bin.

Before you begin, make sure the semester file is open.

1 Double-click the **ARTH 102** folder.

Windows displays the folder contents. It holds three pictures you moved previously.

2 Select files with ⌈Shift⌋+click:

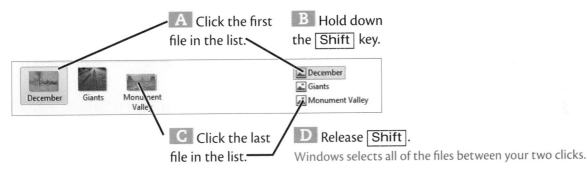

A Click the first file in the list.

B Hold down the ⌈Shift⌋ key.

C Click the last file in the list.

D Release ⌈Shift⌋.
Windows selects all of the files between your two clicks.

3 Tap ⌈Delete⌋ on the keyboard.

Windows may ask you to confirm the Delete command. This is a safeguard to protect against accidental deletions.

4 Choose **Yes** to confirm the deletion, if necessary.

The files disappear from the right panel and have been sent to the Recycle Bin. The folder is now empty.

 If you deleted the picture files from a USB flash drive, the files are not sent to the Recycle Bin. (You still have copies of them in the ecs-L03 folder, however.)

5 Go **back** ⬅ to the semester folder.

6 Delete a folder with the right-click method:

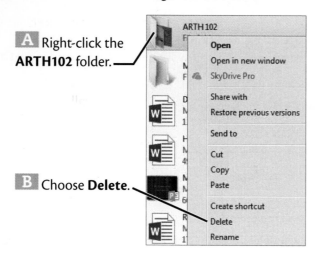

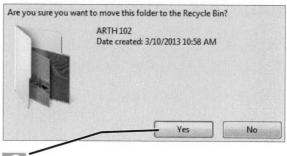

A Right-click the **ARTH102** folder.

B Choose **Delete**.

C Choose **Yes** if asked for confirmation.

The ARTH 102 folder disappears and is moved to the Recycle Bin. (Exception: The folder is not in the Recycle Bin if it was deleted from a USB flash drive.)

7 **Close** ☒ the semester folder window if you use a USB flash drive to store your exercise files. Leave the window open if you store your files in the Documents folder.

> ⚠️ **NOTE** **Skip the rest of this exercise if you use a USB flash drive as your file storage location. Files deleted from USB flash drives *are not* sent to the Recycle Bin.**

Now you will view your files from within the Recycle Bin. Any file in the Recycle Bin can be restored (undeleted) to the location from which it was deleted.

8 **Minimize** ▬ the semester folder.

9 Double-click the **Recycle Bin** on the Desktop.

Windows displays the Recycle Bin. Depending on the type of storage location you deleted from, the three files deleted in step 3 may be visible. Additional files may also be there.

10 Attempt to open **Giants** with a double click.

The file does not open, but a Properties window does. You can't open files in the Recycle Bin.

11 Click **Cancel** on the Properties window.

Emptying Files from the Recycle Bin

 Video

Files located in the Recycle Bin are permanently deleted from your computer when you issue an Empty Recycle Bin command, or automatically when the Recycle Bin runs out of space to keep deleted files. Depending on your computer's configuration, the Recycle Bin is set to store a certain number of files. Once that limit is reached, the oldest files in the Recycle Bin are automatically and permanently deleted to make room for additional files.

Restoring Files from the Recycle Bin

Files cannot be opened if they are located in the Recycle Bin. If you decide you need a file you previously deleted, and it hasn't been permanently deleted from the Recycle Bin, you can restore the file to its original location by right-clicking the file and choosing Restore from the pop-up menu. The Recycle Bin also has a Restore All Items command to restore all files it presently contains.

Recovering Accidentally Deleted Files

If you accidentally empty one or more files or folders from the Recycle Bin, you may still be able to recover them. However, you should not try to do this yourself. Instead, get assistance from an information technology (IT) professional. IT experts have special software that may be able to recover some or all of the lost files.

If you need help recovering files, don't use the drive again until the recovery attempt is made.

Restore Files and Folders

Guide Me   In this exercise, you will restore the files and folders you deleted in the previous exercise.

 NOTE   **Skip this exercise if you use a USB flash drive as your file storage location. Items deleted from a flash drive aren't sent to the Recycle Bin.**

1 Double-click the **Recycle Bin** icon on the Desktop if the Recycle Bin window is not open.

2 Select files in the Recycle Bin:

Your Recycle Bin may have more items, but we are only concerned with the files deleted in the previous exercise.

A Click the **December** file.

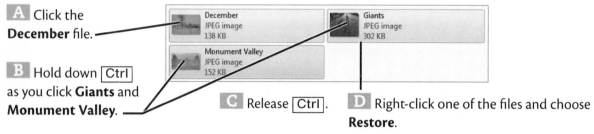

B Hold down Ctrl as you click **Giants** and **Monument Valley**.

C Release Ctrl.

D Right-click one of the files and choose **Restore**.

The files disappear from the right panel as Windows restores them to their original location.

3 **Close** the Recycle Bin.

4 Click to make the semester folder active.

Notice that the ARTH 102 folder has reappeared. It was recreated when you restored the picture files that were deleted from it.

5 Double-click to open the **ARTH 102** folder.

The three restored picture files are visible.

6 **Close** the ARTH 102 folder window.

The Windows Desktop is now empty.

Backing Up Flash Drives

 Video

It is critical to *back up* your flash drive regularly. USB flash drives are extremely compact and convenient. They are also easily lost! The last thing you want is to lose an entire semester's work on your flash drive. The best way to avoid a loss is to make regular backups of your flash drive onto your computer's hard drive, or onto some form of cloud storage. Then, at most, you might lose a day or two of work—but not weeks or months.

Make a backup of your coursework files at least once a week, or even more often.

Storing Backups

Creating a special folder in your Documents folder for flash drive backups is a great idea. That way the backup is easy to find. You could even rename the backup folder with the date you made the backup. This can help you keep track of how recently you backed up your files. Or you can create an "A" and a "B" backup, alternating between the two. This provides extra protection against the loss of a file through corruption or an accidental overwriting.

Flash Drive Backup A
File folder

Flash Drive Backup B
File folder

An example of two sets of flash drive backups.

---

develop your skills | ecs-0309

Back Up Flash Drive Files

 Guide Me

In this exercise, you will copy all the files from your USB flash drive to a hard drive.

Skip this exercise if you are not using a USB flash drive.

1 If necessary, carefully insert your USB flash drive into a USB port.

2 Click the **File Explorer**.

3 Double-click **Computer** if necessary, to display drives below it.

4 Double-click your flash drive.

5 Click **Organize** and choose **Select All**.

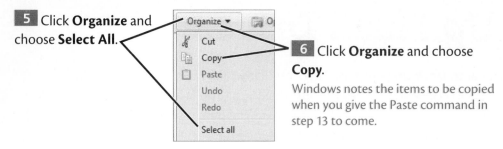

6 Click **Organize** and choose **Copy**.

Windows notes the items to be copied when you give the Paste command in step 13 to come.

7 If necessary, scroll up.

8 Choose **Libraries**.

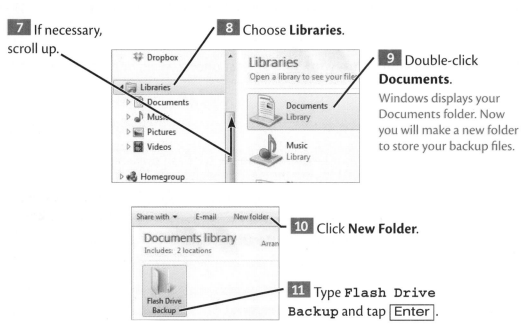

9 Double-click **Documents**.

Windows displays your Documents folder. Now you will make a new folder to store your backup files.

10 Click **New Folder**.

11 Type Flash Drive Backup and tap Enter.

12 Double-click to open the new **Flash Drive Backup** folder.

Now that you are at the destination, you can paste the copied files.

13 Choose **Organize→Paste** from the toolbar (or press Ctrl + V on the keyboard).

All of the files and folders from your flash drive appear in the backup folder.

14 Go **back** to the Documents folder.

Your Flash Drive Backup folder appears in the file/folder list. If you are studying on a public computer, you should delete your files from the Documents folder.

 Skip the rest of this exercise if the files in your Documents folder will remain private. (Ask your instructor if you are unsure.)

15 Delete a folder:

A Make sure the **Flash Drive Backup** folder is selected.

B Tap Delete .

C Choose **Yes** to confirm the deletion.

16 **Close** ▬ X ▬ the Documents window.

17 Empty the Recycle Bin:

A Double-click the **Recycle Bin**.

B Click **Empty the Recycle Bin**.

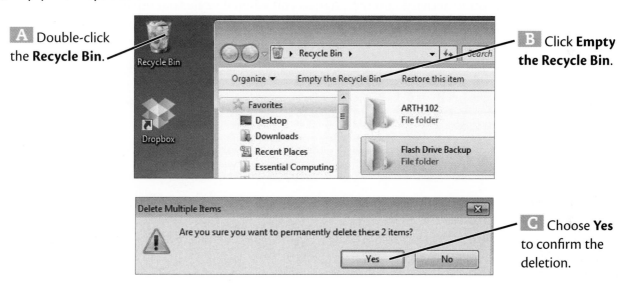

C Choose **Yes** to confirm the deletion.

18 **Close** ▬ X ▬ the Recycle Bin.

Safely Removing Hardware

 Video

Some devices, such as a USB flash drive, require extra care for removal, or you could lose one or more files on them. In an extreme case, a USB flash drive itself could be corrupted and most of the files on it lost.

Always take care when removing a USB flash drive. Never remove it if it is showing activity (usually via a flashing light on the drive).

Safely Remove Hardware Command

Window's Safely Remove Hardware command ensures that a drive or device is inactive and can be removed without risk. The command checks for any open files or other activity, and then signals you when it's safe to remove the device. The command also signals when it's not safe to remove a device.

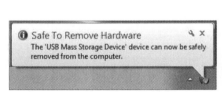

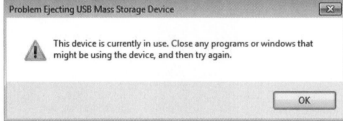

Notification Area

The notification area is on the taskbar just to the left of the date/time display. It may contain hidden icons.

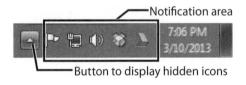

Notification area

Button to display hidden icons

Remove a Flash Drive

 Guide Me   In this exercise, you will safely eject your USB flash drive.

 Skip this exercise if you are not using a USB flash drive.

1 Click **Show Hidden Icons** in the notification area.

2 Click the **Safely Remove Hardware** icon.

3 Click your USB flash drive (the name will likely differ from this one).

Windows determines if your USB flash drive is still in use. You'll see a prompt when it can be safely removed.

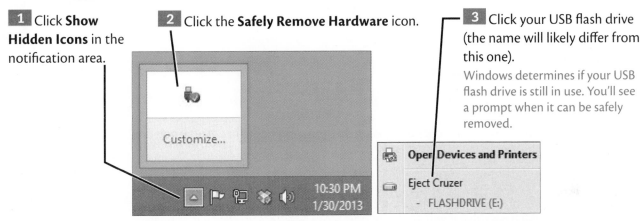

4 Remove the USB flash drive if the Safe to Remove Hardware prompt appears, and skip the rest of this exercise. Otherwise, go to the next step.

5 If a problem is signaled, check to see if you have any open files in an application, and then repeat the steps to safely remove the USB flash drive.

To check your knowledge of the key concepts introduced in this lesson, complete the Concepts Review quiz by choosing the appropriate access option below.

concepts review

If you are...	Then access the quiz by...
Using eLab	Logging in, choosing Content, and navigating to the Concepts Review quiz for this lesson
Not using eLab	Going to the Student Resource Center (see the inside front cover)

reinforce your skills | ecs-0301

Browse, Move, and Copy Files

In this exercise, you will browse files, create folders, and move and copy files. And if you are using one, you will also safely eject a USB flash drive.

Browse Files

1 Insert your USB flash drive if you are using one; **close**  AutoPlay if it appears.

2 Open the **File Explorer**.

3 Display your file storage location.

Flash drive

Documents folder
If you are using another location, ask your instructor for help if necessary.

4 Open the **Essential Computing Skills** folder and then open the **ecs-L03** folder.

5 Click the **More Options** ▼ menu button and change the view to **List**.

6 Use the **More Options** ▼ menu button to change the view three more times:

- Large Icons
- Tiles
- Details

7 Click **Back** ⬅.

8   Drag to create a new link in Favorites for the **ecs-L03** folder below **Recent Places**. Release the mouse button when you see a line in the Favorites list.

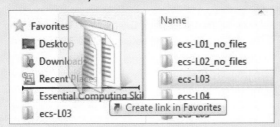

9   Right-click the new Favorites link and choose **Rename**; rename the folder `Lesson 3 Files`.

10   Click the new Favorites link to display the folder.

Open Files

11   Double-click to open **Movie Rentals**.

12   **Close** ☒ PowerPoint. Choose **Don't Save** if asked to save the file.

13   Start **PowerPoint** again via the **Start** menu.

14   Open **Movie Rentals** from the **Recent** list, and then **close** ☒ PowerPoint.

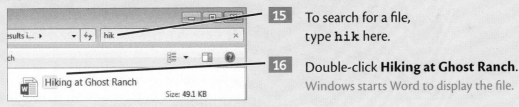

15   To search for a file, type `hik` here.

16   Double-click **Hiking at Ghost Ranch**.
Windows starts Word to display the file.

17   **Close** ☒ Word. Choose **Don't Save** if asked to save the file.

18   Click the "x" in the Search box to close the search.

Create Folders

19   Click **Back** ⬅ twice.
You should be viewing the base level of your file storage location.

20   Click **New Folder** on the toolbar, and name the new folder `Folders Practice`.

21   Double-click **Folders Practice** to open the folder.

22   Click the **New Folder** button, and name the new folder `Docs`.

23   Use the **New Folder** button to create two more new folders: `Pictures` and `Other`.

Move and Copy Files

24 Click **Lesson 3 Files** in Favorites.

25 Choose **Organize→Select All** from toolbar.

26 Choose **Organize→Copy**.

27 Click **Back**  twice and then double-click **Folders Practice**.

28 Choose **Organize→Paste**.
Notice that the copied files are still selected.

29 Click once on a clear area to deselect the copied files.

30 Choose **More Options ▼→Medium Icons**.
Now you will select all of the Word documents in preparation to Cut and Paste.

31 Click (do not double-click)
Destinations.

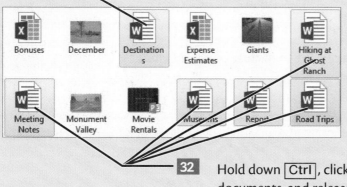

32 Hold down Ctrl, click the remaining Word documents, and release Ctrl.

33 Press Ctrl+X on the keyboard to cut the selection.

34 Double-click the **Docs** folder to open it, and then press Ctrl+V to paste the selection.

35 Click **Back**  and then click a clear area to deselect the Docs folder.

36 Use the Ctrl+click method to select all **Excel** files (but not the Docs folder).
If you click a file/folder you don't want in the selection, just click it again while holding down Ctrl.

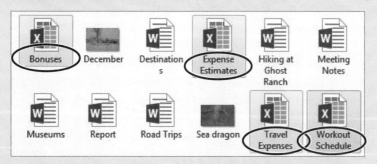

37 Use Ctrl+C to copy the **Excel** files.

38 Double-click to open the **Other** folder, and then use Ctrl+V to paste the Excel files.

39 Click **Back** and then click a clear area to deselect the Other folder.

40 Use the Ctrl+click method to select the picture files.

41 Press Ctrl+X to cut the files, double-click the **Pictures** folder, and press Ctrl+V to paste the files.

42 Click **Back**.

43 Use Ctrl+X to cut the **Pictures** folder.

44 Double-click to open the **Docs** folder, and then use Ctrl+V to paste the Pictures folder.

45 Double-click the **Pictures** folder.

Notice that all the pictures were pasted along with the folder.

46 **Close** X the File Explorer window.

 Skip the rest of this exercise if you are not using a USB flash drive.

Safely Remove Hardware

Properly ejecting your flash drive is a good habit.

47 Click **Show Hidden Icons** in the notification area.

48 Click **Safely Remove Hardware**. (It might appear in a different spot than shown here.)

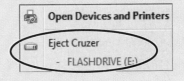

49 Click your USB flash drive (the name will likely differ from the one shown).

Windows determines if your USB flash drive is still in use. You'll see a prompt when it can be safely removed.

50 Remove the USB flash drive if the Safe to Remove Hardware prompt appears, and skip the rest of this exercise. Otherwise, go to the next step.

51 If a problem is signaled, check to see if you have any open files in an application, and then repeat the steps to safely remove the USB flash drive.

Rename and Delete Files and Folders

In this exercise, you will rename and delete files and folders. And if you are using one, you will safely remove your USB flash drive.

Copy Files

Before you can practice the skills in this exercise, you need to copy files into a new folder.

1. Insert your USB flash drive, if you are using one.

2. Open the **File Explorer** and display your file storage location (such as a USB flash drive, the Documents folder, or another location).

3. Open **Essential Computing Skills** and then open **ecs-L03**.

4. Press Ctrl + A to select everything in the folder, and then press Ctrl + C to copy.

5. Click **Back** twice.

   You should now be at the base of your file storage location.

6. Click the **New Folder** button on the toolbar and name the new folder **File Management Practice**.

7. Open the new folder and then press Ctrl + V to paste the copied files.

8. Click a clear area below the last file to deselect the copied files.

Rename Files and Folders

9. Right-click **Giants** and choose **Rename** from the menu. Rename the file **A Boy and His Dog** and tap Enter.

10. Click **Back** and then click a clear area to deselect the File Management Practice folder.

11. Click once (don't double-click) the **File Management Practice** folder name, pause one second, and click again.

    Windows highlights the name, ready for you to rename the folder.

12. Type **Delete Practice** and tap Enter.

Delete Files and Folders

13. Open the **Delete Practice** folder.

14. Click the **More Options** ▼ menu button and change the view to **Medium Icons**.

15. Click the **Bonuses** file and then hold down Ctrl and click **Expense Estimates**.

16 Keep holding down Ctrl and click once on **Travel Expenses** and **Workout Schedule**.

All Excel files should now be highlighted.

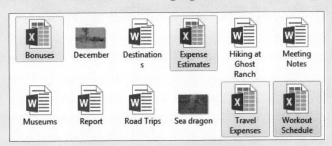

17 Tap the Delete key on the keyboard.

18 Choose **Yes** if asked to confirm the deletion.

The Excel files disappear to the Recycle Bin or are permanently deleted from a USB flash drive.

19 Use the **New Folder** button on the toolbar to create a new folder named `Pictures`.

20 While taking care not to select the Pictures folder and using the Ctrl +click method, select these pictures:

- A Boy and His Dog
- December
- Monument Valley
- Sea Dragon

21 Use Ctrl + C to copy the selection.

22 Double-click to open the **Pictures** folder, and then use Ctrl + V to paste the pictures.

23 Click **Back** .

24 Click once to select the **Pictures** folder and tap Delete . Choose **Yes** if asked to confirm the deletion.

The folder disappears.

25 **Minimize** the **File Explorer** window.

26 Double-click to open the **Recycle Bin**.

You won't see any of the files you just deleted if you are using a USB flash drive. (Files and folders deleted from USB flash drives aren't moved to the Recycle Bin.)

 Skip to step 30 if you are using a USB flash drive.

27 Select the **Pictures** folder.

28 Right-click **Pictures** if it was visible in the previous step and choose **Restore**.

29 Click to make the **File Explorer** window active, and then click **Delete Practice**.

Notice that the Pictures folder has returned if you were able to restore it in the previous step.

Back Up a Flash Drive

 Skip the rest of this exercise if you are not using a USB flash drive.

30 Display your USB flash drive.

31 Use Ctrl+A to select all contents, and then use Ctrl+C to copy it.

32 Display the **Documents** folder.

33 Use the **New Folder** button to create a new folder named `Backup of Flash Drive`.

34 Open the **Backup of Flash Drive** folder and press Ctrl+V.

Windows copies the entire contents of the flash drive into the folder.

35 Click **Back** ⬅.

Let's assume you don't want to leave the contents of your flash drive on the computer. You will delete the backup folder.

36 Click a clear area below the folders and files to deselect Backup of Flash Drive.

37 Click the **Backup of Flash Drive** folder and tap Delete. Choose **Yes** to confirm the deletion.

38 **Close** ✕ the File Explorer window.

39 Open the **Recycle Bin** and click **Empty the Recycle Bin**. Choose **Yes** to confirm.

40 **Close** ✕ the Recycle Bin window.

Safely Remove Hardware

Properly ejecting your flash drive is a good habit.

41 Click **Show Hidden Icons** in the notification area, and then choose **Safely Remove Hardware**. (It might appear in a different spot than shown here.)

42 Choose your USB flash drive.

43 Remove the USB flash drive if the Safe to Remove Hardware prompt appears, and skip the rest of this exercise. Otherwise, go to the next step.

44 If a problem is signaled, check to see if you have any open files in an application, and then repeat the steps to safely remove the USB flash drive.

Browse, Copy, and Move Files

You recently started a term paper project, and the number of files you have collected has already begun to grow. In this exercise, you will organize your files in folders to make them easier to keep track of.

Browse Files

1 Display the contents of the **AYS 3-1** folder within the **ecs-L03** folder in your file storage location.

2 Use the **Snipping Tool** to take a picture of the **File Explorer** window. Save the snip to your file storage location as `ECS03-A01a-Browse-[FirstInitialLastName]`.

Open Files

3 Open **Water Fluoridation Report - 1st Draft** from within the **AYS 3-1** folder.

4 Use the **Snipping Tool** to take a picture of the **Word** window. Save the snip to your file storage location as `ECS03-A01b-Open-[FirstInitialLastName]`.

5 Close the **Word** window.

Create Folders

6 In the base of your file storage location (not in the AYS 3-1 folder), create a folder named `Fluoride Report`.

7 Create these folders within **Fluoride Report**: `Images`, `Old Drafts`, and `Research`.

8 Use the **Snipping Tool** to take a picture of the **File Explorer** window. Save the snip to your file storage location as `ECS03-A01c-Folders-[FirstInitialLastName]`.

Move and Copy Files

9 Copy all files in the **AYS 3-1** folder and paste them in the **Fluoride Report** folder.

10 Move the 1st, 2nd, and 3rd draft report documents into the **Old Drafts** folder.

11 Move the image files into **Images**.

12 Copy (don't move) the PDF files into **Research**.

13 Display the following folders and use the **Snipping Tool** to take a picture of each. Save your snips to your file storage location using the filenames shown.

Folder	Snip Filename
Fluoride Report	`ECS03-A01d1-Copy-[FirstInitialLastName]`
Old Drafts	`ECS03-A01d2-Copy-[FirstInitialLastName]`
Research	`ECS03-A01d3-Copy-[FirstInitialLastName]`
Images	`ECS03-A01d4-Copy-[FirstInitialLastName]`

14 **Close** ▬X▬ the File Explorer window.

15 Give the **Safely Remove Hardware** command and eject your USB flash drive, if applicable.

16 Submit your snipped files based on the guidelines provided by your instructor.

---

apply your skills | ecs-0302

Rename and Delete Files

While working on a project, you find that you need to reorganize and rename some items and to delete unnecessary files. You want to also create a backup copy of the files, just to be safe. In this exercise, you will clean up and organize your project files.

Rename Files and Folders

1 Display the contents of your **ecs-L03** folder in your file storage location.

2 Copy the entire contents of the folder to a new folder named `Rename & Delete Test` at the base level of your file storage location.

3 Rename the **Report** document `Report to Trustees`.

4 Create a new folder named `Nonprofit Organization`. Then rename the folder `Conservation Trust`.

5 Use the **Snipping Tool** to take a picture of the **File Explorer** window. Save the snip to your file storage location as `ECS03-A02a-Rename-[FirstInitialLastName]`.

Delete Files and Folders

6 Delete all pictures in the **Rename & Delete Test** folder.

7 Use the **Snipping Tool** to take a picture of the **File Explorer** window. Save the snip to your file storage location as `ECS03-A02b1-Delete-[FirstInitialLastName]`.

8 Display the **Recycle Bin**.

If you deleted the files from your USB flash drive, they won't be in the Recycle Bin. That's okay.

9 Use the **Snipping Tool** to take a picture of the **Recycle Bin**. Save the snip to your file storage location as `ECS03-A02b2-Delete-[FirstInitialLastName]`.

Back Up a Flash Drive

 Skip steps 10–12 if you are not using a USB flash drive.

10 Copy the contents of your USB flash drive to a new folder in **Documents** named `Flash Drive Backup Test`.

11 Use the **Snipping Tool** to take a picture of **Flash Drive Backup Test** folder. Save the snip to your file storage location as `ECS03-A02c-Backup-[FirstInitialLastName]`.

12 Delete the **Flash Drive Backup Test** folder then empty the **Recycle Bin**.

Safely Remove Hardware

13 Give the **Safely Remove Hardware** command and eject your USB flash drive.

14 **Close** [X] the **File Explorer** window.

15 Submit your snipped files based on the guidelines provided by your instructor.

---

apply your skills | ecs-0303

Do It All

You are starting a new job. Your predecessor's computer has all sorts of files in one folder, and you decide to reorganize them into function-related folders. In this exercise, you will examine the contents of some files and rename them as necessary. You will delete unnecessary files or folders and create a backup copy of your USB flash drive (if you are using one).

Browse Files

1 Display the contents of the **ecs-L03** folder on your file storage location.

2 Use the **Snipping Tool** to take a picture of the **File Explorer** window. Save the snip to your file storage location as `ECS03-A03a-Browse-[FirstInitialLastName]`.

Open Files

3 Open **Museums** from within the **ecs-L03** folder.

4 Use the **Snipping Tool** to take a picture of the Word window. Save the snip to your file storage location as `ECS03-A03b-Open-[FirstInitialLastName]`.

5 Close the **Word** window.

Create Folders

6 In the base of your file storage location, create a folder named `Do It All Test`.

7 Create the following folders within **Do It All Test**: `Documents`, `Pictures`, and `Other Files`.

8 Use the **Snipping Tool** to take a picture of the **File Explorer** window. Save the snip to your file storage location as `ECS03-A03c-Folders-[FirstInitialLastName]`.

Move and Copy Files

9   Copy these files from the **ecs-L03** folder into the **Do It All Test** folder:

- December
- Destinations
- Hiking at Ghost Ranch
- Meeting Notes
- Monument Valley
- Road Trips
- Sea Dragon

10   Move these files from **Do It All Test** into **Pictures**:

- December
- Monument Valley
- Sea Dragon

11   Display the following folders and use the **Snipping Tool** to take a picture of each. Save your snips to your file storage location using the filenames shown.

Folder	Snip Filename
Do It All Test	ECS03-A03d1-Copy-[FirstInitialLastName]
Pictures	ECS03-A03d2-Copy-[FirstInitialLastName]

Rename Files and Folders

12   Go back to the **Do It All Test** folder.

13   Rename the **Meeting Notes** document `Session Report`.

14   Rename the **Documents** folder `Word Files`.

15   Use the **Snipping Tool** to take a picture of the **File Explorer** window. Save the snip to your file storage location as `ECS03-A03e-Rename-[FirstInitialLastName]`.

Delete Files and Folders

16   Delete the **Pictures** folder.

17   Use the **Snipping Tool** to take a picture of the **File Explorer** window. Save the snip to your file storage location as `ECS03-A03f1-Delete-[FirstInitialLastName]`.

18   Delete **Destinations** from the **Do It All Test** folder.

19   Use the **Snipping Tool** to take a picture of the **File Explorer** window. Save the snip to your file storage location as `ECS03-A03f2-Delete-[FirstInitialLastName]`.

20   Display the **Recycle Bin**.

If you deleted the files from your USB flash drive, they won't be in the Recycle Bin. That's okay.

21   Use the **Snipping Tool** to take a picture of the **Recycle Bin**. Save the snip to your file storage location as `ECS03-A03f3-Delete-[FirstInitialLastName]`.

Back Up a Flash Drive

 Skip steps 22–24 if you are not using a USB flash drive.

22   Copy the contents of your USB flash drive to a new folder in the **Documents** folder named `Flash Drive Do It All Test`.

23   Use the **Snipping Tool** to take a picture of the files and folders within the **Flash Drive Do It All Test** folder. Save the snip to your file storage location as `ECS03-A03g-Backup-[FirstInitialLastName]`.

24   Delete the **Flash Drive Do It All Test** folder and then empty the **Recycle Bin**.

Safely Remove Hardware

25   Give the **Safely Remove Hardware** command and eject your USB flash drive.

26   Submit your snipped files based on the guidelines provided by your instructor.

Organize Your Coursework

In this exercise, you will create folders to store files for courses you are enrolled in this term. Then you will copy and paste files from their current locations into the new folders.

- Create a folder in your file storage location for the current term (Fall 2014, for instance). Within this folder, create additional folders for all courses you are enrolled in this term. If you are enrolled in fewer than three courses, create folders for the previous term until you have at least three folders. Or, simply make up course names.

- Copy files for each course from their current location into the new folders you've created.

- Create a backup copy of your current term folder in a second location. For example, create a backup folder on the hard drive of your own computer, or in the Documents folder of your lab computer.

- Take a screen snip of the current term folder's contents. Take one snip of the contents of each course folder. Take one snip of the contents of the backup folder. Renaming as necessary, name the snips in a logical fashion your instructor will understand.

Submit your snipped screens according to the guidelines provided by your instructor.

Prepare for a New Project

In this exercise, you will create folders for a professional project. You will also copy some files into selected folders.

- Create a new Project folder of your choice on your file storage location. Then create new folders within it according to this diagram.

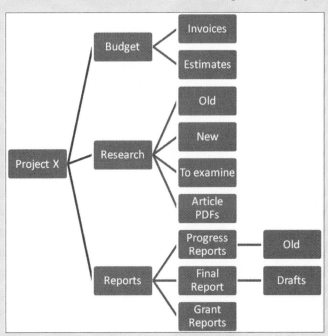

- Copy files from the ecs-L03 folder into the new folder structure according to these instructions.

File Type	Folder
Spreadsheet (Excel) files	Budget folder
Word files	Research folder
Picture files	Research/Old folder
Presentation files	Reports/Progress Reports folder

- Create a backup copy of the Project folder in a second location. For example, create a backup folder on the hard drive of your own computer, or in the Documents folder of your lab computer.

- Take a screen snip of the Project folder's contents. Take one snip of the contents of each project folder into which you copied files. Take a snip of the backup copy folder contents too. (You don't have to take snips of folders within the backup copy folder.) Renaming as necessary, name the snips in a logical fashion your instructor will understand.

Submit your snipped screens according to the guidelines provided by your instructor.

Windows 8.1

Managing Files

4

in this lesson

When you begin working with a computer, you will have just a few files to keep track of. As your use of computers grows, so will the number of files you must manage. After several months, you may have more than one hundred files; after a year, hundreds more. Windows gives you a very effective tool for managing files: folders. With folders, you can group related files. You can even create folders inside of other folders. In this lesson, you will find files, organize them into folders, and move them from one location to another.

Creating Folders for a New Semester

Esmeralda is taking five courses at her community college, one of which will require her to submit a term paper. In preparation for the work, Esmeralda creates folders on her computer to organize files as she does her research. She also creates a folder for each of her classes—as well as folders inside the class folders to further organize her files. For example, she creates Project folders for the different word processor documents she will create. Esmeralda also creates a Term Paper folder to hold files, web pages, and notes related to her large research paper. She even creates an Old Stuff folder (not shown below) for everything she thinks she doesn't need but does not yet want to delete.

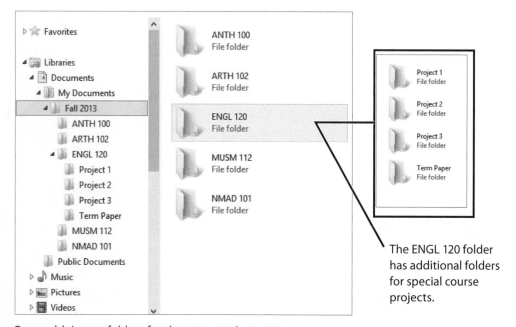

The ENGL 120 folder has additional folders for special course projects.

Esmerelda's new folders for the semester's courses.

What Is File Management?

File management is the organization of your work and entertainment data for easy access and security. The convenience of digital devices such as cameras, smartphones, and tablets makes the accumulation of large numbers of files inevitable. The consequences of lost files (or files you simply can't find) make file-management skills essential.

File-Management Tasks

To perform file management effectively, there are several tasks you will (or should) undertake regularly.

- **Finding files:** Look for files in various storage locations. Sometimes you'll need to find a file you don't recall the exact location of. For example, a paper or report you worked on six months ago.

- **Organizing files:** Organize files into logical groups. The primary tool for organizing files is folders. For example, organizing files for a college course or work project.

- **Moving and copying files:** Move/copy files to reorganize and share them. For example, copying files to a USB flash drive to share them with someone.

- **Backing up files:** Regularly back up important files. For example, digital photos, tax records, and ongoing coursework. Increasingly, these backups can be made automatically online, but sometimes you'll want a secure local backup copy as well.

Secure storage of digital photos is a good example of file management in action. Ten years from now, the program used to view or tag these photos may not exist, but a rational folder organization will.

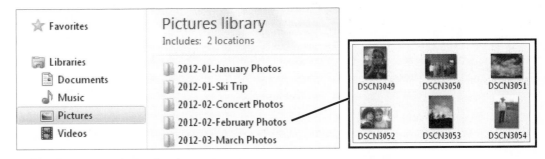

Folders organize photos for the ages.

Browsing Files

Video

Browsing to locate files is a key skill. You can accumulate a lot of files as you use a computer. If you have a digital camera, for example, you can end up with thousands of photo files within a year. Being a student requires the creation of numerous files each semester. There will be times when you need to locate a file you haven't used in months. File Explorer is the primary tool to locate files on your computer, flash drives, and cloud storage.

File Explorer

The File Explorer lets you navigate to various parts of the computer system, for example, to a specific folder, USB flash drive, or other storage location. Take care not to confuse the *File Explorer* with *Internet Explorer*. Internet Explorer is a program for browsing web pages, not the computer system.

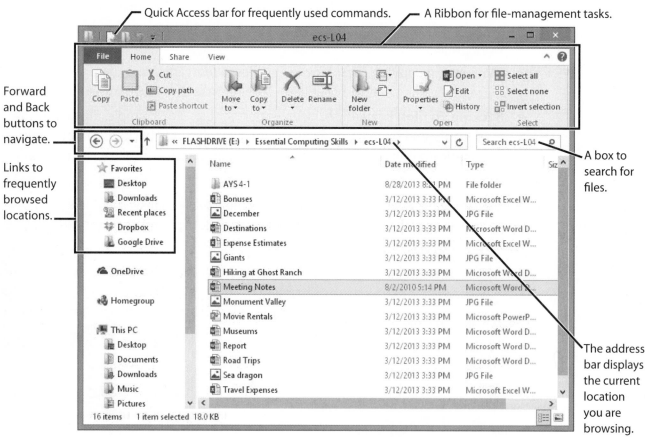

Windows 8.1 File Explorer.

The File Storage Hierarchy

 Video

Windows 8.1 introduces changes to file organization compared to Windows 7. The four levels are listed below.

File Storage Hierarchy

Level	Definition	Examples
Cloud	This is Internet-based storage and is covered in detail in Lesson 8.	• OneDrive • Dropbox • Google Drive
This PC	This location displays folders and storage drives located on your physical computer or tablet.	• Documents • Music • Pictures • Videos • USB Flash Drive
Folder	This is an electronic location in which you store groups of related files. It is also possible to place folders inside of other folders. Folders are often grouped into libraries.	• A folder to store all files for the Word program • A folder to store papers you've written for a course
File	This is a collection of computer data that has some common purpose.	• A paper you've typed • A photo you've taken

Changes from Windows 7 and Windows 8.0

Windows 8.1 introduced a fundamental reorganization of some familiar storage locations. For example, the Libraries folder is gone.

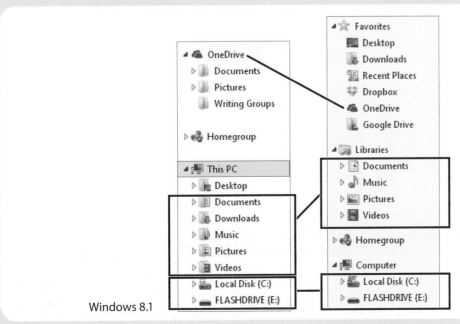

Windows 8.1 organizes familiar storage locations.

Open File Explorer

Guide Me   In this exercise, you will open File Explorer and view the lesson folder.

Before You Begin: Download the student exercise files from the Student Resource Center. Instructions for downloading the files are included there.

1 If necessary, start the computer and sign on to **Windows**.

2 Carefully insert your USB flash drive, if you are using one as your file storage location. Otherwise, skip to step 4.

3 Ignore any flash drive message.

FLASHDRIVE (E:)
Tap to choose what happens with removable drives.

4 Open the **File Explorer** and display your file storage location:

USB Flash Drive

A Click the **File Explorer**.

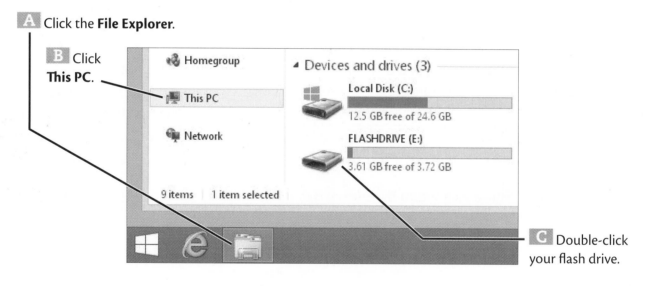

B Click **This PC**.

C Double-click your flash drive.

Documents Folder

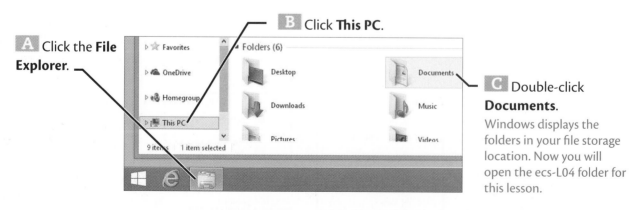

A Click the **File Explorer**.

B Click **This PC**.

C Double-click **Documents**.

Windows displays the folders in your file storage location. Now you will open the ecs-L04 folder for this lesson.

5 Maximize the window, if necessary.

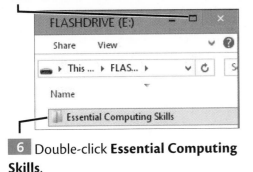

6 Double-click **Essential Computing Skills**.

A list of folders for course lessons appears.

▸ This PC ▸ FLASHDRIVE (E:) ▸ Essential Computing Skills ▸

Name	Date modified
ecs-L01_no_files	12/29/2012 10:36 …
ecs-L02_no_files	12/29/2012 10:36 …
ecs-L03	12/29/2012 12:16 …
ecs-L04	12/29/2012 12:16 …
ecs-L05	3/9/2013 1:01 PM

8 The address bar displays your location, including the drive letter.

7 Double-click **ecs-L04**.

Windows displays the contents of the ecs-L04 folder.

Changing the View

You can change the way files and folders are displayed in the File Explorer window. For example, you can display files as large thumbnails or lists.

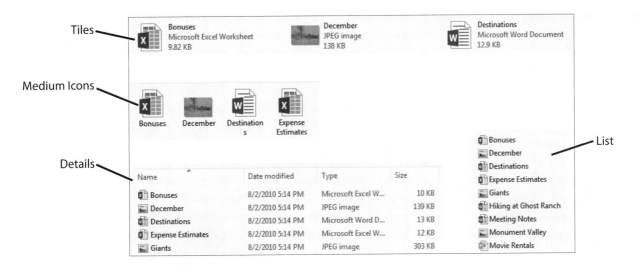

Opening Files

 Video

When you double-click a file's icon, Windows launches the program used to create or edit that file and displays it in the program window. This is a convenient way to start working with a file after you find it.

Creating Favorites Locations

The *Favorites* section of the File Explorer window has links to frequently browsed locations. You can add your own links to this list.

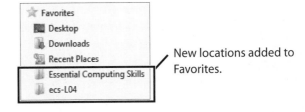

New locations added to Favorites.

develop your skills | ecs-0402

Open Document Files

Guide Me   In this exercise, you will open a file in the ecs-L04 folder. You will also add new locations to Favorites.

1 Change the view of files:

A Click **View**.

B Choose **Small Icons**.

C Choose **Details**.

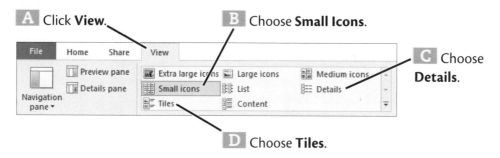

D Choose **Tiles**.

2 Examine the files in the File Explorer:

A Notice the different icons for specific file types (Word, Excel, etc.).

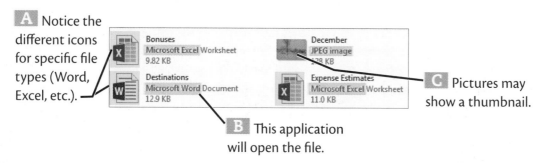

C Pictures may show a thumbnail.

B This application will open the file.

3 To open the **Meeting Notes** file, double-click the icon.

Windows starts Word and displays the file. Windows knows to start Word because Word was used to create the file.

4 Click **File** on the Ribbon.

5 Choose **Close**. Choose **Don't Save** if prompted to save changes.

The Meeting Notes file closes, but Word remains open.

6 Close **Word**.

The ecs-L04 folder window should be visible again. Now you will add the folder to Favorites.

7 Click **Back**.

8 Click the triangle if items aren't displayed below Favorites.

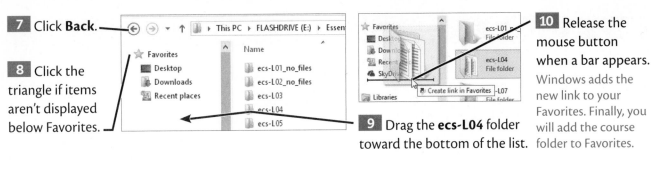

9 Drag the **ecs-L04** folder toward the bottom of the list.

10 Release the mouse button when a bar appears. Windows adds the new link to your Favorites. Finally, you will add the course folder to Favorites.

11 Click **Back**.

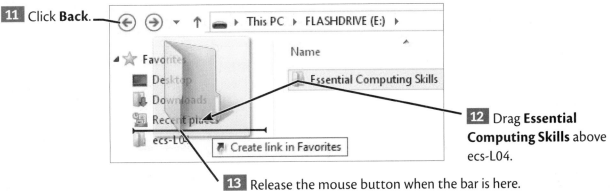

12 Drag **Essential Computing Skills** above ecs-L04.

13 Release the mouse button when the bar is here.

Opening Recently Used Files

▶️ **Video**

Applications such as Word and Excel can display your most recently used files. If you recall the program you used to create it, this is often a more convenient way to locate a file you've worked on.

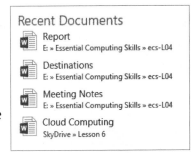

Word displays recently saved files.

Searching for Files

If you recall the name or part of the name of a file, Windows can search for it. You can limit a search to a specific folder, or search the entire computer system.

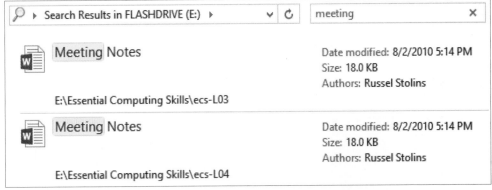

You can search on parts of a filename in specific locations.

a closer look

About Drive Letters

Windows identifies each storage drive on the computer with a *drive letter*. When you attach a USB flash or external drive to the computer, Windows assigns it the next available drive letter. Thus, your USB flash drive may have a different drive letter on different computers. This makes no difference in terms of the files you store on the drive.

Cloud Storage

Depending on the computer's configuration, you may see a Dropbox, OneDrive, or some other sort of cloud-based storage drive in Favorites. Because they aren't physical locations, these drives do not receive drive letters.

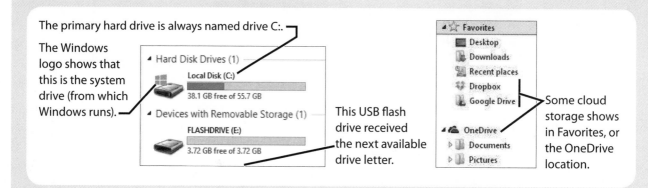

The primary hard drive is always named drive C:.

The Windows logo shows that this is the system drive (from which Windows runs).

This USB flash drive received the next available drive letter.

Some cloud storage shows in Favorites, or the OneDrive location.

develop your skills | ecs-0403

Find Files

Guide Me   In this exercise, you will open a file in your lesson folder. You will also search for and open a file.

1 Display the **ecs-L04** folder using the link in Favorites.

2 Double-click the **Report** document.
Word displays the document.

3 Click the **FILE** tab.

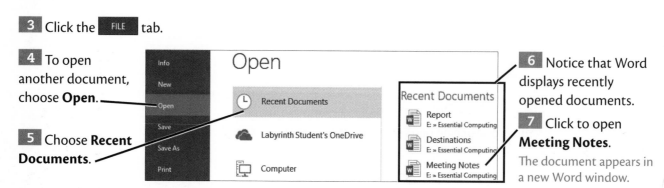

4 To open another document, choose **Open**.

5 Choose **Recent Documents**.

6 Notice that Word displays recently opened documents.

7 Click to open **Meeting Notes**.
The document appears in a new Word window.

8 **Close** ☒ Word. Choose **Don't Save** if asked to save.

9 **Close** ☒ Word again. Choose **Don't Save** if asked to Save.
Word closes the Report document.

10 Use ⌈Alt⌉+⌈Tab⌉ to display the **ecs-L04** folder.

11 Search for a file:

A Type **expense**.

B Double-click **Expense Estimates**.
Excel displays the spreadsheet.

12 **Close** ☒ Excel. Choose **Don't Save** if asked to save the file.

13 **Close** ☒ the search box to return to the normal (nonsearch) file display.
Windows closes the search and displays files normally.

Creating Folders

🎬 Video

A *folder* is an electronic location where you store groups of related files and folders. Folders are important tools for organizing files. Over time, you can accumulate hundreds and thousands of files. If you create new folders as you need them, you'll always feel well-organized.

Folders help you divide your files into easy-to-find groups. What if you could only view your files in a single, long list? This would be similar to finding a book in a library that had only one long bookshelf. You could find the book eventually, but it would no doubt take you a long time.

Folder Hierarchy

Folders form a hierarchy on a storage drive or Documents window. You can create new folders inside of other folders to add multiple layers to your file organization.

Displays files physically stored on your computer. (Earlier versions of Windows called this "My Computer".)

The Documents folder on your local storage drive

A white triangle indicates that this folder contains additional folders.

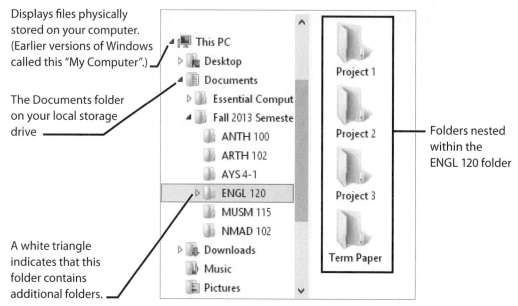

Folders nested within the ENGL 120 folder

The *This PC* section is a significant change introduced in Windows 8.1. It includes folders that used to be in the Libraries section of the File Explorer in Windows 7 and 8.0.

Windows 8.1

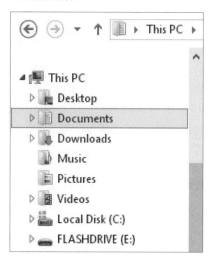

Windows 8.0, Windows 7

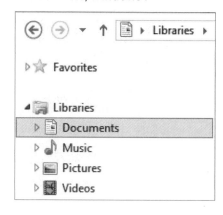

develop your skills | ecs-0404

Create Folders

Guide Me In this exercise, you will create six folders on your file storage location.

The ecs-L04 folder should be on the screen.

1 Return to the base level of your file storage location:

- USB Flash Drive
- Documents Folder

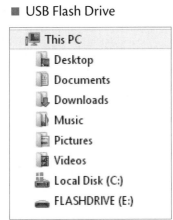 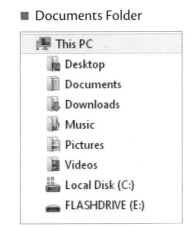

If you are using a different storage location, ask your instructor for help if necessary.

Now that the location where you wish to create a new folder is displayed, you can begin. The figures in the rest of this exercise show the My Documents location. Your screen may display some other location.

2 Create a new folder:

A Choose **Home→New→New Folder**.

A new folder appears. Its name is selected, ready for you to type the new name.

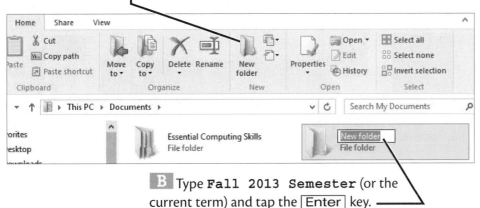

B Type **Fall 2013 Semester** (or the current term) and tap the |Enter| key.

3 Double-click your new folder. It's empty now, but you will place files in it later.

Notice that the address bar displays the folder you are viewing. Now you will create some folders within the semester folder.

4 Choose **Home→New→ New Folder**.

5 Name the folder **ANTH 100**.

6 Create another new folder, this one named **ARTH 102**.

7 Create three more folders with the names shown here.

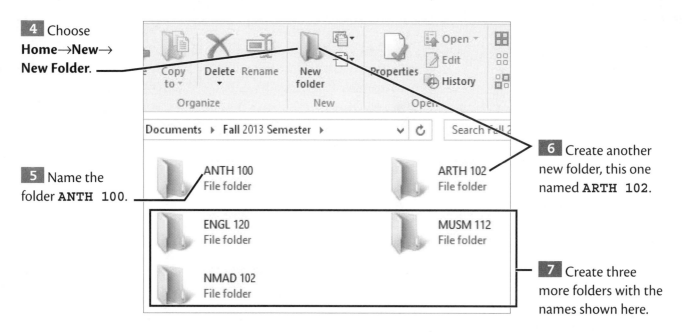

8 Double-click the **ENGL 120** folder.

Notice the folder name in the address bar. The new project folders you create next will be placed within the ENGL 120 folder.

9 Choose **Home→New→New Folder**.

10 Name the folder **Project 1**.

11 Create three more new folders with these names.

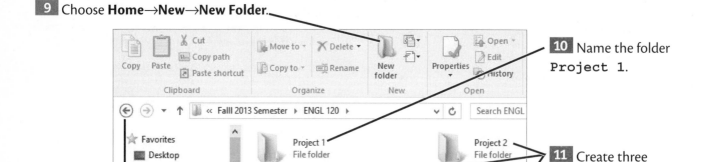

12 Go **Back** to the semester folder.

Windows displays the course folders.

Moving and Copying Files

 Video

Windows lets you move and copy files from one drive to another and from one folder to another using several techniques. This lesson will teach two methods.

- **Copy and Paste:** Copies files into a new location
- **Cut and Paste:** Moves files to a new location

Selecting Multiple Files for Commands

You can move and copy a single file or dozens of files with the same command. Before you give the Cut or Copy command, select the file(s) you wish to be affected by the command. To select a single file, simply click it. The two easiest methods for selecting multiple files use the Ctrl and Shift keys. Combine these two techniques as you like.

You can select nonconsecutive files for Cut and Copy commands.
In this example, only picture files are selected.

Selecting Files with Ctrl and Shift	
Method	**How It Works**
Ctrl+click	Adds a new item to your selection with each click, or deselects any already selected item.
Shift+click	Selects all the items between two clicks.

develop your skills | ecs-0405

Copy and Move Files

Guide Me   In this exercise, you will use the Cut, Copy, and Paste commands to move files.

1 Navigate to the **ecs-L04** folder from your Favorites list.

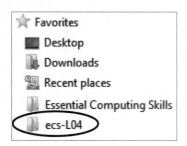

2 Select and copy all files in the ecs-L04 folder:

A Choose **Home→Select→Select All**. ———

B Notice that everything is highlighted (selected).

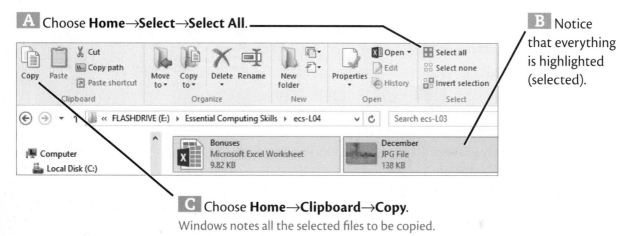

C Choose **Home→Clipboard→Copy**.

Windows notes all the selected files to be copied.

3 Go **Back** to the semester folder.

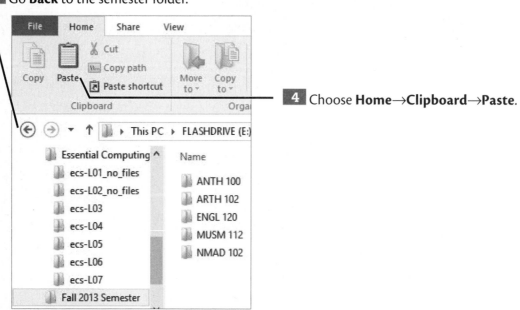

4 Choose **Home→Clipboard→Paste**.

Windows pastes all of the files you copied in step 2. Now you will cut a file for pasting.

5 Click once (do not double-click) **Bonuses**. **6** Choose **Home→ Clipboard→Cut**.

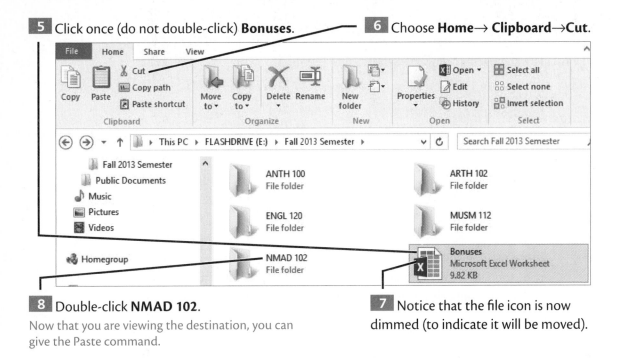

8 Double-click **NMAD 102**.

Now that you are viewing the destination, you can give the Paste command.

7 Notice that the file icon is now dimmed (to indicate it will be moved).

9 Choose **Home→Clipboard→Paste**.

Windows pastes the file into the folder.

10 Go **Back** to confirm that the file was moved.

Notice that a different file has taken the place of the Bonuses you moved.

11 Select and cut multiple files:

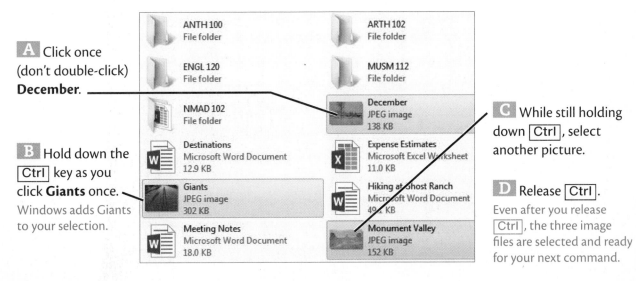

A Click once (don't double-click) **December**.

B Hold down the Ctrl key as you click **Giants** once.

Windows adds Giants to your selection.

C While still holding down Ctrl, select another picture.

D Release Ctrl.

Even after you release Ctrl, the three image files are selected and ready for your next command.

12 Choose **Home**→**Clipboard**→**Cut** and notice that the file icons are dimmed.

13 Double-click **ARTH 102** and then choose **Paste** from the Ribbon.

The files appear in the window as they are pasted.

14 Go **Back** ⬅ to the semester folder.

Notice that the three image files no longer appear in the semester folder.

Renaming Files and Folders

 Video

There may be times you'll want to rename a file or folder. You can rename files from the File Explorer window or from within a program. For example, if you save a file with a default name like Document1 or Workbook1, you'll want to rename it. Windows gives you plenty of flexibility for creating filenames.

File-Naming Rules

There are two important rules for naming Windows files.

- **Length:** Filenames can be a maximum of 260 characters.
- **Special characters:** Many special characters are permitted in filenames, such as ( ) **& + −** . These characters can't be used: **\ / ? : * " > < |**.

Changing a Filename from Within a Program

You may want to change the name of a file while you are working on it. For example, you can open a previously written letter, then change its name to create a new version of the same letter to someone else.

develop your skills | ecs-0406

Rename Files and a Folder

 Guide Me   In this exercise, you will rename files and folders using three methods.

Before you begin, make sure the semester folder is on the screen.

1 Double-click the **NMAD 102** folder.

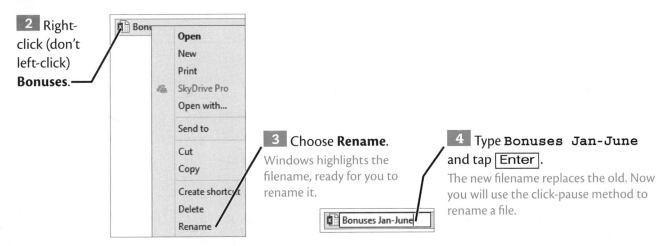

2 Right-click (don't left-click) **Bonuses.**

Open
New
Print
SkyDrive Pro
Open with...
Send to
Cut
Copy
Create shortcut
Delete
Rename

3 Choose **Rename**.
Windows highlights the filename, ready for you to rename it.

☒ Bonuses Jan-June

4 Type **Bonuses Jan-June** and tap `Enter`.
The new filename replaces the old. Now you will use the click-pause method to rename a file.

5 Click a clear area of the window to deselect the file.

6 Click once on the **Bonuses Jan-June** filename (not the icon).

7 Pause one second and click again.
The filename is highlighted for editing.

☒ Bonuses Jan-June

8 Tap the `←` key until the *insertion point* is blinking to the left of the B in *Bonuses*.
Arrow keys move the insertion point without deleting any part of the filename.

☒ Bonuses Jan-June

9 Type **Company**, tap `Spacebar`, and tap `Enter`.

☒ Company Bonuses Jan-June

10 Go **Back** ⬅ to the semester folder.

11 Rename the **MUSM 112** folder to **MUSM 115**.

12 Double-click the **Meeting Notes** document.

13 Click **FILE**.

14 Save the document with a new name:

A Choose **Save As**.   **B** Choose **Computer**.

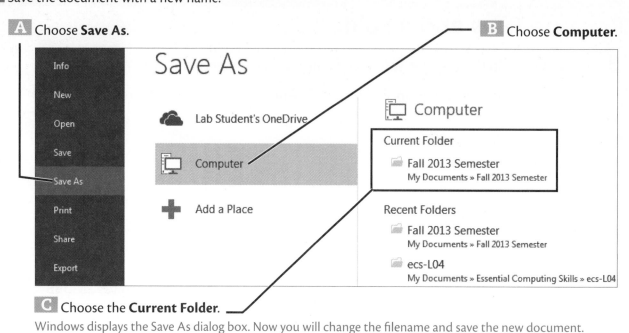

C Choose the **Current Folder**.

Windows displays the Save As dialog box. Now you will change the filename and save the new document.

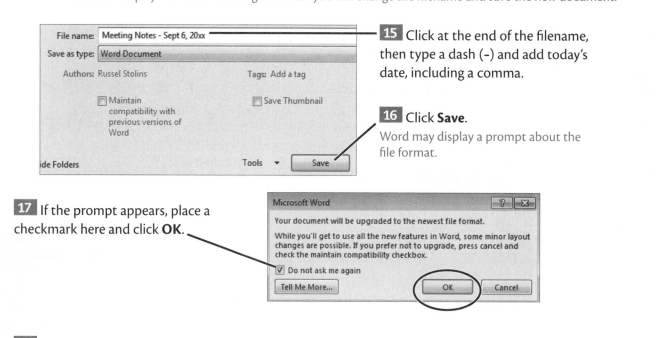

15 Click at the end of the filename, then type a dash (–) and add today's date, including a comma.

16 Click **Save**.

Word may display a prompt about the file format.

17 If the prompt appears, place a checkmark here and click **OK**.

18 Notice the new filename displayed in the title bar.

19 **Close** ☒ Meeting Notes. Choose **Don't Save** if prompted to save the file.

Deleting Files and Folders

 Video

You can delete unneeded files and folders to free up space on a storage drive. When you delete a folder, any other folders and files inside that folder are deleted as well. However, the Delete command doesn't necessarily mean erase. Windows takes steps to help avoid the loss of files you may not have meant to delete.

What Happens to Deleted Files and Folders?

Windows does not physically erase a deleted file from the hard drive. Instead, the file is placed in the Recycle Bin. (Exception: See the Warning below.) The Recycle Bin holds the deleted files until you give a command to empty it, or until it runs out of the space allotted to store deleted files.

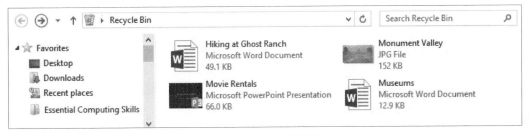

Recently deleted files and folders reside in the Recycle Bin.

 Files and folders deleted from *USB flash drives* or a network drive *are not* sent to the Recycle Bin! They are *immediately deleted* when you issue the Delete command.

Restoring Files and Folders

If you delete files or folders from a local storage drive, you can usually restore them to their previous locations from the Recycle Bin. For example, you might accidentally delete some photo files and realize your mistake. You could look for these files in the Recycle Bin and restore them.

develop your skills | ecs-0407

Delete Files and a Folder

Guide Me   In this exercise, you will delete some files. Then you will delete a folder and view the contents of the Recycle Bin.

Before you begin, make sure the semester file is open.

1 Double-click the **ARTH 102** folder.

Windows displays the folder contents. It holds three pictures you moved previously.

2 Select files with [Shift]+click:

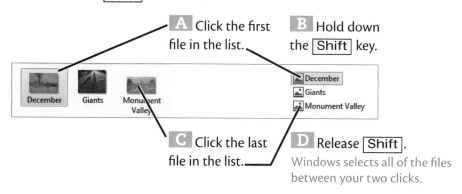

A Click the first file in the list.

B Hold down the [Shift] key.

C Click the last file in the list.

D Release [Shift].
Windows selects all of the files between your two clicks.

3 Tap [Delete] on the keyboard.

Windows may ask you to confirm the Delete command. This is a safeguard to protect against accidental deletions.

4 Choose **Yes** to confirm the deletion, if necessary.

The files disappear from the right panel and have been sent to the Recycle Bin. The folder is now empty.

If you deleted the picture files from a USB flash drive, the files are not sent to the Recycle Bin. (You still have copies of them in the ecs-L04 folder, however.)

5 Go **back** ⬅ to the semester folder.

6 Delete a folder with the right-click method:

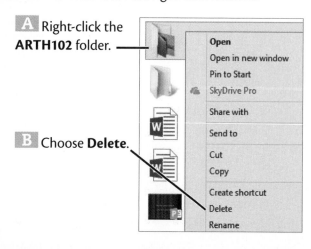

A Right-click the **ARTH102** folder.

B Choose **Delete**.

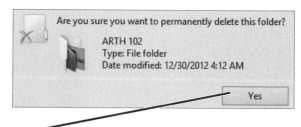

Are you sure you want to permanently delete this folder?

ARTH 102
Type: File folder
Date modified: 12/30/2012 4:12 AM

Yes

C Choose **Yes** if asked for confirmation.

The ARTH 102 folder disappears and is moved to the Recycle Bin. (Exception: The folder is not in the Recycle Bin if it was deleted from a USB flash drive.)

7 **Close** ☒ the semester folder window if you use a USB flash drive to store your exercise files. Leave the window open if you store your files in the Documents folder.

Skip the rest of this exercise if you use a USB flash drive as your file storage location. Files deleted from USB flash drives *are not* sent to the Recycle Bin.

Now you will view your files from within the Recycle Bin. Any file in the Recycle Bin can be restored (undeleted) to the location from which it was deleted.

8 **Minimize** ⬜ the semester folder.

9 Double-click the **Recycle Bin** on the Desktop.

Windows displays the Recycle Bin. Depending on the type of storage location you deleted from, the three files deleted in step 3 may be visible. Additional files may also be there.

10 Attempt to open **Giants** with a double click.

The file does not open, but a Properties window does. You can't open files in the Recycle Bin.

11 Click **Cancel** on the Properties window.

Emptying Files from the Recycle Bin

 Video

Files located in the Recycle Bin are permanently deleted from your computer when you issue an Empty Recycle Bin command, or automatically when the Recycle Bin runs out of space to keep deleted files. Depending on your computer's configuration, the Recycle Bin is set to store a certain number of files. Once that limit is reached, the oldest files in the Recycle Bin are automatically and permanently deleted to make room for additional files.

Restoring Files from the Recycle Bin

Files cannot be opened if they are located in the Recycle Bin. If you decide you need a file you previously deleted, and it hasn't been permanently deleted from the Recycle Bin, you can restore the file to its original location by right-clicking the file and choosing Restore from the pop-up menu. The Recycle Bin also has a Restore All Items command to restore all files it presently contains.

Recovering Accidentally Deleted Files

If you accidentally empty one or more files or folders from the Recycle Bin, you may still be able to recover them. However, you should not try to do this yourself. Instead, get assistance from an information technology (IT) professional. IT experts have special software that may be able to recover some or all of the lost files.

If you need help recovering files, don't use the drive again until the recovery attempt is made.

develop your skills | ecs-0408

Restore Files and Folders

Guide Me   In this exercise, you will restore the files and folders you deleted in the previous exercise.

Skip this exercise if you use a USB flash drive as your file storage location. Items deleted from a flash drive aren't sent to the Recycle Bin.

1 Double-click the **Recycle Bin** icon on the Desktop if the Recycle Bin window is not already open.

2 Select files in the Recycle Bin:

Your Recycle Bin may have more items, but we are only concerned with the files deleted in the previous exercise.

A Click the **December** file.

B Hold down Ctrl as you click **Giants** and **Monument Valley**.

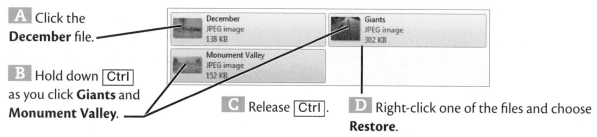

December
JPEG image
138 KB

Giants
JPEG image
302 KB

Monument Valley
JPEG image
152 KB

C Release Ctrl.

D Right-click one of the files and choose **Restore**.

The files disappear from the right panel as Windows restores them to their original location.

3 **Close** [x] the Recycle Bin.

4 Click to make the semester folder active.

Notice that the ARTH 102 folder has reappeared. It was recreated when you restored the picture files that were deleted from it.

5 Double-click to open the **ARTH 102** folder.

The three restored picture files are visible.

6 **Close** [x] the **ARTH 102** folder window.

The Windows Desktop is now empty.

Backing Up Flash Drives

 Video

It is critical to **_back up_** your flash drive regularly. USB flash drives are extremely compact and convenient. They are also easily lost! The last thing you want is to lose an entire semester's work on your flash drive. The best way to avoid a loss is to make regular backups of your flash drive onto your computer's hard drive, or onto some form of cloud storage. Then, at most, you might lose a day or two of work—but not weeks or months.

 Make a backup of your coursework files at least once a week, or even more often.

Storing Backups

Creating a special folder in your Documents folder for flash drive backups is a great idea. That way the backup is easy to find. You could even rename the backup folder with the date you made the backup. This can help you keep track of how recently you backed up your files. Or you can create an "A" and a "B" backup, alternating between the two. This provides extra protection against the loss of a file through corruption or an accidental overwriting.

An example of two sets of flash drive backups.

Back Up Flash Drive Files

 Guide Me In this exercise, you will copy all the files from your USB flash drive to a storage drive.

 Skip this exercise if you are not using a USB flash drive.

1 If necessary, carefully insert your USB flash drive into a USB port.

2 Click the **File Explorer**. **3** Click **This PC**. **4** Click your flash drive.

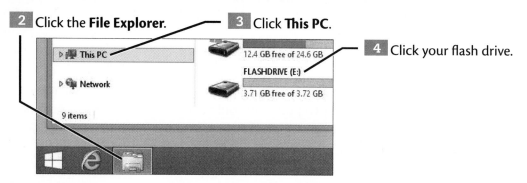

5 Click **Home**. **6** Click **Select All**.

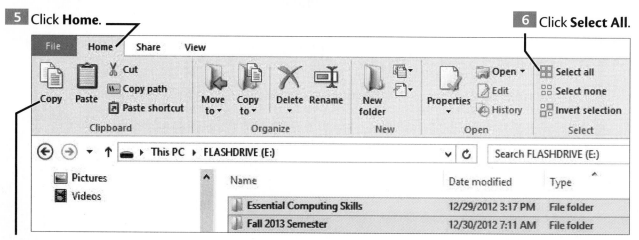

7 Click **Copy**.

Windows notes all the items to be copied when you give the Paste command at the Documents folder, which you will navigate to now.

8 Click **Documents**.

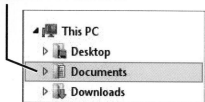

Windows displays your Documents folder. Now you will make a new folder to store your backup files.

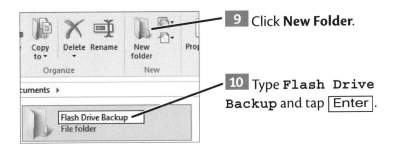

9 Click **New Folder**.

10 Type `Flash Drive Backup` and tap `Enter`.

11 Double-click to open the new **Flash Drive Backup** folder.

Now that you are at the destination, you can paste the copied files.

12 Choose **Paste** from the Ribbon (or press `Ctrl` + `V` on the keyboard).

All files and folders from your flash drive appear in the backup folder.

13 Go **back** ⬅ to the Documents folder.

Your Flash Drive Backup folder appears in the file/folder list. If you are studying on a public computer, you should delete your files from the Documents folder.

 Skip the rest of this exercise if the files in your Documents folder will remain private. (Ask your instructor if you are unsure.)

14 Delete a folder:

A Make sure the **Flash Drive Backup** folder is selected.

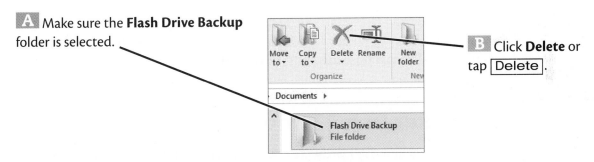

B Click **Delete** or tap `Delete`.

15 **Close** ☒ the Documents window.

16 Empty the Recycle Bin:

A Double-click the **Recycle Bin**.

B Click **Empty Recycle Bin**.

C Choose **Yes** to confirm the deletion.

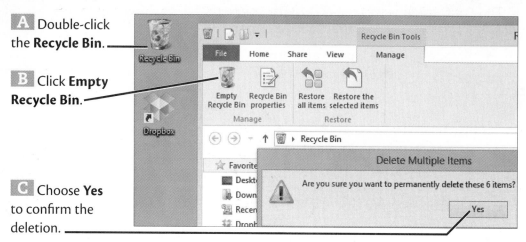

17 **Close** ▨ the Recycle Bin.

Safely Removing Hardware

 Video

Some devices, such as a USB flash drive, require extra care for removal, or you could lose one or more files on them. In an extreme case, a USB flash drive itself could be corrupted and most of the files on it lost.

 Always take care removing a USB flash drive. Never remove it if it is showing activity (usually via a flashing light on the drive).

Safely Remove Hardware Command

Window's Safely Remove Hardware command ensures that a drive or device is inactive and can be removed without risk. The command checks for any open files or other activity, then signals you when it's safe to remove the device. The command also signals when it's not safe to remove a device.

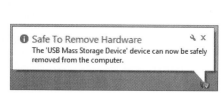

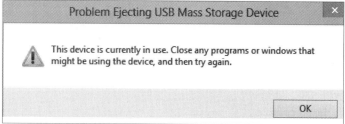

Notification Area

The notification area is on the taskbar just to the left of the date/time display. It may contain hidden icons.

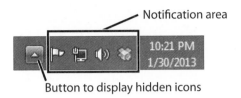

Notification area

Button to display hidden icons

Remove a Flash Drive

 Guide Me   In this exercise, you will safely eject your USB flash drive.

Skip this exercise if you are not using a USB flash drive.

NOTE

1 Click **Show Hidden Icons** in the notification area.

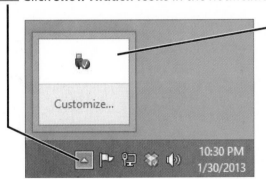

2 Click the **Safely Remove Hardware** icon.

3 Choose your USB flash drive (the name will likely differ from this one).

Windows determines if your USB flash drive is still in use. You'll see a prompt when it can be safely removed.

	Open Devices and Printers
	Eject VBOX HARDDISK
	- Local Disk (C:)
	Eject Cruzer
	- FLASHDRIVE (E:)

4 Remove the USB flash drive if the Safe to Remove Hardware prompt appears, and skip the rest of this exercise. Otherwise, continue to the next step.

Safe To Remove Hardware
The 'USB Mass Storage Device' device can now be safely removed from the computer.

5 If a problem is signaled, check to see if you have any open files in an application, then repeat the steps to safely remove the USB flash drive.

concepts review

To check your knowledge of the key concepts introduced in this lesson, complete the Concepts Review quiz by choosing the appropriate access option below.

If you are...	Then access the quiz by...
Using eLab	Logging in, choosing Content, and navigating to the Concepts Review quiz for this lesson
Not using eLab	Going to the Student Resource Center (see the inside front cover)

reinforce your skills | ecs-0401

Browse, Move, and Copy Files

In this exercise, you will browse files, create folders, and move and copy files. And if you are using one, you will also safely eject a USB flash drive.

Browse Files

1   Display the **Desktop**.

2   Insert your USB flash drive if you are using one; ignore any flash drive message.

3   Open the **File Explorer**.

4   Display your file storage location:

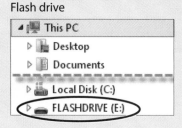

Flash drive   Documents folder

  Click the white triangle if the location you need isn't visible.

If you are using another location, ask your instructor for help if necessary.

5   Open the **Essential Computing Skills** folder, then open the **ecs-L04** folder.

6   Choose **View→Layout→List** from the Ribbon to change the view of files.

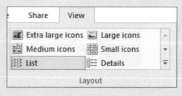

7   Change the view three more times:

■ View→Layout→Large Icons

■ View→Layout→Tiles

■ View→Layout→Details

8 Click **Back** ⬅.

9 Drag to create a new link in Favorites for the **ecs-L04** folder below **Recent Places**. Release the mouse button when you see a line in the Favorites list.

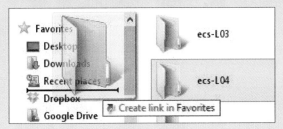

10 Right-click the new Favorites link and choose **Rename**; rename the folder **Lesson 4 Files**.

11 Click the new Favorites link to display the folder.

Open Files

12 Double-click to open **Movie Rentals**.

13 **Close** ☒ PowerPoint. Choose **Don't Save** if asked to save the file.

14 Start **PowerPoint** again via the **Start screen**. Go to the **All Apps** screen if necessary.

15 Open **Movie Rentals** from the **Recent** list, then **close** ☒ PowerPoint.

16 To search for a file, type **hik** here.

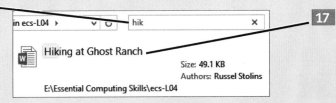

17 Double-click **Hiking at Ghost Ranch**.
Windows starts Word to display the file.

18 **Close** ☒ Word. Choose **Don't Save** if asked to save the file.

19 Click the "x" in the search box to close the search.

Create Folders

20 Click **Back** ⬅ twice.
You should be viewing the base level of your file storage location.

21 Choose **Home→New→New Folder** and name the new folder **Folders Practice**.

22   Double-click **Folders Practice** to open the folder.

23   Choose **Home→New→New Folder** and name the new folder `Docs`.

24   Choose **Home→New→New Folder** to create two more folders: `Pictures` and `Other`.

Move and Copy Files

25   Click **Lesson 4 Files** in Favorites.

26   Choose **Home→Select→Select All**.

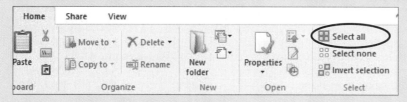

27   Choose **Home→Clipboard→Copy**.

28   Click **Back** ⬅ twice and then double-click **Folders Practice**.

29   Choose **Home→Clipboard→Paste**.
Notice that the copied files are still selected.

30   Click once on a clear area to deselect the copied files.

31   Choose **View→Layout→Medium Icons** to change the view.
Now you will select all of the Word documents in preparation to Cut and Paste.

32   Click (do not double-click) **Destinations**.

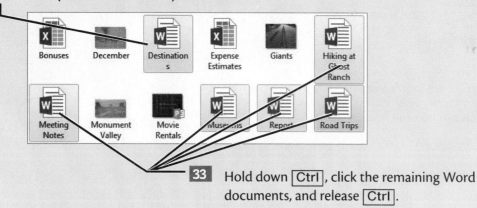

33   Hold down ⎡Ctrl⎤, click the remaining Word documents, and release ⎡Ctrl⎤.

34   Press ⎡Ctrl⎤+⎡X⎤ on the keyboard to cut the selection.

35   Double-click the **Docs** folder to open it, then press ⎡Ctrl⎤+⎡V⎤ to paste the selection.

36   Click **Back** ⬅ and then click a clear area to deselect the Docs folder.

37 Use the ⌈Ctrl⌉+click method to select all **Excel** files (but not the Docs folder).

If you click a file/folder you don't want in the selection, just click it again while holding down ⌈Ctrl⌉.

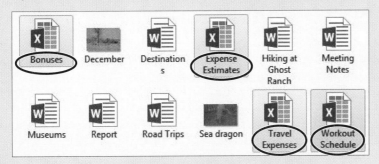

38 Use ⌈Ctrl⌉+⌈C⌉ to copy the **Excel** files.

39 Double-click to open the **Other** folder, then use ⌈Ctrl⌉+⌈V⌉ to paste the Excel files.

40 Click **Back** ⟲ and then click a clear area to deselect the other folder.

41 Use the ⌈Ctrl⌉+click method to select the picture files.

42 Press ⌈Ctrl⌉+⌈X⌉ to cut the files, double-click the **Pictures** folder, and press ⌈Ctrl⌉+⌈V⌉ to paste the files.

43 Click **Back** ⟲ .

44 Use ⌈Ctrl⌉+⌈X⌉ to cut the **Pictures** folder.

45 Double-click to open the **Docs** folder, then use ⌈Ctrl⌉+⌈V⌉ to paste the Pictures folder.

46 Double-click the **Pictures** folder.

Notice that all the pictures were pasted along with the folder.

47 **Close** ⌧ the File Explorer window.

 Skip the rest of this exercise if you are not using a USB flash drive.

Safely Remove Hardware

Properly ejecting your flash drive is a good habit.

48 Click **Show Hidden Icons** in the notification area.

49 Click **Safely Remove Hardware**. (It might appear in a different spot than shown here.)

50   Click your USB flash drive (the name will likely differ from the one shown).

Windows determines if your USB flash drive is still in use. You'll see a prompt when it can be safely removed.

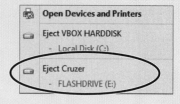

51   Remove the USB flash drive if the Safe to Remove Hardware prompt appears, and skip the rest of this exercise. Otherwise, continue to the next step.

52   If a problem is signaled, check to see if you have any open files in an application, then repeat the steps to safely remove the USB flash drive.

---

reinforce your skills | ecs-0402

Rename and Delete Files and Folders

In this exercise, you will rename and delete files and folders. And if you are using one, you will safely remove a USB flash drive.

Copy Files

Before you can practice the skills in this exercise, you need to copy files into a new folder.

1   Insert your USB flash drive, if you are using one.

2   Display the Desktop. Then, open the **File Explorer** and display your file storage location (such as a USB flash drive, the Documents folder, or another location).

3   Open **Essential Computing Skills** and then open **ecs-L04**.

4   Press Ctrl+A to select all files in the folder, and then press Ctrl+C to copy them.

5   Click **Back** ← twice.

You should now be at the base of your file storage location.

6   Choose **Home→New→New Folder** and name the new folder `File Management Practice`.

7   Open the new folder and then press Ctrl+V to paste the copied files.

8   Click a clear area below the last file to deselect the copied files.

Rename Files and Folders

9   Right-click **Giants** and choose **Rename** from the menu. Rename the file `A Boy and His Dog` and tap `Enter`.

10   Click **Back** ⬅ and then click a clear area to deselect the File Management Practice folder.

11   Click once (don't double-click) the **File Management Practice** folder name, pause one second, and click again.

Windows highlights the name, ready for you to rename the folder.

12   Type `Delete Practice` and tap `Enter`.

Delete Files and Folders

13   Open the **Delete Practice** folder.

14   Choose **View→Layout→Medium Icons**.

15   Click the **Bonuses** file and then hold down `Ctrl` and click **Expense Estimates**.

16   Keep holding down `Ctrl` and click once on **Travel Expenses** and **Workout Schedule**.

All Excel files should now be highlighted.

17   Tap the `Delete` key on the keyboard.

18   Choose **Yes** if asked to confirm the deletion.

The Excel files disappear to the Recycle Bin or are permanently deleted from a USB flash drive.

19   Choose **Home→New→New Folder** and name the new folder `Pictures`.

20   While taking care not to select the Pictures folder and using the `Ctrl` key, select these pictures:

- A Boy and His Dog
- December
- Monument Valley
- Sea Dragon

21   Use `Ctrl`+`C` to copy the selection.

22   Double-click to open the **Pictures** folder then use `Ctrl`+`V` to paste the pictures.

23   Click **Back** ⬅.

24 Click once to select the **Pictures** folder and tap Delete . Choose **Yes** if asked to confirm the deletion.
The folder disappears.

25 **Minimize** the **File Explorer** window.

26 Double-click to open the **Recycle Bin**.
You won't see any of the files you just deleted if you are using a USB flash drive.
(Files and folders deleted from USB flash drives aren't moved to the Recycle Bin.)

 Skip to step 29 if you are using a USB flash drive.

27 Select the **Pictures** folder.

28 Right-click **Pictures** if it was visible in the previous step and choose **Restore**.

29 Click to make the **File Explorer** window active, then click **Delete Practice**.
Notice that the Pictures folder has returned if you were able to restore it in the previous step.

Back Up a Flash Drive

 Skip the rest of this exercise if you are not using a USB flash drive.

30 Display your USB flash drive.

31 Use Ctrl + A to select all contents and then use Ctrl + C to copy it.

32 Display the **Documents** folder.

33 Choose **Home→New→New Folder** and name the new folder Backup of Flash Drive.

34 Open **Backup of Flash Drive** and press Ctrl + V .
Windows copies the entire contents of the flash drive into the folder.

35 Click **Back** .
Let's assume you don't want to leave the contents of your flash drive on the computer. You will delete the backup folder.

36 Click a clear area below the folders and files to deselect Backup of Flash Drive.

37 Click the **Backup of Flash Drive** folder and tap Delete . Choose **Yes** to confirm the deletion.

38 **Close** the File Explorer window.

39 Open the **Recycle Bin** and choose **Manage→Manage→Empty Recycle Bin**.

40 Choose **Yes** to confirm the deletion.

41 **Close** the Recycle Bin.

Safely Remove Hardware

Properly ejecting your flash drive is a good habit.

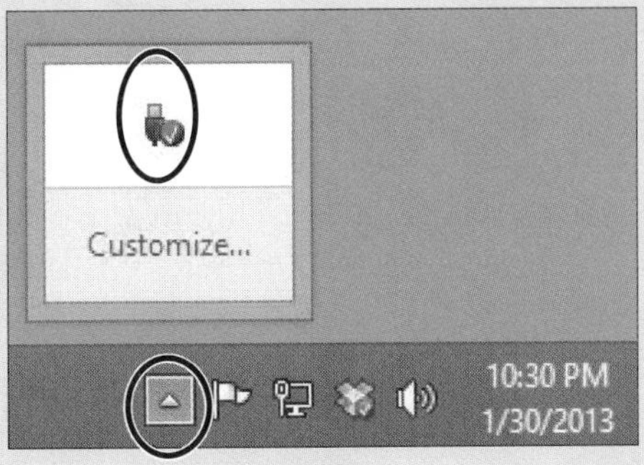

42 Click **Show Hidden Icons** in the notification area and then choose **Safely Remove Hardware**. (It might appear in a different spot than shown here.)

43 Choose your USB flash drive.

44 Remove the USB flash drive if the Safe to Remove Hardware prompt appears, and skip the rest of this exercise. Otherwise, continue to the next step.

45 If a problem is signaled, check to see if you have any open files in an application, then repeat the steps to safely remove the USB flash drive.

apply your skills | ecs-0401

Browse, Copy, and Move Files

You recently started a term paper project, and the number of files you have collected has already begun to grow. In this exercise, you will organize the files in folders to make them easier to keep track of.

Browse Files

1 Display the contents of the **AYS 4-1** folder within the **ecs-L04** folder in your file storage location.

2 Use the **Snipping Tool** to take a picture of the **File Explorer** window. Save the snip to your file storage location as `ECS04-A01a-Browse-[FirstInitialLastName]`.

Open Files

3 Open **Water Fluoridation Report - 1st Draft** from within the **AYS 4-1** folder.

4 Use the **Snipping Tool** to take a picture of the **Word** window. Save the snip to your file storage location as `ECS04-A01b-Open-[FirstInitialLastName]`.

5 Close the **Word** window.

Create Folders

6 In the base of your file storage location (not in the AYS 4-1 folder), create a folder named `Fluoride Report`.

7 Create these folders within **Fluoride Report**: `Images`, `Old Drafts`, and `Research`.

8 Use the **Snipping Tool** to take a picture of the **File Explorer** window. Save the snip to your file storage location as `ECS04-A01c-Folders-[FirstInitialLastName]`.

Move and Copy Files

9 Copy all files in the **AYS 4-1** folder to the **Fluoride Report** folder.

10 Move the 1st, 2nd, and 3rd draft report documents into the **Old Drafts** folder.

11 Move the image files into **Images**.

12 Copy (don't move) the PDF files into **Research**.

13 Display the following folders and use the **Snipping Tool** to take a picture of each. Save your snips to your file storage location using the filenames shown.

Folder	Snip Filename
Fluoride Report	`ECS04-A01d1-Copy-[FirstInitialLastName]`
Old Drafts	`ECS04-A01d2-Copy-[FirstInitialLastName]`
Research	`ECS04-A01d3-Copy-[FirstInitialLastName]`
Images	`ECS04-A01d4-Copy-[FirstInitialLastName]`

14   **Close** [X] the File Explorer window.

15   Give the **Safely Remove Hardware** command and eject your USB flash drive, if applicable.

16   Submit your snipped files based on the guidelines provided by your instructor.

apply your skills | ecs-0402

Rename and Delete Files

While working on a project, you find that you need to reorganize and rename some items, and delete unnecessary files. You want to also create a backup copy of the files, just to be safe. In this exercise, you will clean up and organize your project files.

Rename Files and Folders

1   Display the contents of the **ecs-L04** folder in your file storage location.

2   Copy the entire contents of the folder to a new folder named `Rename & Delete Test` at the base level of your file storage location.

3   Rename the **Report** document to `Report to Trustees`.

4   Create a new folder named `NonProfit Organization`. Then, rename the folder `Conservation Trust`.

5   Use the **Snipping Tool** to take a picture of the **File Explorer** window. Save the snip to your file storage location as `ECS04-A02a-Rename-[FirstInitialLastName]`.

Delete Files and Folders

6   Delete all the pictures in the **Rename & Delete Test** folder.

7   Use the **Snipping Tool** to take a picture of the **File Explorer** window. Save the snip to your file storage location as `ECS04-A02b1-Delete-[FirstInitialLastName]`.

8   Display the **Recycle Bin**.
If you deleted the files from your USB flash drive, they won't be in the Recycle Bin. That's okay.

9   Use the **Snipping Tool** to take a picture of the **Recycle Bin**. Save the snip to your file storage location as `ECS04-A02b2-Delete-[FirstInitialLastName]`.

Back Up a Flash Drive

Skip steps 10–12 if you are not using a USB flash drive.

10   Copy the contents of your USB flash drive to a new folder in **Documents** named `Flash Drive Backup Test`.

11 Use the **Snipping Tool** to take a picture of **Flash Drive Backup Test** folder. Save the snip to your file storage location as `ECS04-A02c-Backup-[FirstInitialLastName]`.

12 Delete the **Flash Drive Backup Test** folder, then empty the **Recycle Bin**.

Safely Remove Hardware

13 Give the **Safely Remove Hardware** command and eject your USB flash drive.

14 **Close** ☒ the **File Explorer** window.

15 Submit your snipped files based on the guidelines provided by your instructor.

---

apply your skills | ecs-0403

Do It All

You are starting a new job. Your predecessor's computer has all sorts of files in one folder, and you decide to reorganize them into function-related folders. In this exercise, you will examine the contents of some files and rename them as necessary. You will delete unnecessary files or folders and create a backup copy of your USB flash drive (if you are using one).

Browse Files

1 Display the contents of the **ecs-L04** folder on your file storage location.

2 Use the **Snipping Tool** to take a picture of the **File Explorer** window. Save the snip to your file storage location as `ECS04-A03a-Browse-[FirstInitialLastName]`.

Open Files

3 Open **Museums** from within the **ecs-L04** folder.

4 Use the **Snipping Tool** to take a picture of the Word window. Save the snip to your file storage location as `ECS04-A03b-Open-[FirstInitialLastName]`.

5 Close the **Word** window.

Create Folders

6 In the base of your file storage location, create a folder named `Do It All Test`.

7 Create the following folders within **Do It All Test**: `Documents`, `Pictures`, and `Other Files`.

8 Use the **Snipping Tool** to take a picture of the **File Explorer** window. Save the snip to your file storage location as `ECS04-A03c-Folders-[FirstInitialLastName]`.

Move and Copy Files

9 Copy these files from the **ecs-L04** folder into the **Do It All Test** folder:

- December
- Destinations
- Hiking at Ghost Ranch
- Meeting Notes
- Monument Valley
- Road Trips
- Sea Dragon

10 Move these files from **Do It All Test** into **Pictures**:

- December
- Monument Valley
- Sea Dragon

11 Display the following folders and use the **Snipping Tool** to take a picture of each. Save your snips to your file storage location using the filenames shown.

Folder	Snip Filename
Do It All Test	ECS04-A03d1-Copy-[FirstInitialLastName]
Pictures	ECS04-A03d2-Copy-[FirstInitialLastName]

Rename Files and Folders

12 Go back to the **Do It All Test** folder.

13 Rename the **Meeting Notes** document to Session Report.

14 Rename the **Do It All Test** folder to Word Files.

15 Use the **Snipping Tool** to take a picture of the **File Explorer** window. Save the snip to your file storage location as ECS04-A03e-Rename-[FirstInitialLastName].

Delete Files and Folders

16 Delete the **Pictures** folder.

17 Use the **Snipping Tool** to take a picture of the **File Explorer** window. Save the snip to your file storage location as ECS04-A03f1-Delete-[FirstInitialLastName].

18 Delete **Destinations** from the **Word Files** folder.

19 Use the **Snipping Tool** to take a picture of the **File Explorer** window. Save the snip to your file storage location as ECS04-A03f2-Delete-[FirstInitialLastName].

20 Display the **Recycle Bin**.

If you deleted the files from your USB flash drive, they won't be in the Recycle Bin. That's okay.

21 Use the **Snipping Tool** to take a picture of the **Recycle Bin**. Save the snip to your file storage location as `ECS04-A03f3-Delete-[FirstInitialLastName]`.

Back Up a Flash Drive

  Skip steps 22–24 if you are not using a USB flash drive.

22 Copy the contents of your USB flash drive to a new folder in the **Documents** Library named `Flash Drive Do It All Test`.

23 Use the **Snipping Tool** to take a picture of files and folders within the **Flash Drive Do It All Test** folder. Save the snip to your file storage location as `ECS04-A03g-Backup-[FirstInitialLastName]`.

24 Delete the **Flash Drive Do It All Test** folder, and then empty the **Recycle Bin**.

Safely Remove Hardware

25 Give the **Safely Remove Hardware** command and eject your USB flash drive.

26 Submit your snipped files based on the guidelines provided by your instructor.

Organize Your Coursework

In this exercise, you will create folders to store files for courses you are enrolled in this term. Then you will copy and paste files from their current locations into the new folders.

- Create a folder in your file storage location for the current term (Fall 2014, for example). Within this folder, create additional folders for all courses you are enrolled in this term. If you are enrolled in fewer than three courses, create folders for the previous term until you have at least three folders. Or simply make up course names.

- Copy files for each course from their current location into the new folders you've created.

- Create a backup copy of your current term folder in a second location. For example, create a backup folder on the hard drive of your own computer, or in the Documents folder of your lab computer.

- Take a screen snip of the current term folder's contents. Take one snip of the contents of each course folder. Take one snip of the contents of the backup folder. Renaming as necessary, name the snips in a logical fashion your instructor will understand.

Submit your snipped screens according to the guidelines provided by your instructor.

Prepare for a New Project

In this exercise, you will create folders for a professional project. You will also copy some files into selected folders.

- Create a new Project folder of your choice on your file storage location. Then, create new folders within it according to this diagram.

- Copy files from the ecs-L04 folder into the new folder structure according to these instructions.

File Type	Folder
Spreadsheet (Excel) files	Budget folder
Word files	Research folder
Picture files	Research/Old folder
Presentation files	Reports/Progress Reports folder

- Create a backup copy of the Project folder in a second location. For example, create a backup folder on the hard drive of your own computer, or in the Documents folder of your lab computer.

- Take a screen snip of the Project folder's contents. Take one snip of the contents of each project folder into which you copied files. Take a snip of the backup copy folder contents too. (You don't have to take snips of folders within the backup copy folder.) Renaming as necessary, name the snips in a logical fashion your instructor will understand.

Submit your snipped screens according to the guidelines provided by your instructor.

The Internet

5 Searches and Web 2.0

in this lesson

Searching the web effectively is a necessity in any serious academic or professional work. Web browser programs now typically integrate powerful search capabilities in their address or search bar. Web 2.0 offers new levels of interactivity, allowing online discussions and meetings. In this lesson, you will learn about additional web search techniques and tools for interactivity.

Searching for a Destination

You're planning a road trip for semester break. You look for places to visit, but it's not always easy to sift through the millions of search results that come up in a basic web search. You try narrowing your search by using more specific terms. And you use tabbed browsing to quickly view several search results.

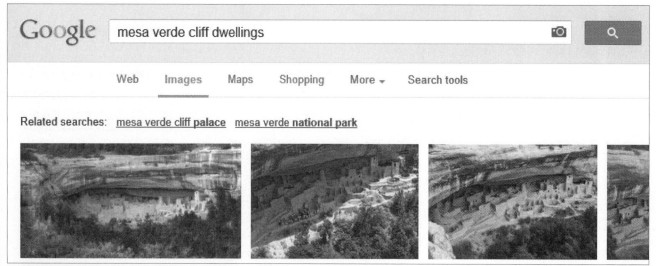

A search engine helps you locate some good photos.

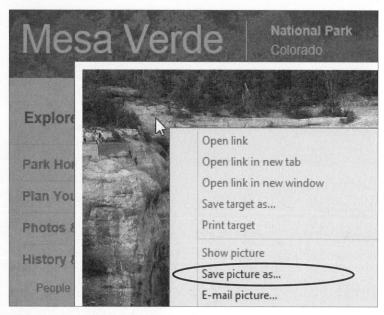

Saving a picture to your storage drive.

Browsing the Web

 Video   Just twenty years after its creation, the *web (Word Wide Web)* is a universal medium for communication. Whether on your phone, at a library or an Internet café, or traveling, access to the web is a necessity. It's likely you're experienced with web browsing. This topic reviews a few basics about your browser and web browsing.

The Homepage

When you first start a browser program, it automatically displays its homepage. You can set the homepage to any page you prefer. For example, there may be a favorite web page you like to check every day. Some browsers allow you to set more than one homepage.

Internet Explorer Tablet App and Application

Windows 8.1 effectively has two different versions of Internet Explorer installed.

- **Internet Explorer 11 Application:** This runs on the traditional Desktop.
- **Internet Explorer 11 Tablet App:** This runs as a full-screen Win 8 tablet app.

---

develop your skills | ecs-0501

Start Internet Explorer

 Guide Me   In this exercise, you will start the Internet Explorer browser and view the homepage.

1 **Windows 8.1 Only:** Display the **Desktop**.

2 Start Internet Explorer:

Windows 7   Windows 8.1

The browser window appears and displays the homepage.

3 **Maximize** ▣ / ▭ the Internet Explorer window if necessary.
Windows 7 Users: Skip the rest of this exercise.

The next steps let Windows 8.1 users compare the app and application (traditional Desktop) versions of Internet Explorer.

4 Display the **Start screen** and then start **Internet Explorer**.
Notice how the app fills the entire screen. (There are no quick sizing buttons.) The address bar appears at the bottom of the screen rather than the top.

5 Click on a non-link area of the page.

The address bar disappears. The entire screen displays the web page.

6 Right-click (don't left-click) on a non-link area.

The address bar and a page navigation display appear.

7 Use Alt + Tab to flip back to **Internet Explorer** on the Desktop.

You are back at the traditional Desktop version. You'll use this version for the remaining web browser exercises.

Web Browser Features

 Video

A *web browser* (from here on referred to simply as a browser) is an application optimized for viewing web pages. As with other types of applications, a variety of companies compete to make the best and most popular web browser. Microsoft's Internet Explorer browser comes installed on every Windows computer. Other popular browsers include Firefox, Safari, and Chrome. The following figure displays the primary features of a web browser.

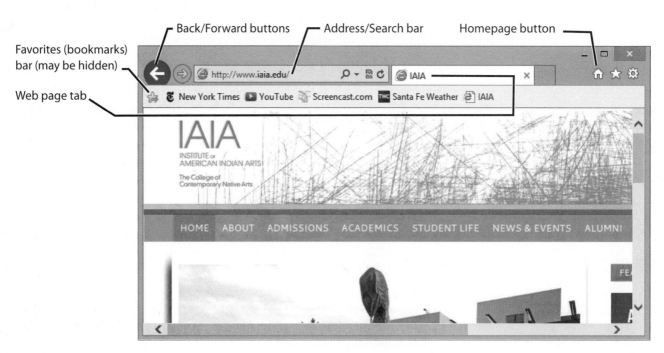

URLs

A *URL (Uniform Resource Locator)*, pronounced "you are el," is the address for a web page. Every URL contains a *domain name*. A URL may also contain file and folder names that point to a specific web page. If page names and folder names are part of a URL, each is separated by a forward slash (/).Below is an illustration of a typical URL.

http://www.nasa.gov/mission_pages/mars/main/index.html

| Protocol | Domain name | Folder names | Page name |

a closer look

Top-Level Domain Names

The top-level domain name in a URL can give useful clues about the *website*'s origins. The following table displays several typical top-level domain names and their usages. The usage of some top-level domains is controlled very tightly. For example, the .edu top-level domain is closely reserved for institutions of higher learning. The .com domain doesn't require such stringent standards.

Top-level Domain Name	Common Usage
.com	A commercial enterprise or business
.gov	An official U.S. government website
.org	A nonprofit or noncommercial organization
.edu	An accredited postsecondary educational institution
.info	A generic informative website
.ca	A Canadian website
.cn	A Chinese website

Mesa Verde National Park – Vacations, Tours, Hiking in Southwest …
Cliff dwellings. **Cliff dwelling**. Arrowheads found at **Mesa Verde**. **Mesa Verde** Heritage …
Mesa Verde Tours. **Cliff dwellings**. Durango Narrow Gauge Railroad …
Far View Lodge - Lodging - Morefield Campground
www.visit**mesaverde**.com/ - Cached - Similar

Despite its web page label, this website's .com top-level domain name indicates it is most likely for a business and is not an official National Park system site.

develop your skills | ecs-0502

Navigate with the Address Bar

 Guide Me   In this exercise, you will navigate to the Student Resource Center for this book.

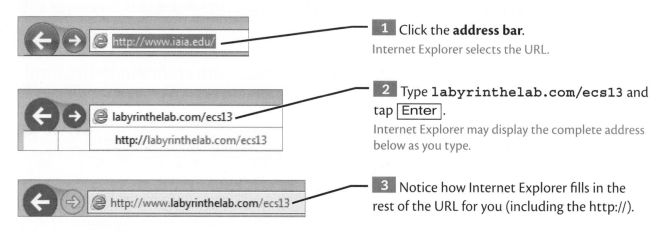

1 Click the **address bar**.
Internet Explorer selects the URL.

2 Type **labyrinthelab.com/ecs13** and tap **Enter**.
Internet Explorer may display the complete address below as you type.

3 Notice how Internet Explorer fills in the rest of the URL for you (including the http://).

4 From the left navigation bar, click the link for this lesson.
The student resource center for this book contains links to exercises you'll perform.

Searching the Web

Video   When you search the web, you usually just want a short list of what you're looking for. Since there are billions of web pages available for viewing, finding the right ones can be a challenge. Internet search engines help. The most popular search engine is Google.com. There are also search engines that provide results from multiple search engines simultaneously (called a metasearch). Search engines constantly seek out new web pages to improve the accuracy of search results.

Address Bar Search

Internet Explorer features a hybrid address/search bar. If you don't type a URL in the address bar, Internet Explorer treats it as search keywords.

NOTE   **In this lesson, the address/search bar will simply be called the address bar.**

Keyword Suggestions

Search engines can display suggestions as you type keywords. This shows popular searches others have made using similar keywords. It reduces typing, since you can click directly on the displayed keywords.

Search suggestions send information to search engines, which many consider a privacy issue.

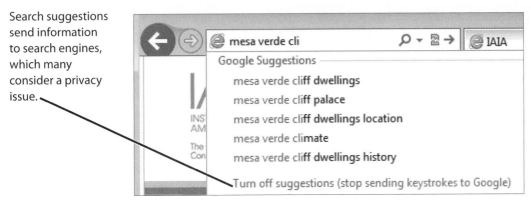

Search suggestions appear when you type keywords in the address bar.

Perform a Web Search

 Guide Me   In this exercise, you will use the search box to perform a quick web search.

 Use the Guide Me to work through this exercise. Go to the Student Resource Center (URL on inside front cover) or your eLab course and click the Guide Me link for this exercise. If you are using an eBook, just click the Guide Me icon under the exercise title.

1 Click once on the **address bar**, then type `mesa verde cli`.

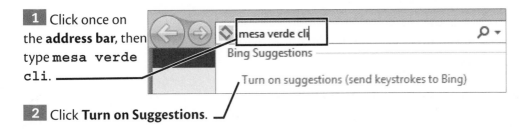

2 Click **Turn on Suggestions**.

3 Click **Mesa Verde Cliff Dwellings**.

Search results appear. These may contain links to ads near the top or on the right side of the page.

4 View search result types:

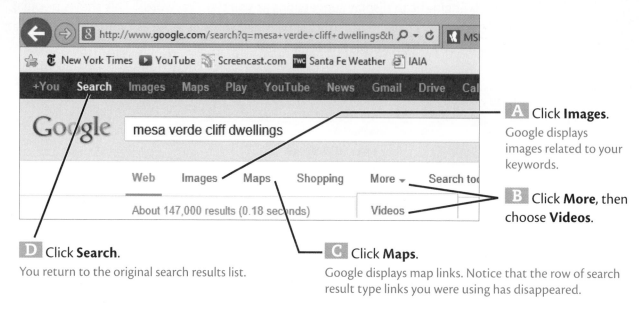

A Click **Images**.
Google displays images related to your keywords.

B Click **More**, then choose **Videos**.

D Click **Search**.
You return to the original search results list.

C Click **Maps**.
Google displays map links. Notice that the row of search result type links you were using has disappeared.

Adding Search Providers

 Video

You can add search providers to the Internet Explorer's address bar. You can switch from one provider to another from the address bar. For example, you might use Google as a general search engine and switch to a different search engine for a more specialized search. There are search providers for shopping, news, music, and other needs.

Setting a Default Search Provider

You can change the search provider Internet Explorer uses by default. Keyword searches in the address bar use the default provider unless you choose a different one.

Default search provider

Currently chosen provider

Internet Explorer displays its installed search providers.

develop your skills | ecs-0504

Add a Search Provider

Guide Me   In this exercise, you will add a search provider to Internet Explorer.

Use the Guide Me to work through this exercise.

1 Click the **search** ▼ menu button. ──────

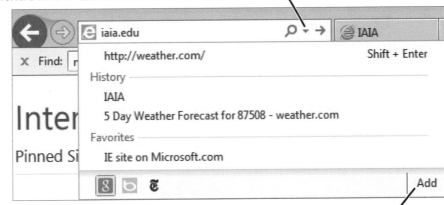

2 Click **Add**. ──────

The Internet Explorer gallery page appears. It lists search providers and other features you can add to Internet Explorer.

3 Choose **Most Popular**. ──────

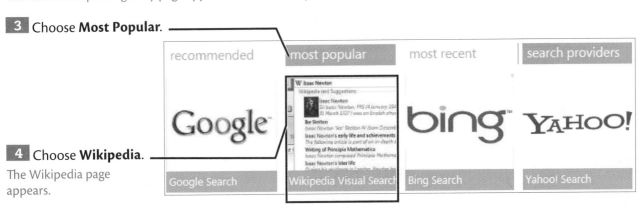

4 Choose **Wikipedia**. ──────

The Wikipedia page appears.

5 Click **Add to Internet Explorer**.

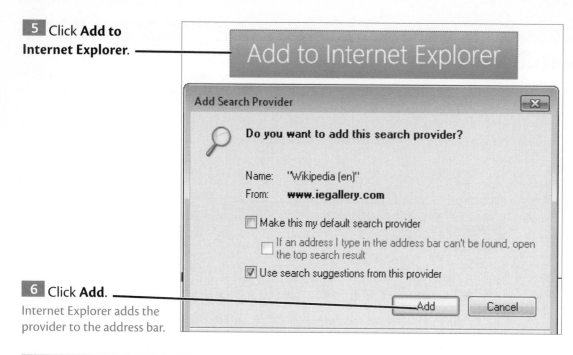

6 Click **Add**.

Internet Explorer adds the provider to the address bar.

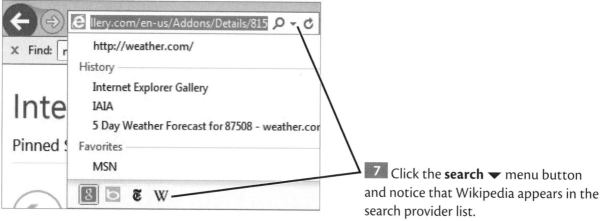

7 Click the **search** ▼ menu button and notice that Wikipedia appears in the search provider list.

8 Set the default search provider:

A Click **Settings**.

B Choose **Manage Add-Ons**.
The Manage Add-Ons window appears.

C Choose **Search Providers**.

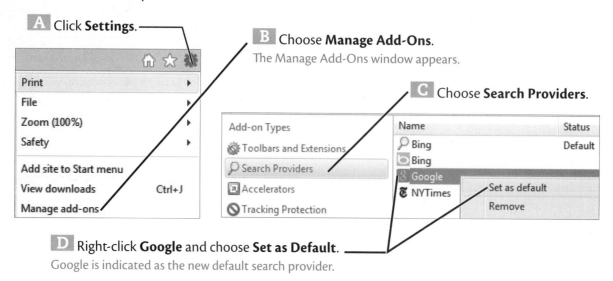

D Right-click **Google** and choose **Set as Default**.
Google is indicated as the new default search provider.

9 **Close**  Manage Add-Ons.
Now you will verify the default setting.

10 Click the **search** ▼
menu button. ———

Notice that Google is
now set as the default
search provider.

11 Click the **search** ▼
menu button again to
dismiss the search menu.———

12 Close the **Internet Explorer Gallery** tab.

Using Tabbed Browsing

▐▣◖ Video

Web browsers can display multiple web pages in the same window. Each web page
has a tab. You navigate tabs via the mouse, keyboard, or touch. *Tabbed browsing*
lets you jump quickly between web pages.

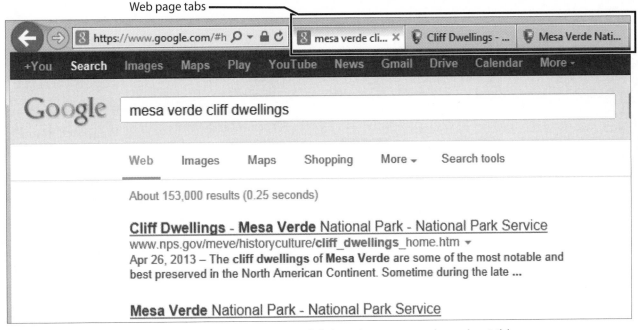

Tabbed browsing allows you to open new web pages while keeping your search results visible.

Use Tabbed Browsing

Guide Me   In this exercise, you will work with Internet Explorer tabs.

Use the Guide Me to work through this exercise.

1 Open a search result in a new tab:

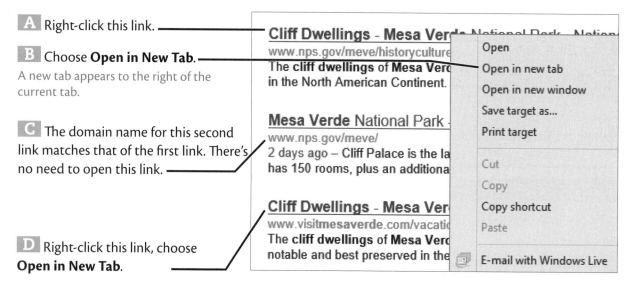

A Right-click this link.

B Choose **Open in New Tab**.
A new tab appears to the right of the current tab.

C The domain name for this second link matches that of the first link. There's no need to open this link.

D Right-click this link, choose **Open in New Tab**.

Cliff Dwellings - Mesa Verde National Park - National
www.nps.gov/meve/historyculture
The **cliff dwellings** of **Mesa Verde** in the North American Continent.

Mesa Verde National Park -
www.nps.gov/meve/
2 days ago – Cliff Palace is the la has 150 rooms, plus an additional

Cliff Dwellings - Mesa Verde
www.visitmesaverde.com/vacatio
The **cliff dwellings** of **Mesa Verde** notable and best preserved in the

Open
Open in new tab
Open in new window
Save target as...
Print target

Cut
Copy
Copy shortcut
Paste

E-mail with Windows Live

2 Navigate the new tabs with the mouse:

A Click this tab.   **B** Click this tab.

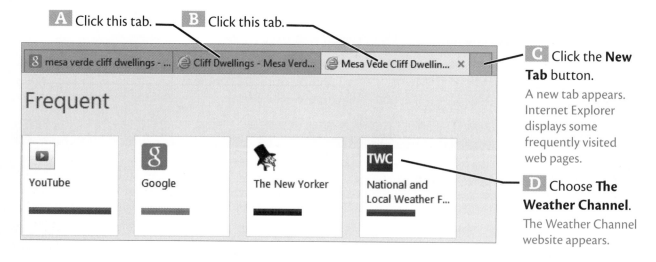

8 mesa verde cliff dwellings - ...   Cliff Dwellings - Mesa Verd...   Mesa Vede Cliff Dwellin... ✕

Frequent

YouTube   Google   The New Yorker   National and Local Weather F...

C Click the **New Tab** button.
A new tab appears. Internet Explorer displays some frequently visited web pages.

D Choose **The Weather Channel**.
The Weather Channel website appears.

3 Navigate tabs using the keyboard:

- Hold down [Ctrl] and tap [Tab] to jump forward to the search results tab.
  This keyboard shortcut is a convenient way to jump from tab to tab.

- Hold down [Ctrl] and tap [Tab] again.

- Use [Ctrl]+[Tab] again.

- Press [Ctrl]+[Shift] and tap [Tab] to jump backward.

4 Click the "x" to close the tab. ———

5 Right-click this tab and choose **Close Other Tabs**. ———

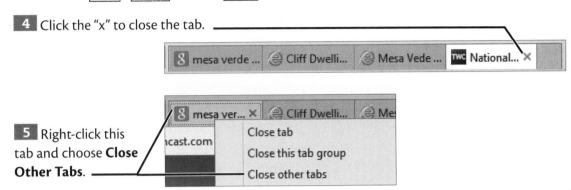

Saving Images from the Web

 Video

You can save images from the web. Saving an image from a web page is an example of *downloading*. Once you save the image, you can work with it like any other file on your computer. For example, you can save an image and insert it into a PowerPoint presentation.

Copyright

Photos and other items you find on the web typically have copyright restrictions. Just because you can save it doesn't mean you own it. Look for any copyright restrictions the website may define.

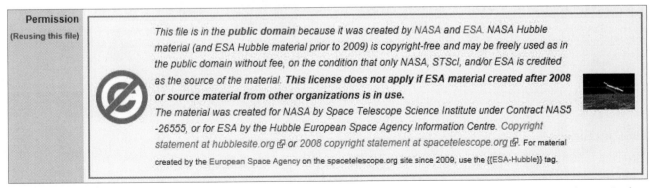

A permission statement accompanies a photo on Wikipedia. Many photos created by government agencies are in the public domain and may be used freely.

Fair Use

The principle of fair use allows teachers and students to use a portion of copyrighted material for educational, nonprofit use without having to seek permission. For example, you can quote a passage from an article or illustrate a class presentation with a photo.

In college coursework, *always* cite the source of any quoted text or images that are not your own. Do this regardless of the item's copyright status.

---

develop your skills | ecs-0506

Save an Image

 Guide Me   In this exercise, you will display a file and save it to your computer.

 Use the Guide Me to work through this exercise.

1 Click **Images**. _____

2 Point at (don't click) the first image. _____
Details for the image appear.

3 Notice that the image is from a government website (.gov). _____

4 Click the image. _____

Google displays the image on top of the page it came from. Since the image came from a government agency, it's safe to assume it may be copied and used freely.

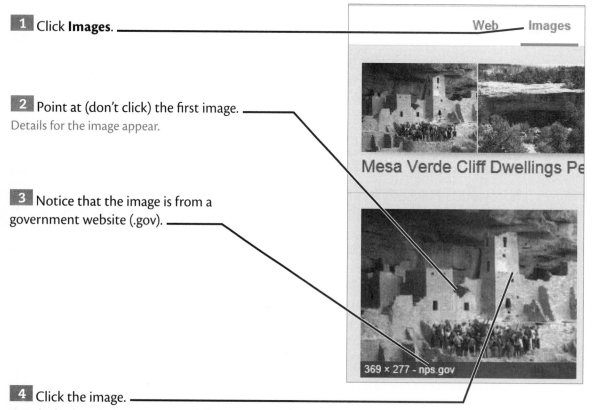

5 Click **View Original Image.**

Google displays the original image. Depending on its size, it may appear the same or larger.

6 Right-click the photo and choose **Save Picture As.**

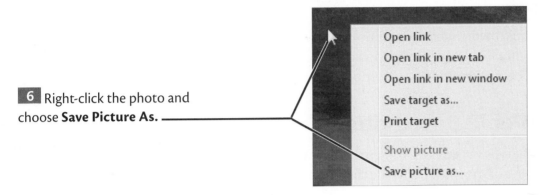

7 If necessary, click the **white triangle** to display items below **This PC.**

8 Click **Pictures.**

9 Type this Filename.

10 Click Save.

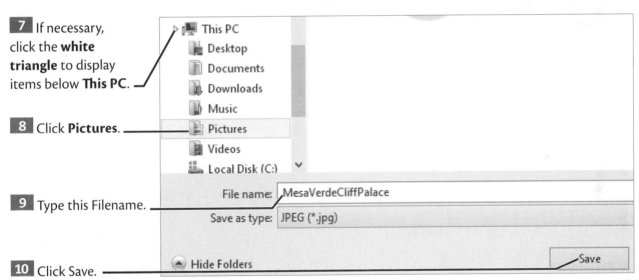

11 Click **Back** ◄ twice to return to the search results page.

What Is Web 2.0?

 Video

Web 2.0 is a generation of web creations focused on interactivity. Web pages were originally one-way communication media; you could view web pages but could not "talk back." Web 2.0 applications make it easy for viewers to interact with others. The term Web 2.0 doesn't indicate a change in the network that transmits web pages.

Social media such as Facebook and Twitter are classic examples of Web 2.0 technology. Anyone with an account can actively participate in conversations, post photos and messages, and more.

Web 2.0 Activities

The types of interactivity enabled by Web 2.0 continue to grow. This lesson covers some of the most popular activities.

Web 2.0 Activities		
Activity	**Description**	**Examples**
Threaded discussion	Place where you can post messages and reply directly to others' messages so additional people can follow and join in on the correspondence.	Google Groups
Online conferencing	Services that support group meetings online, including viewing attendee screens, voice communications, and sometimes webcam video.	GoToMeeting, WebEx, Skype
Blog	Short for web log. A place where you can post writings. Readers can post comments on your writings. There are numerous free blogging websites.	WordPress, Blogspot, Blogger

Threaded Discussions

 Video   A threaded discussion is an online space where participants can post a series of linked messages and responses. The linked messages form a "thread" that you can follow. A threaded discussion is like a conversation that takes place over the course of hours, days, or perhaps weeks.

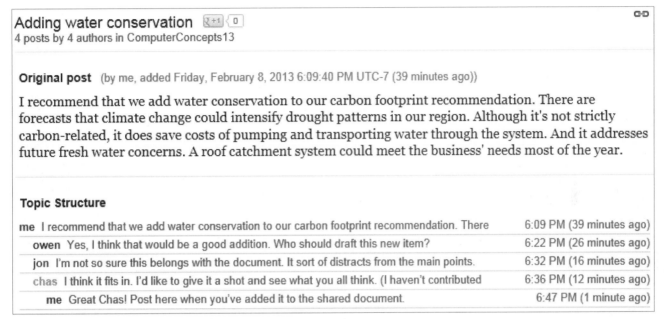

A threaded discussion on Google Groups.

 There are free and paid threaded discussion services. Free services tend to use online ads.

Two Types of Online Communications

There are two basic types of online communication. Each has its advantages.

- **Asynchronous:** Group members don't need to be logged in at the same time. Threaded discussions and email are examples of asynchronous communications.

- **Synchronous:** Group members must be logged in at the same time. Online chats and meetings are examples of synchronous communications.

develop your skills | ecs-0507

Participate In a Threaded Discussion

 Guide Me   In this exercise, you will sign in to Google Groups and post a blog entry.

Use the Guide Me to work through this exercise.

1 Start **Internet Explorer** and type this URL in the address bar.

Brooke is a member of an online discussion group hosted by Google Groups.

2 Click **Sign In.**

3 Type **brooke@gmail.com.**

4 Type **changeme.**

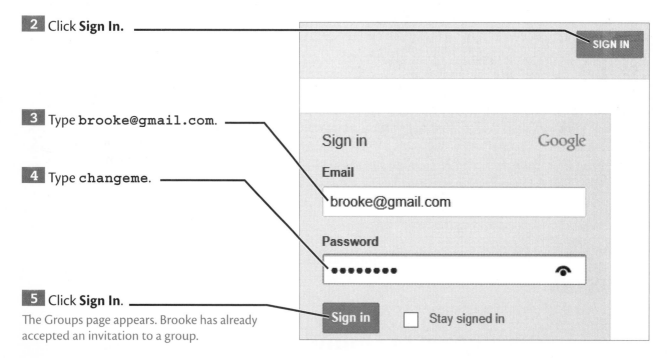

5 Click **Sign In.**
The Groups page appears. Brooke has already accepted an invitation to a group.

6 Click **My Groups.**

7 Click **ComputerConcepts13.**
There are no topics yet; you will add one next.

8 Click **New Topic**.

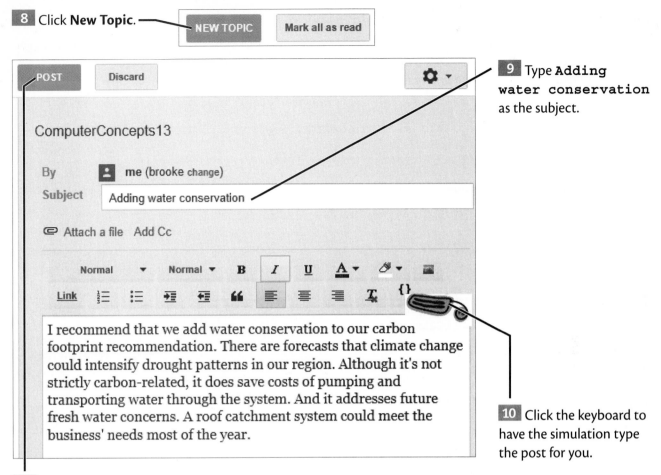

9 Type **Adding water conservation** as the subject.

10 Click the keyboard to have the simulation type the post for you.

11 Click **Post**.

Google Groups creates the post and sends an email message to group members.

12 Click **Adding Water Conservation**.

The post appears as others will see it.

13 Click **Next Day**.

Imagine that a day has passed and you are checking in on the discussion. Now you will reply to another posting.

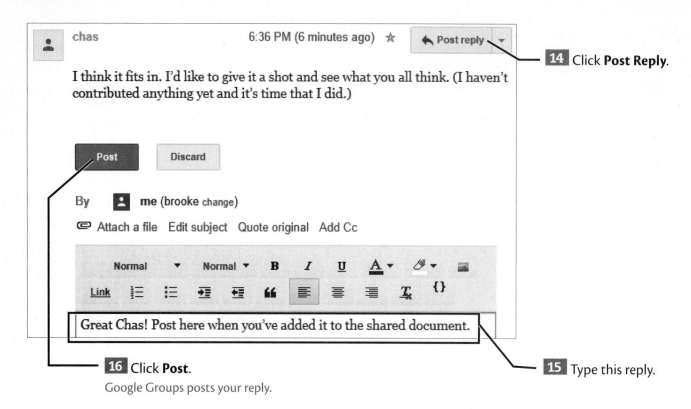

14 Click **Post Reply**.

15 Type this reply.

16 Click **Post**.

Google Groups posts your reply.

17 Click **Overview**.

Google Groups displays the threaded discussion in a condensed format.

Conducting Online Meetings

 Video

Online meeting services, such as GoToMeeting, allow small groups to hold virtual meetings. The presenter's screen is visible to everyone. Audio can be handled via the mic and speakers on your computer. Depending on the service used, you may even see each attendee's face on his or her webcam.

Joining a Meeting

Joining an online meeting is free and takes just a few minutes. The meeting host sends you an invitation with details on how to join the meeting. For example, it may have a link you can click to login to the meeting via the web. Joining a meeting may require the download of a small program to give you access.

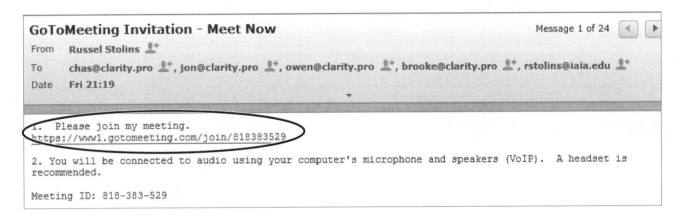

Hosting Meetings

Many online meeting services require a monthly or annual subscription to host meetings. Only the host has to pay; attendees join free. Some services may use online ads instead of a subscription.

Participate In an Online Meeting

Guide Me   In this exercise, you will briefly join a simulated online meeting. As you begin, you will be viewing a meeting invitation in an email.

Use the Guide Me to work through this exercise.

1 Click the join-meeting link.

> 1.   Please join my meeting.
>   https://www1.gotomeeting.com/join/818383529

After a pause, GoToMeeting prompts you to install a small file.

2 Click **Run**.

Do you want to run or save **Citrix Online Launcher.exe** from **download.citrixonline.com**?   Run   Save ▼   Cancel   ✕

An online meeting launcher appears and displays the connection progress.

3 Choose **Yes** to install the program.

Once the launcher finishes installing and making a meeting connection, a new window appears in which you enter your personal information.

4 Type **Jon** as the name.

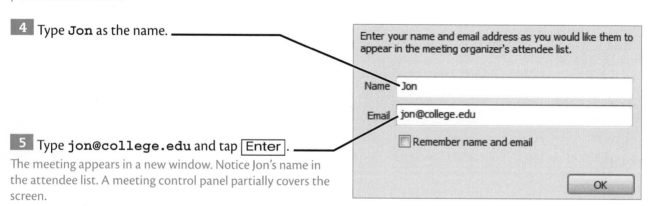

Enter your name and email address as you would like them to appear in the meeting organizer's attendee list.

Name Jon

Email jon@college.edu

☐ Remember name and email

OK

5 Type **jon@college.edu** and tap Enter.

The meeting appears in a new window. Notice Jon's name in the attendee list. A meeting control panel partially covers the screen.

6 Click the arrow to hide the control panel.

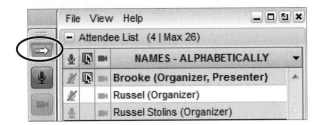

The meeting is in progress. You'll be able to speak and hear via your computer's or tablet's built-in webcam and microphone.

7 Leave the meeting:

A Show the control panel.

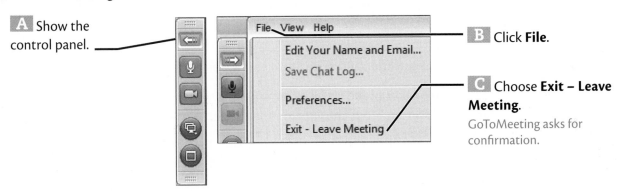

B Click **File**.

C Choose **Exit – Leave Meeting**.
GoToMeeting asks for confirmation.

8 Click **Yes**.

The meeting window disappears.

concepts review

To check your knowledge of the key concepts introduced in this lesson, complete the Concepts Review quiz by choosing the appropriate access option below.

If you are...	Then access the quiz by...
Using eLab	Logging in, choosing Content, and navigating to the Concepts Review quiz for this lesson
Not using eLab	Going to the Student Resource Center (see the inside front cover)

reinforce your skills | ecs-0501

Search the Web

In this exercise, you will search for information and open and close tabs as you view search results.

This exercise takes place on "live" web pages, which means the pages you see may look different from the figures shown here. That's okay; the features should still work.

Browse the Web

1. **Windows 8.1 Only:** Display the **Desktop**.

2. Start **Internet Explorer**.

3. Click in the address bar, type **si.edu**, and tap [Enter].
   The Smithsonian Institution website appears.

4. Click **Museums and Zoo** or any other menu link you find of interest.

Explore	Visit	Get Involved	Connect	Educators	Kids
Home	Museums and Zoo	Research Centers	Cultural Centers

5. Navigate to a museum you find interesting. Take a few minutes to explore the museum's contents.

Search the Web

6 Click the **address bar** ▼ menu button.

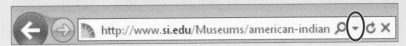

7 Click any installed search provider near the lower-left corner of the menu.

8 Click in the address bar, type one or more search keywords related to the Smithsonian museum you've just browsed, and tap Enter.

Internet Explorer displays search results from the chosen provider.

9 Open one of the search results and then go **Back** ◀ to the search results page.

10 Open another search result.

Add a Search Provider

11 Click the **address bar** ▼ menu button and then choose **Add** at the bottom-right corner of the menu.

12 Choose a search provider type (All, Videos, Music, etc.) from the list on the left side of the page.

13 Click any search provider to display information about it.

14 Click **Add to Internet Explorer** and then click **Add**.

15 Click the **address bar** ▼ menu button and then choose the new search provider.

16 Type one or more keywords in the address bar and tap Enter.

Internet Explorer displays search results from your newly installed search provider.

Use Tabbed Browsing

17 Right-click a search result and choose **Open in New Tab**.

A new tab appears but you remain on the search results page.

18 Right-click another search result and choose **Open in New Tab**.

19 Navigate tabs with the keyboard:

- Press Ctrl+Tab to jump to first search result you opened.

- Press Ctrl+Tab again, and the second search result appears.

- Press Ctrl+Tab one more time to return to the search results page.

- Press Shift+Ctrl and tap Tab, and you move back to the previous search result.

20 Right-click the current tab and choose **Close Other Tabs**.

Save an Image

21   Click the **address bar** ▼ menu and choose **Bing**.

This search provider selection remains active until you choose another search provider, or until you close all Internet Explorer windows and then restart the application.

22   Click the address bar, type **new york skyline**, and tap Enter.

23   Click to display the **Images** search results.

24   Click any picture.

The search engine displays the picture. There may be a delay before the picture displays clearly.

25   Right-click the picture and choose **Save Picture As**.

26   Choose the **Pictures** folder and click **Save**.

Leave Internet Explorer open for the next exercise.

reinforce your skills | ecs-0502

Use Web 2.0

Guide Me   In this exercise, you will practice using two primary Web 2.0 tools.

Use the Guide Me to work through this exercise.

Threaded Discussions

You are already logged in to Google Groups and are participating in two discussions.

1   Click the **CloudComputing2** group.

2   Click the **New Topic** button and type the subject **Sharing a Folder**.

3   Click the keyboard icon in the message area to "type" a new message.

4   Click the **Online Meetings** message.

5 Click the **Click Here to Reply** box below the message.

Google Groups opens a message composition box where you can type a reply.

6 Click the keyboard icon in the message area to "type" and then click **Post** (not Post Reply).

This ends the threaded discussions section of the simulation.

Online Meetings

You are now in a phone call with a meeting organizer who gives you instructions to join a meeting-in-progress. The Budget-Projection spreadsheet is open on your Desktop, ready to display to meeting participants.

7 Click its taskbar button to start **Internet Explorer** and then type `joingotomeeting.com` in the address bar.

GoToMeeting asks for a meeting ID, which you get from the meeting organizer over the phone. (Meeting IDs can also be shared via email.)

8 Type the meeting ID **319-858-520** and click **Continue**.

You've participated in a meeting before, so the small GoToMeeting program is already installed on your computer. The launcher displays the progress of connecting to the meeting.

9 Type your name, leave the email address box blank, and click **OK**.

10 Click **Zoom** and then choose **Full Screen**.

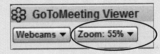

The meeting fills your screen.

11 Tap Esc on the keyboard or on the simulation screen.

The meeting returns to a normal window. You see an invitation to become the presenter.

12 Click **Show My Screen**.

The GoToMeeting window disappears. Others can see your screen now. The GoToMeeting control panel covers part of your screen, so you will make it smaller.

13 Click the **Hide Control Panel** button.

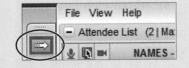

The control panel collapses to a narrow set of buttons.

14 Click the **Budget Summary Data** tab.

Meeting attendees see the new view of the spreadsheet. Your part of the presentation is finished, so you return control of the meeting to the organizer.

15   Return control of the meeting:

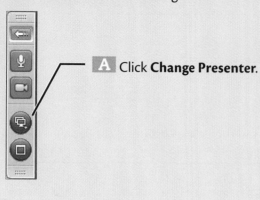

A Click **Change Presenter**.

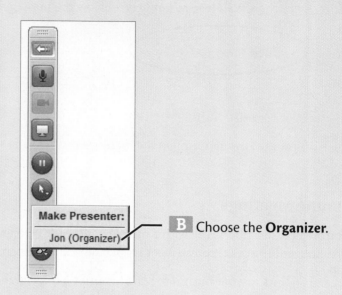

B Choose the **Organizer**.

16   Click the **Show Control Panel** button.

The full control panel reappears.

17   Choose **File→Exit – Leave Meeting**.
This ends the online meeting section of the simulation.

18   **Close** ✕ Internet Explorer.

Browse and Search the Web

You are working as an intern for an online publication. In this exercise, you will look up the latest news about certain topics.

Your instructor will provide you with the following details.

New Search Provider: _____

Search Topic A: _____

Search Topic B: _____

Search Topic C: _____

Browse the Web

1 **Windows 8.1 Only:** Display the **Desktop**.

2 Start **Internet Explorer** and type `mars.jpl.nasa.gov/msl` in the address bar.

3 Use the **Snipping Tool** to take a picture of the page, including the address bar. Save the snip to your file storage location as `ECS05-A01a-Browse-[FirstInitialLastName]`.

Search the Web

4 Search the web for Topic A.

5 Use the **Snipping Tool** to take a picture of the search results page, including the address bar. Save the snip to your file storage location as `ECS05-A01b-Search-[FirstInitialLastName]`.

Add a Search Provider

6 Add a search provider (specified by your instructor) to the address bar.

7 Perform a search on Topic B using the new search provider.

8 Use the **Snipping Tool** to take a picture of your search results. Save the snip to your file storage location as `ECS05-A01c-Provider-[FirstInitialLastName]`.

Use Tabbed Browsing

9 Open three links to search results in their own tabs.

10 Use the **Snipping Tool** to take a picture of the search results page, including the three tabs you just opened. Save the snip to your file storage location as `ECS05-A01d-Tabbed-[FirstInitialLastName]`.

Save an Image

11   Search the web for images on Topic C.

12   Save one image to your USB flash drive or the **Pictures** folder.

13   Rename the picture to **ECS05-A01e-Image-[FirstInitialLastName]**.

At the end of the exercise, your screen should appear like the figure below (Windows 8.1). The exact images displayed depend on your instructor's search Topic C.

14   **Close** [X] Internet Explorer.

15   Submit your snipped screens according to the guidelines provided by your instructor.

Use Web 2.0

You are working as an intern for an online publication. In this exercise, you will participate in an online discussion and an online meeting about the latest news topics. You can perform this exercise even if the Outlook application on your computer is not set up for email.

This exercise requires that invitations to an online discussion group and an online meeting be sent to you. Ask your instructor for assistance, if necessary.

Threaded Discussions

1   Check your email for an invitation to an online discussion group, and join it.

2   Make a post to the discussion on a topic designated by your instructor.

3 Use the **Snipping Tool** to take a picture of your discussion posting. Save the snip to your file storage location as `ECS05-A02a-Post-[FirstInitialLastName]`.

4 Make a reply to one classmate's post.

5 Use the **Snipping Tool** to take a picture of your reply. Save the snip to your file storage location as `ECS05-A02b-Reply-[FirstInitialLastName]`.

Online Meeting

6 Check your email for an invitation to an online meeting, and join it.

7 Use the **Snipping Tool** to take a picture during the meeting. Save the snip to your file storage location as `ECS05-A02c-Meeting-[FirstInitialLastName]`.

8 Submit your snipped screens according to the guidelines provided by your instructor.

---

apply your skills | ecs-0503

Do It All

You are working as an intern for an online publication. In this exercise, you will research various topics for articles and participate in online interactions with other staff members. You can perform this exercise even if the Outlook application on your computer is not set up for email.

 A portion of this exercise requires that invitations to an online discussion group and an online meeting be sent to you. Ask your instructor for assistance, if necessary.

Your instructor will provide you with the following details.

New Search Provider: _____

Search Topic A: _____

Search Topic B: _____

Search Topic C: _____

Browse the Web

1 **Windows 8.1 Only:** Display the **Desktop**.

2 Start **Internet Explorer** and type `americanart.si.edu` in the address bar.

3 Use the **Snipping Tool** to take a picture of the page, including the address bar. Save the snip to your file storage location as `ECS05-A03a-Browse-[FirstInitialLastName]`.

Search the Web

4   Search the web for Topic A.

5   Use the **Snipping Tool** to take a picture of the search results page, including the address bar. Save the snip to your file storage location as `ECS05-A03b-Search-[FirstInitialLastName]`.

Add a Search Provider

6   Add a search provider (specified by your instructor) to the address bar.

7   Search for Topic B using the new search provider.

8   Use the **Snipping Tool** to take a picture of your search results. Save the snip to your file storage location as `ECS05-A03c-Provider-[FirstInitialLastName]`.

Use Tabbed Browsing

9   Open three links to search results in their own tabs.

10   Use the **Snipping Tool** to take a picture of the search results page, including the three tabs you just opened. Save the snip to your file storage location as `ECS05-A03d-Tabbed-[FirstInitialLastName]`.

Save an Image

11   Search the web for images on Topic C.

12   Save one image to your USB flash drive or the **Pictures** folder.

13   Rename the picture to `ECS05-A03e-Image-[FirstInitialLastName]`.

Threaded Discussions

14   Check your email for an invitation to an online discussion group, and join it.

15   Make a post to the discussion on a topic designated by your instructor.

16   Use the **Snipping Tool** to take a picture of your discussion posting. Save the snip to your file storage location as `ECS05-A03f-Post-[FirstInitialLastName]`.

17   Make a reply to one classmate's post.

18   Use the **Snipping Tool** to take a picture of your reply. Save the snip to your file storage location as `ECS05-A03g-Reply-[FirstInitialLastName]`.

Online Meeting

19   Check your email for an invitation to an online meeting, and join it.

20   Use the **Snipping Tool** to take a picture during the meeting. Save the snip to your file storage location as `ECS05-A03h-Meeting-[FirstInitialLastName]`.

21   Submit your snipped screens based on the guidelines provided by your instructor.

Save a Tabbed Search

In this exercise, you will perform a search on a topic of your choice.

- Choose any topic that interests you. For example, you might search about a hobby, volunteer community service activity, musician, or virtually any other topic.

- Use any search engine to search for information, images, and videos related to your topic. Open at least six promising search results in tabs.

- Save the tabbed search as a tabbed group Favorite using Favorites→Favorites menu→Add Tabbed Group to Favorites.

- Open the saved search from the tabbed group Favorites. Use the Snipping Tool to take a picture of the search page and the six search results you opened in tabs.

Submit your snipped screens according to the guidelines provided by your instructor.

Recommend a Device and Vendor

In this exercise, you will shop online for a computer, printer, or some other piece of office equipment. You will compare prices of various online vendors and prepare a recommendation on which vendor to purchase from.

You will submit screen snips of four pages at the end of the project, so keep track of where you've been using Favorites/Bookmarks.

- You've been asked to do research on a new device for your office. It could be a printer, computer, tablet, digital camera, or another device used in a business setting.

- Find reviews of the device. The best reviews are likely to be from well-known publications (e.g., PCWorld) and on websites with specialist interest in that type of device. You may also see reviews on vendor websites.

- Look on the web for vendors selling the device that rated highly in the reviews.

- Write a one or two paragraph memo that recommends a model of the device and a vendor from which to purchase it. Base your recommendation on price, return policy, reliability, or similar criteria.

- Use the Snipping Tool to take screen snips of the following:
  - Device page at the recommended vendor website
  - The vendor's return policy page
  - One page of a review of the device
  - One page of a vendor website you did not recommend

Submit your snipped screens according to the guidelines provided by your instructor.

The Cloud

6 Storing Files and Sharing Online

Skills YOU Will Learn

- Define cloud computing
- Use cloud-based file storage
- Describe sync and watched folders
- Share a file or folder online
- Describe an online application

in this lesson

Carrying your files with you on a device is becoming a thing of the past. Cloud storage based on the Internet allows access to documents, music, photos, and data from almost any connected device. The cloud also supports new ways to interact with classmates and coworkers. In this lesson, you will learn about online file storage, sync, sharing, and online applications.

Collaborating on a Cloud

You are taking an online writing course. One of your first assignments is a collaborative writing project. The instructor assigns you to a group with three other students. Although your online course supports email exchanges, one group member suggests forming a cloud-based online study group. She explains that it's a way to share documents and information without constantly passing email messages back and forth.

You establish the online study group and create a document for the group paper on your cloud drive. You share a link to this document so everyone can edit it.

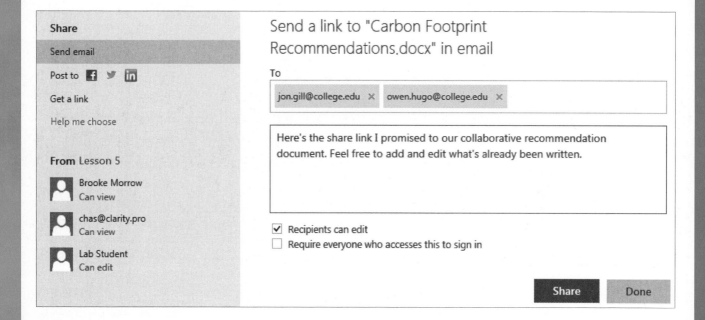

What Is the Cloud?

 Video

The *cloud* is services and storage (typically running via the Internet) with an unknown physical location. You can use the cloud to store files, run software, or access additional computing power. The cloud enables new levels of collaboration. Since the physical location doesn't matter, you can share files and other information with anyone anywhere.

Servers

A server is a computer that stores files in the cloud and transfers them to and from local devices. Most servers reside in huge server farm warehouse installations containing thousands of computers/storage drives.

A Google server farm somewhere in the U.S.

Services

The cloud supports numerous services. New services are added constantly. A few have become popular quite rapidly.

- **Cloud-based storage:** Online storage space from 2 gigabytes (GB) on up.
- **Cloud-based** *file sharing*: The ability to share files and/or folders with a link, without sending them via email or other means.
- **Cloud-based** *synchronization (sync)*: Files, settings, and program data that are automatically updated between multiple computers/devices.
- **Cloud-based workspaces:** Online spaces where teams can share files, calendars, and other information.

Storing Files Online

 Video

Storing files online places them in the cloud. These files are available wherever you have an Internet connection. Most online storage systems offer a basic level of free storage, with the option to pay for additional storage. You'll have the opportunity to practice using three popular cloud storage services in this lesson: OneDrive, Dropbox, and Google Drive.

Watched Folders

A *watched folder* is a location on your local computer that responds to file/folder activity. *Cloud storage* services usually set up a watched folder on your computer. When you store a file or folder there, a copy uploads to online storage automatically.

Checkmarks indicate files
successfully synchronized with
cloud storage.

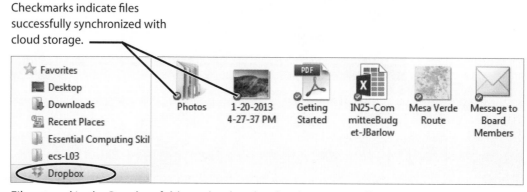

Files stored in the Dropbox folder upload to the cloud automatically.

Modifying Watched Folders

You can modify watched folders as you would any local folder on your computer. For example, you can create new folders inside a watched folder. You can move and copy files to the watched folder with normal file management commands. The cloud-storage service copies all modifications.

develop your skills | ecs-0601

Create a Watched Folder

 Guide Me In this exercise, you will create a new folder in a watched folder.

 Use the Guide Me to work through this exercise. Go to the Student Resource Center (URL on inside front cover) or your eLab course and click the Guide Me link for this exercise. If you are using an eBook, just click the Guide Me icon under the exercise title.

1 **Windows 8.1 Only:** Display the **Desktop**.

2 Carefully insert your USB flash drive.

3 Dismiss any prompt from Windows:

■ **Windows 7: Close** [X] AutoPlay if it appears.

■ **Windows 8.1:** Ignore any flash drive message.

4 Open the **File Explorer** and display the **OneDrive** watched folder.

The OneDrive folder has three folders created with the account. You open them like normal storage drive folders.

5 Double-click the **Documents** folder.
The folder is likely to be empty.

6 Click **Back** .

7 Create a new folder named `Lesson 6`.

Windows 7

Windows 8.1

Synchronized Storage

 Video   Synchronized storage makes sure the latest versions of your files are available on all your devices. When you log in to your computer, the service checks files stored online against the ones in the watched folder. If files online are newer, the service downloads them. Older online files are replaced with new versions uploaded from your computer.

Files as they appear in OneDrive on your computer (with checkmarks).

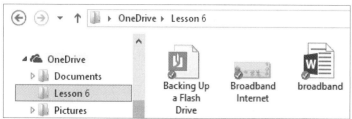

Copies of the files as they appear in OneDrive on the web.

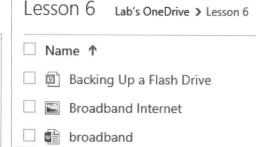

OneDrive displays a checkmark by each up-to-date (synchronized) file and folder.

---

develop your skills | ecs-0602

Copy Files to a Watched Folder

 Guide Me   In this exercise, you will add files to OneDrive by copying.

NOTE   **Use the Guide Me to work through this exercise.**

1 Display your USB flash drive.

2 Double-click **Essential Computing Skills** and then **ecs-L06**.

3 Use Ctrl + A from the keyboard to select all files.

4 Use Ctrl + C to copy the selection.

5 Display **OneDrive**.

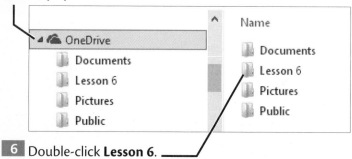

6 Double-click **Lesson 6**.

7 Change the view to **Medium Icons**.

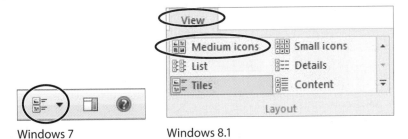

Windows 7   Windows 8.1

8 Use Ctrl + V to paste.

Windows pastes copies of the files. Notice that checkmarks gradually appear on the file icons. This signals that the files are copied to the cloud.

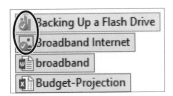

9 Click **Back**   /   .

Notice the checkmark on the folder icon. (It might take a moment or two for this to appear, depending on the speed of your Internet connection.)

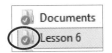

Saving to a Watched Folder

🎦 **Video**   You save your work from applications to watched folders as you would with normal (local storage drive) folders. Office 2013 applications have OneDrive access built into them. You can also save to watched folders for other cloud storage services.

develop your skills | ecs-0603

Save to a Watched Folder

 Guide Me   In this exercise, you will save a Word document to OneDrive.

Use the Guide Me to work through this exercise.

1 Start **Word**, then create a new blank document.

2 Type this text: `Document saved to a watched folder.`

3 To save the document to OneDrive, first click .

4 Choose **Save As**.

5 Choose **Lab Student's OneDrive**.

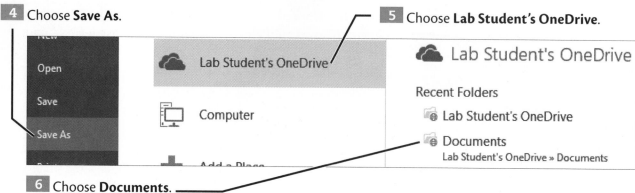

6 Choose **Documents**.

7 Confirm that the correct filename was entered from the document text.

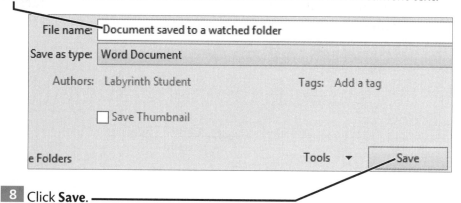

8 Click **Save**.

9 **Close** ☒ Word.
The OneDrive window reappears.

10 Double-click **Documents**.
The document just saved is visible.

11 Click **Back** ⟲ / ⟲.

Web Access to Cloud Storage

📹 **Video**

Cloud storage gives you *web access*, or access to your files wherever you have an Internet connection. When you're not at your computer, or using some other device such as a tablet or smartphone, you can access your files via a web browser or an app on the device.

For example, imagine you are doing research at a library and need to look over some notes and diagrams. You start a web browser and type the URL for your cloud storage service. You log in to your account and then open the folder for your research project. You display a mind map you created about your research.

Navigating Cloud Storage

Cloud storage services let you view and open various folders. There will usually be links along the top of the page to help you move back to the base level of your cloud storage.

Link to the base level of online storage. ─┐   ┌─ Links to folders you've opened.

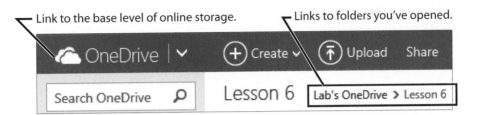

 Windows 8.1 Users: The OneDrive tablet app on the Start screen functions differently from the web browser interface. Because the web browser interface has more commands and versatility, this lesson concentrates on the browser rather than the Windows 8.1 tablet app.

---

develop your skills | ecs-0604

Browse Cloud Storage via the Web

 Guide Me In this exercise, you will view files in a OneDrive folder. As the exercise begins, you are logged in as a guest at a library computer.

 Use the Guide Me to work through this exercise.

1 Open a web browser window.

2 Type **onedrive.live.com**.

3 Type **labstudent11@gmail.com** as the account name.

4 Type **changeme** as the password.

5 Click **Sign In** or tap Enter.

OneDrive displays the contents of your cloud storage.

6 Click the **Lesson 6** tile.

OneDrive displays the files you copied in a previous exercise. Pictures appear as small versions at the bottom of the folder list. However, it doesn't list the filenames.

7 Change to the list view.

OneDrive transforms the view from tiles to a list.

8 Click **Computer System Mind Map**.

OneDrive displays the mind map picture.

9 Return to the folder view.

OneDrive transforms the view from tiles to a list.

10 Click **Lab's OneDrive** to navigate back to the cloud storage base level.

11 Click **Lesson 6**.

12 Display the tile view.

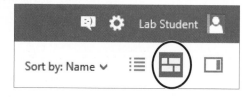

Downloading and Uploading

 Video   As you work with cloud-based storage, you may need to transfer files and folders from one storage location to another. Some commands will only work with files stored on a physical drive on a computer or tablet. While watched folders make file transfer commands for you automatically, sometimes you'll need to transfer files manually with download and upload commands.

- *downloading*: Transfers a file from a remote server to your local computer.
- *uploading*: Sends a file from your local computer to a remote server.

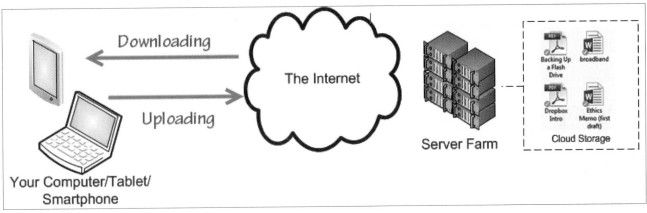

Download and upload commands transfer files between local and remote storage.

develop your skills | ecs-0605

Download and Upload Files

 Guide Me   In this exercise, you will download from and upload to OneDrive.

Use the Guide Me to work through this exercise.

1 Place a checkmark on the **Cloud Upload & Downloading** figure.

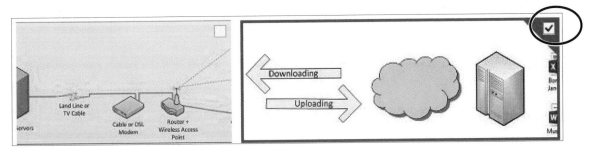

2 Click **Download**

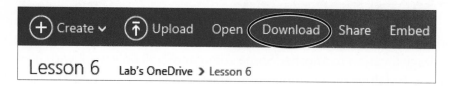

3 Click the **Save menu** and choose **Save As.**

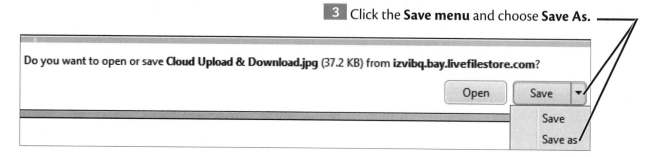

4 Display your USB flash drive.

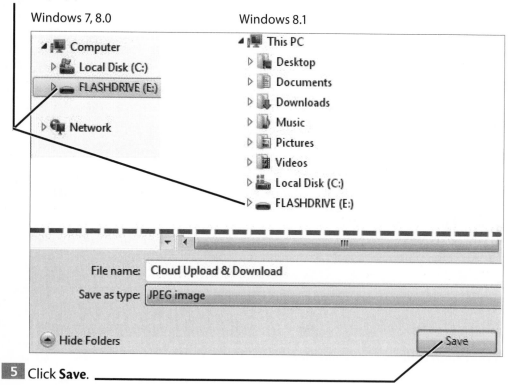

5 Click **Save.**

OneDrive downloads the picture to your USB flash drive.

6 **Close** ☒ the download box.

When your watched folder isn't installed on a computer, you can still upload files from a local drive to your cloud storage.

7 Click the base level of your OneDrive, **Lab's OneDrive.**

8 Display your flash drive, then open the **Essential Computing Skills** folder and the **ecs-L06** folder.

Windows 7, 8.0   Windows 8.1

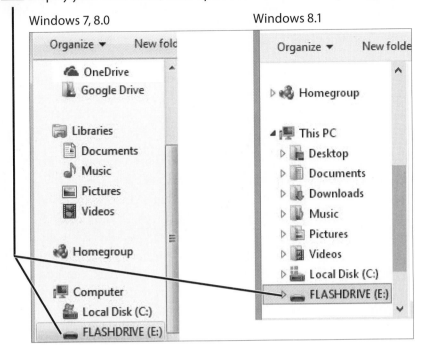

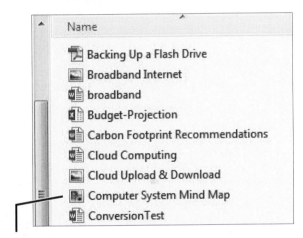

9 Double-click **Computer System Mind Map**.

OneDrive uploads the file to the cloud. It will appear as a new image in your OneDrive web page. When you get back to your computer, the file will be waiting in your watched OneDrive folder.

10 Click the **Lesson 6** folder.

a closer look

Online Storage Privacy

Free online storage often comes at a price. Many services claim nonexclusive ownership and access to any files stored on their servers. This co-ownership may continue even if you delete the files or close your account.

Rights to Your Content

The rights a service has to your files are usually described in their terms of service agreement. There may be additional details in the service's privacy rights statement. These terms define their access to your files and how long that access may last. These terms may change from time to time. Some services may define their rights to last *forever*; that is, anything you upload to their service is theirs to use as they see fit, even if you terminate your account. The terms often give cloud storage services the right to develop new products based on your files, without limitation.

Online Ads

Many services survey your files to target online ads that help fund the free storage. (This is frequently done with free email services, too.) The content of your files may give clues to personal interests and concerns which accumulate in an online profile. The service then offers use of the profile details to advertisers. Revenue is earned every time a targeted ad is displayed, and even more if it is clicked.

Terms of service can vary widely. It pays to review the terms with care. Check out the buzz with a web search related to privacy rights on any service you choose.

Online Applications

 Video

Online applications run off software stored on the cloud rather than on your computer's local storage drives. You can run online applications from any computer/device with an Internet connection. Some online applications allow you to start them when you have an Internet connection and run when you aren't connected.

Capabilities

Online applications tend to be simpler and less capable compared to traditional applications. Since most users don't utilize advanced features of applications, this simplicity isn't that great of a disadvantage. Online applications work fine for basic editing and file creation tasks.

OneDrive's Word Online app.

Word 2013 application.

Google Docs, a web-based word processor.

Edit an Online Document

Guide Me   In this exercise, you will edit an online document using the Word Web App.

Use the Guide Me to work through this exercise.

1 Click to place a checkmark to edit **Cloud Computing**.

2 Choose
Open→Open in Word Web App.

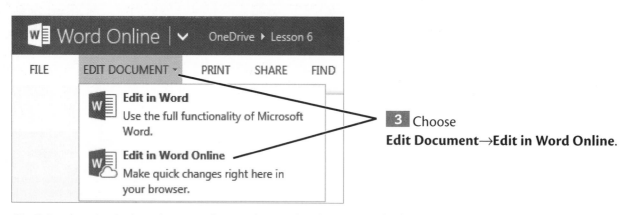

3 Choose
Edit Document→Edit in Word Online.

OneDrive downloads the software and starts the Word Online App in the browser window. You're ready to edit the document.

4 Click here and tap ⬚Enter⬚.

Origin

The term "cloud computing" originated with the use of a cloud to represent the Internet on many network diagrams. Since the physical location of the network server didn't really matter, the cloud symbolized the vague residence of files and other resources accessed via the Internet.

File Transfer

Transferring files is accomplished by uploading and downloading. Watched folders accom￼ uploading and downloading automatically. If you are at a computer without a watched fol￼ upload and download files manually.

5 Click the keyboard to "type" a new heading and paragraph.

6 Tap ⬚Enter⬚.

7 Insert a picture:

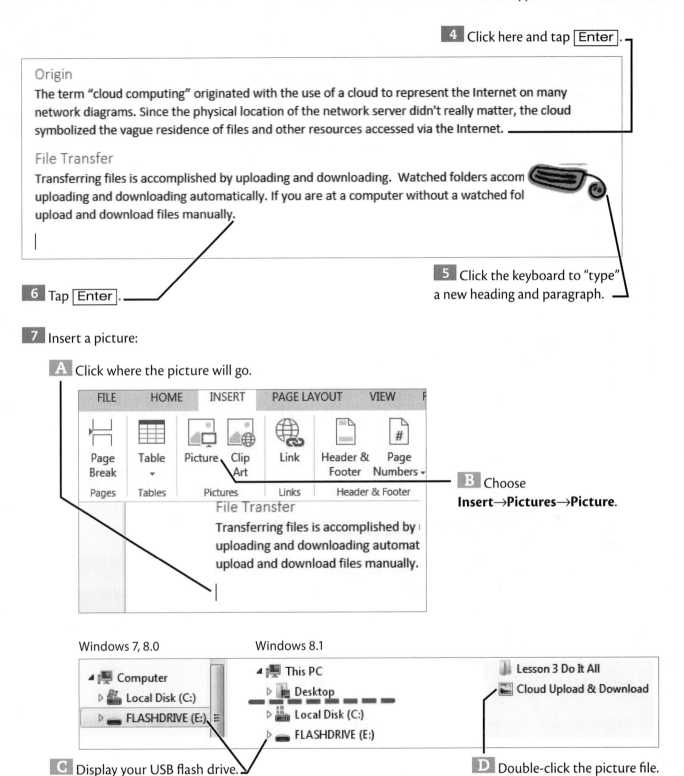

A Click where the picture will go.

B Choose
Insert→Pictures→Picture.

File Transfer

Transferring files is accomplished by ￼ uploading and downloading automat￼ upload and download files manually.

Windows 7, 8.0   Windows 8.1

▲ 🖥 Computer
  ▷ 🖴 Local Disk (C:)
  ▷ ▭ FLASHDRIVE (E:)

▲ 🖥 This PC
  ▷ 🖳 Desktop
  ▷ 🖴 Local Disk (C:)
  ▷ ▭ FLASHDRIVE (E:)

📁 Lesson 3 Do It All
🖼 Cloud Upload & Download

C Display your USB flash drive.

D Double-click the picture file.

Word uploads the picture into the document. The picture is "grayed out," indicating that it's selected for your next command.

8 Choose **Picture Tools→Format→Picture Styles→Drop Shadow Rectangle**.

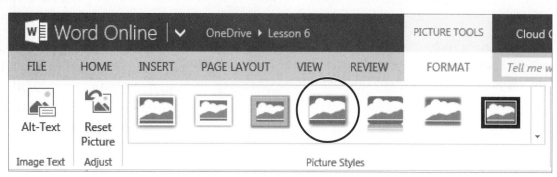

9 Click below the picture.

Word deselects the picture so you can see the picture style effect.

10 Return to the **Lesson 6** folder.

Word closes and the folder displays again. After a pause, the edited Cloud Computing document thumbnail displays the new text and picture you added. Since you're at a public computer, you'll want to sign out.

11 Click your
sign-in ID.

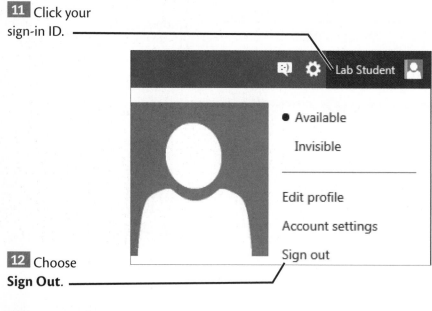

12 Choose
Sign Out.

13 **Close** [X] Internet Explorer.

Sharing Files

 Video

Sharing is the ability to give others online access to items in your cloud storage. As digital files grow in volume and number, sharing can be a great convenience. For example, you can share a folder of photos taken during a recent trip. Since most email services limit the size of attachments to messages, sharing can be the best way to distribute large files.

Types of Sharing

Most cloud storage services support multiple types of sharing. Each type has benefits, depending on the type of interactivity you want. Some services require others to log in with an account regardless of the share level. Other services may allow view-only access without a login.

> Get a link to "Lesson 6"
>
> Create a link to copy and paste in an email, blog, or webpage.
>
> Choose an option
>
> **View only**
> Edit
> Public
>
> **Create link**

OneDrive displays three options for sharing a folder.

 Shared storage on the cloud is evolving rapidly. New types of permissions may have emerged by the time you read this.

Online Shared Document Editing

Some cloud storage services, such as Google Drive and OneDrive, support online applications for editing files without downloading. These services let you give shared users permission to edit files directly online. Otherwise, others must download a shared file in order to edit it. Even if sharing is enabled, online editing may require a user to log in to the same cloud storage service.

develop your skills | ecs-0607

Share a File

Guide Me   In this exercise, you will share a file with two others via email.

Use the Guide Me to work through this exercise.

1 Start the **File Explorer**, display **OneDrive**, and double-click the **Lesson 6** folder.

2 Give the share command:

A Right-click **Cloud Computing**.   B Choose **OneDrive**.

C Choose **Share**.

OneDrive displays a Share form.

3 Click in the **To** box and address the share to these two recipients.

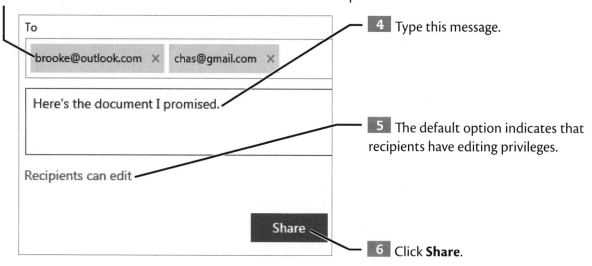

4 Type this message.

5 The default option indicates that recipients have editing privileges.

6 Click **Share**.

After a pause, OneDrive displays the file's new share status.

7 Click **Close**.

8 Click **Switch Chairs**.

You are now at Brooke's computer. Outlook is running and displays the sharing invitation.

9 Click the download prompt.

10 Choose **Download Pictures**.

Outlook displays a document icon.

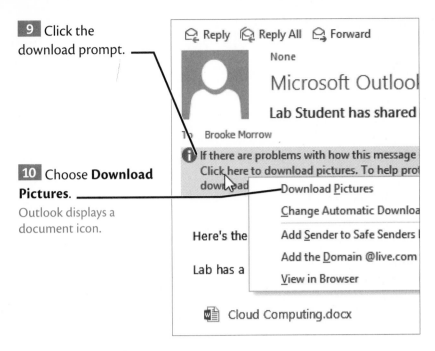

Reply   Reply All   Forward

None

Microsoft Outlool

Lab Student has shared

To   Brooke Morrow

If there are problems with how this message
Click here to download pictures. To help prot
download

| |
| |
| Download Pictures |
| Change Automatic Downloa |
| Add Sender to Safe Senders |
| Add the Domain @live.com |
| View in Browser |

Here's the

Lab has a

Cloud Computing.docx

11 Click the shared document link.

OneDrive displays the document. Brooke has Word 2013 and decides to edit the document with the full application rather than the Word Online.

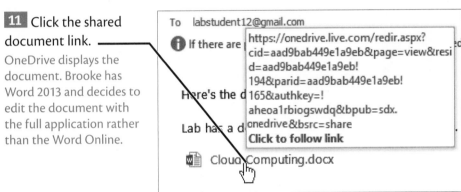

To   labstudent12@gmail.com

If there are

Here's the d

Lab has a d

Cloud Computing.docx

https://onedrive.live.com/redir.aspx?
cid=aad9bab449e1a9eb&page=view&resi
d=aad9bab449e1a9eb!
194&parid=aad9bab449e1a9eb!
165&authkey=!
aheoa1rbiogswdq&bpub=sdx.
onedrive&bsrc=share
Click to follow link

12 Choose
**Edit Document→
Edit in Word**.

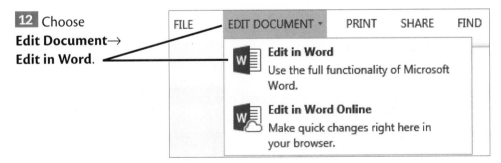

FILE   EDIT DOCUMENT ▾   PRINT   SHARE   FIND

Edit in Word
Use the full functionality of Microsoft Word.

Edit in Word Online
Make quick changes right here in your browser.

OneDrive displays a virus risk warning. Since Brooke trusts the source of the document, she'll continue with the edit command.

13 Click **Yes**.

OneDrive starts Word and displays the document. Note the warning at the top of the screen. Word's Ribbon is not visible.

14 Click **Enable Editing.**

Word's normal editing Ribbon appears. You are ready to edit the document.

15 Type **Definition** in place of *Defined*.

16 Choose **FILE** →**Save**.

OneDrive saves Brooke's document change to the cloud.

17 **Close** ⊠ Word.

A prompt from OneDrive is visible. It asks to confirm that the file opened.

18 Click **My Document Opened Successfully**.

OneDrive displays your cloud storage.

19 Click **Shared**.

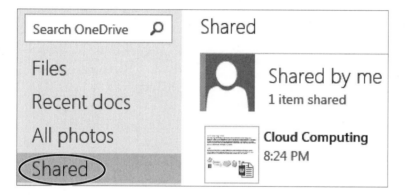

OneDrive displays the status of your shared documents.

Sharing Folders

 Video   Cloud storage allows *folder sharing*. This access can be a link, which allows only viewing and downloading. Or access can be granted for the sharer to modify the contents of the folder.

Shared Sync

Shared sync access requires the sharers to have an account on the same cloud storage service. The storage in the folder will also count against their total free or paid storage. They'll be able to add files to the folder and modify files just as if it were one of their own watched folders.

develop your skills | ecs-0608

Share a Folder

 Guide Me   In this exercise, you will share your OneDrive lesson folder with others.

Use the Guide Me to work through this exercise.

1 Start the **File Explorer**, then display **OneDrive**.

2 To share the folder, right-click **Lesson 6**.   **3** Choose **OneDrive**.

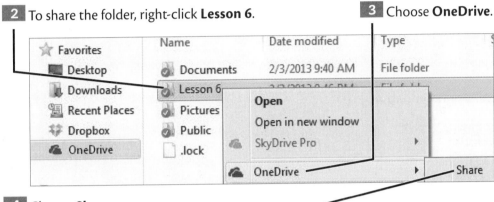

4 Choose **Share**.

OneDrive opens a web browser window to display a Share form.

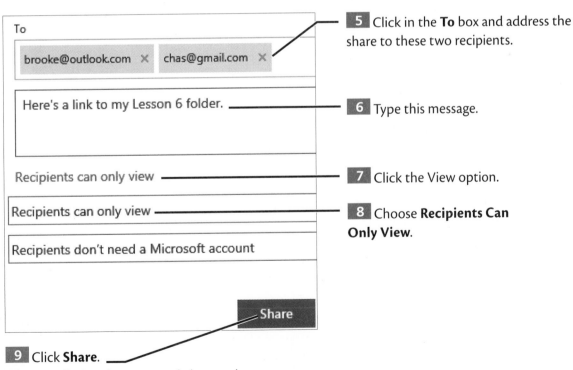

5 Click in the **To** box and address the share to these two recipients.

6 Type this message.

7 Click the View option.

8 Choose **Recipients Can Only View**.

9 Click **Share**.

OneDrive displays the new permissions settings.

10 Click **Close**.

OneDrive returns to a view of your cloud storage.

11 Click **Switch Chairs**.

The WebSim switches you to Chas's computer. She doesn't have a OneDrive account. She views the shared folder invitation in her email.

12 Click **Lesson 6**.

OneDrive displays the folder contents: documents above, pictures below.

13 Click **Carbon Footprint Recommendations**.

OneDrive displays the document in a new tab.

14 **Close** the document tab.

Chas returns to viewing the folder contents. She could continue viewing any and all of the documents in the folder.

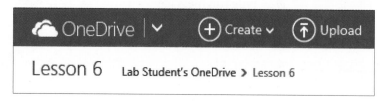

15 Close **Internet Explorer**.

File Compatibility and Conversion

 Video

You want to be sure that others can work with files you share. Every application has a native file format. If others you work with use a different application for the same task, they may not be able to open your files. Most applications can save in a different (nonnative) file format. Most can also open files from different file formats.

Converting a File

Most Microsoft Office programs support *file conversion*. The Save As command displays file formats the application supports. When you save in a different file format, the filename extension is changed to match the new file format. The file also displays a different icon.

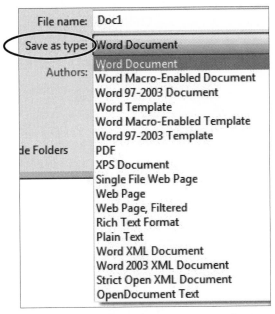

Word displays file types it supports in the Save As window.

The rich text format (.rtf) file format supports rich formatting and can be opened by almost any word processor.

Convert a File

Guide Me   In this exercise, you will convert a file to a different file format.

1 **Windows 8.1 Only:** Display the **Desktop**, if necessary.

2 Insert your USB flash drive, if you are using one, and close any prompt from Windows.

3 Open the **File Explorer** and display your file storage location.

4 Double-click **Essential Computing Skills** and then double-click **ecs-L06**.

5 Open the **Carbon Footprint Recommendations** document.

6 Choose FILE .

Now you are ready to save the file in a new format.

7 Click **Save As**.   **8** Choose **Computer** and then choose **ecs-L06**.

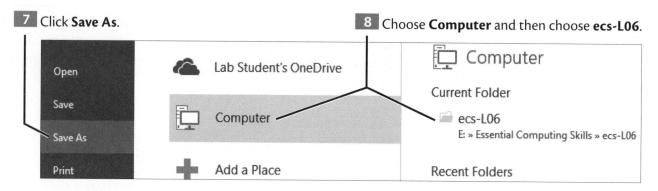

9 Add **-rtf** to the end of the filename.

10 Choose **Rich Text Format** as the type.

11 Click **Save**.

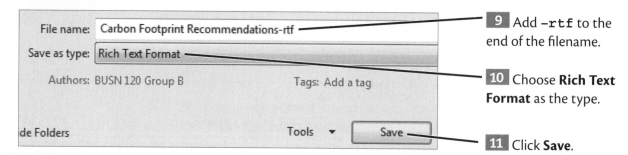

Word indicates that some features of the document won't be supported by the new file type.

12 Click **Continue**.

Notice that an indication ("Compatibility Mode") of the file type appears on the title bar, telling you that the document is not saved in Word's native file format.

13 **Close** ⊠ Word.

14 **Close** x the File Explorer.

concepts review

To check your knowledge of the key concepts introduced in this lesson, complete the Concepts Review quiz by choosing the appropriate access option below.

If you are...	Then access the quiz by...
Using eLab	Logging in, choosing Content, and navigating to the Concepts Review quiz for this lesson
Not using eLab	Going to the Student Resource Center (see the inside front cover)

reinforce your skills | ecs-0601

Use Cloud Storage with Google Drive

 Guide Me   In this exercise, you will practice skills with online file storage and applications using the Google Drive cloud storage service.

NOTE

Use the Guide Me to work through this exercise.

1 Start **Internet Explorer**, navigate to `drive.google.com`, and sign in with your Google account.

2 Download and install **Google Drive** on your computer. (There will be a download button or link for this on the page.)

Store Files Online

3 Carefully insert your USB flash drive, and dismiss any pop-up prompt about it.

4 Open the **File Explorer** and display the **Google Drive** watched folder.

5 Create a new folder named `Lesson 6` in Google Drive:

■ **Windows 7:** Click **New Folder** on the toolbar.

■ **Windows 8.1:** Choose **Home→New→New Folder** from the Ribbon.

Synchronize Storage

6 On the USB flash drive, open **Essential Computing Skills** then **ecs-L06**. Then, use $\boxed{Ctrl}$ + $\boxed{A}$ to select all files.

7 Use $\boxed{Ctrl}$ + $\boxed{C}$ to copy the selection.

8 Navigate to the **Lesson 6** folder on Google Drive.

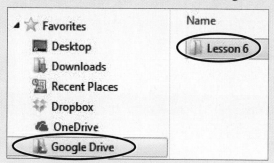

9 Change the view to **Medium Icons**.

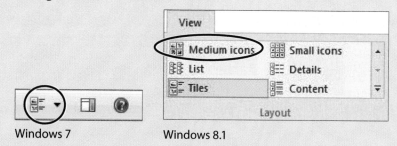

Windows 7   Windows 8.1

10 Use $\boxed{Ctrl}$ + $\boxed{V}$ to paste.
Windows pastes the files. As with OneDrive, there are checkmarks to indicate which files are synced to the cloud.

11 Click **Back** ⬅ / ⬅.
There's a sync checkmark on the folder, too.

Save to a Watched Folder

12 Start **Word 2013** and create a new blank document.

13 Type this text: `Google Drive watched folder save`

14 Choose **FILE** →**Save As**.
Unlike OneDrive, Google Drive isn't built into the design of Word 2013. You must browse for its watched folder on the computer.

15 Choose **Computer**→**Browse**→**Google Drive**.

16 Click **Save**.

17 **Close** ✖ Word.
The Google Drive window reappears.

18 Click **Back** ⟵ / ⟵ .

The document just saved is visible. Since it's been saved to the watched folder, you'll see it when you view Google Drive contents via the web in the next section.

Web Access to Cloud Storage

19 Start **Internet Explorer** and sign in to Google Drive:

A Type **drive.google.com** in the address bar. ⟶

B Type **labstudent11** as the Google ID email address.

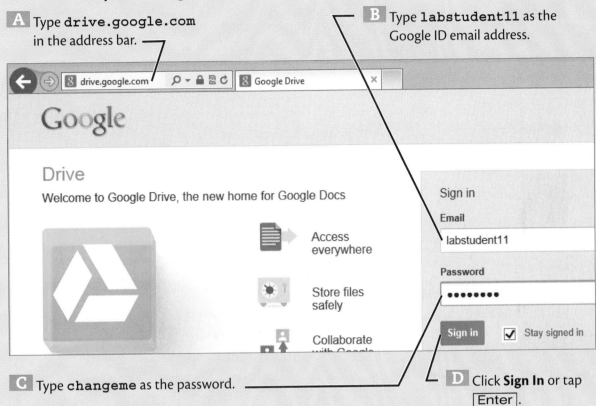

C Type **changeme** as the password.

D Click **Sign In** or tap Enter .

After a pause, Google Drive displays the contents of its cloud storage. Notice that the Word document you just saved is visible. So is the Lesson 6 folder.

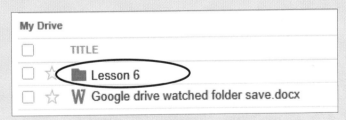

20 Click the **Lesson 6** folder.

The files you copied earlier appear. They are synchronized to your cloud storage.

21   Scroll down, then click the **Computer System Mind Map** picture file.
Google Drive displays the picture in its picture preview app.

22   Taking care not to close Internet Explorer, **close** ☒ the preview.

23   Scroll up, then click **Broadband.docx**.
Google Drive displays the document in its own viewer (it doesn't open the document in Word as OneDrive does).

24   Using the scroll bar on the right side of the screen or the scroll wheel on your mouse, scroll down to view the next page.

25   Click the **Next** icon on the center-right side of the window.

A preview of the next file in the folder appears.

26   Click the **Previous** icon on the center-left side of the window.
You return to a preview of the Broadband document.

27   **Close** ☒ the preview.

28   Click **My Drive** to return to the top level of your Google Drive.

Download and Upload

29 Click the **Lesson 6** folder.

Many web-based applications support the type of pop-up menus you've seen when you right-click filenames and icons in the File Explorer. Let's try this in Google Drive.

30 Scroll down, then right-click the **Cloud Upload & Download** file and choose **Download**.

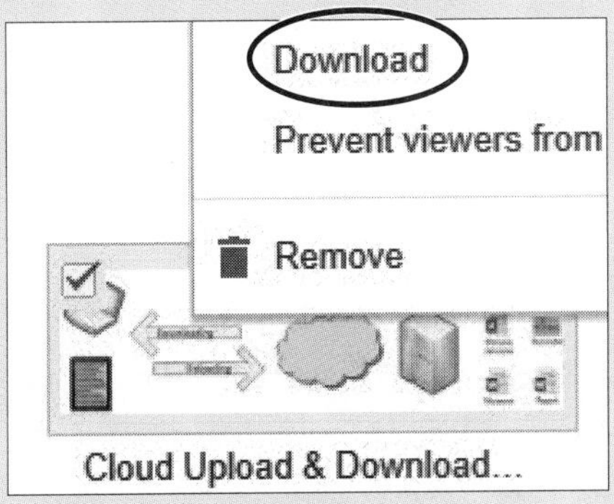

31 Download the file:

A Click the **Save ▾** menu button.

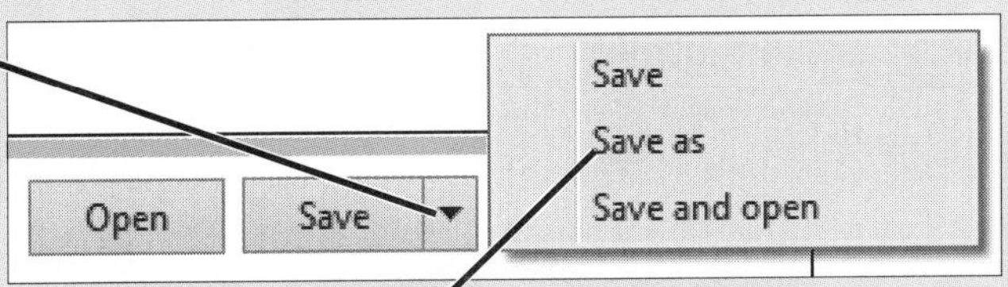

B Choose **Save As.**

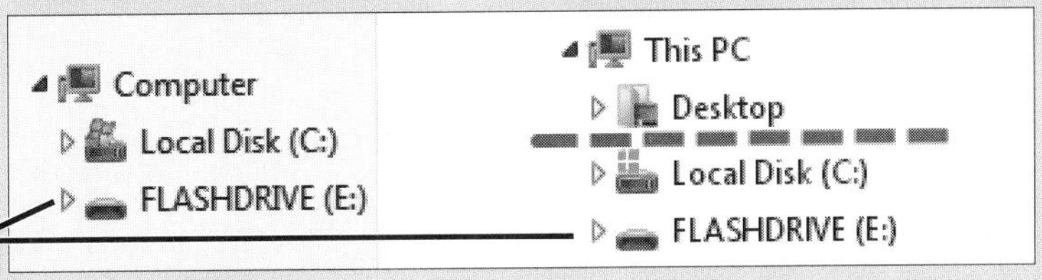

C Choose the flash drive and click **Save.**

Google Drive copies the file from cloud storage to your local drive. Internet Explorer displays download buttons at the bottom of the window.

32 Click the **Open** button.

Windows displays the downloaded picture in a photo viewer. If you are using Windows 8.1, the photo appears in a photo tablet app (not on the traditional Desktop).

33 To return to Internet Explorer, (Windows 7) **close** [X] the picture or (Windows 8.1) press [Alt]+[Tab].

The empty tab you opened to download the picture appears.

34   **Close** ☒ the tab.

Now that you are back to the base level of Google Drive, you will upload a file.

35   Start an upload to Google Drive:

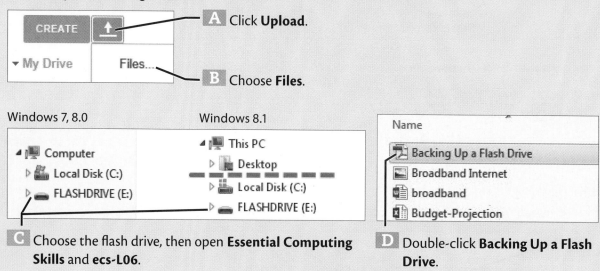

A Click **Upload**.

B Choose **Files**.

Windows 7, 8.0   Windows 8.1

C Choose the flash drive, then open **Essential Computing Skills** and **ecs-L06**.

D Double-click **Backing Up a Flash Drive**.

A new window shows uploading progress.

36   **Close** ☒ the upload window.

Notice the newly uploaded file in your Google Drive.

Online Applications

Google Drive has an online word processor: Google Docs.

37 Click **Carbon Footprint Recommendations**.

38 Edit the memo:

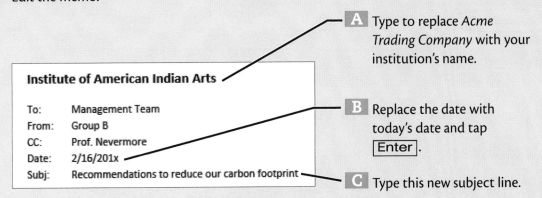

A Type to replace *Acme Trading Company* with your institution's name.

B Replace the date with today's date and tap Enter .

C Type this new subject line.

Institute of American Indian Arts

To: Management Team
From: Group B
CC: Prof. Nevermore
Date: 2/16/201x
Subj: Recommendations to reduce our carbon footprint

Google Docs saves changes as you type. It displays a prompt that changes are saved.

Carbon Footprint Recommendations.docx ☆ 📁

File   Edit   View   Insert   Format   Tools   Table   Help   All changes saved in Drive

39 **Close** ☒ the Carbon Footprint Recommendations tab.

40 **Close** ☒ Internet Explorer and the File Explorer.

---

reinforce your skills | ecs-0602

Use Document Sharing with Dropbox

Guide Me In this exercise, you will practice file sharing using the Dropbox cloud-storage system, which is quite similar to OneDrive and Google Drive. The principles of watched folders and web-based access to your files you learned with OneDrive apply to Dropbox, too.

Use the Guide Me to work through this exercise.

Copy Files to Watched Storage

1 Open the **File Explorer** and display the USB flash drive.

2 Open the **Essential Computing Skills** folder and then the **ecs-L06** folder.

3 Use Ctrl + A to select all and then use Ctrl + C to copy.

4   Click the **Dropbox** watched folder in Favorites.

5   Create a new folder named **Cloud Practice** within your Dropbox.

Synchronized Storage

6   Open the **Cloud Practice** folder and use $\boxed{\text{Ctrl}}$+$\boxed{\text{V}}$ to paste the files you copied earlier.
Windows pastes the files. Similar to OneDrive, Dropbox displays checkmarks as files sync.

7   Click **Back** ⊙ / ⊙.
Dropbox gives the folder a checkmark, too.

8   **Minimize** ▭ the File Explorer window.

9   Click the **Dropbox icon** in the notification area and choose **Dropbox.com**.

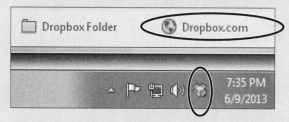

The notification area icon signs on to your Dropbox web access automatically.

10   Open the **Cloud Practice** folder.
The files you copied and pasted earlier are already synchronized from your local Dropbox to cloud storage.

Online Applications

Dropbox doesn't yet have web-based apps like those in OneDrive and Google Drive. Instead, you must download the file, make revisions, and upload the file back to cloud storage.

11   Choose the **Dropbox Cloud Storage** file

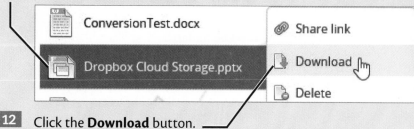

12   Click the **Download** button.

13　Click the **Save ▼** menu button and choose **Save As**.

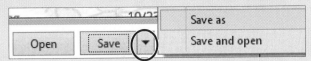

14　Click the **Documents** as shown below, then click **Save**.

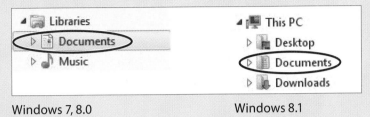

Windows 7, 8.0　　　　　　　Windows 8.1

15　Click the **Open** button near the bottom of the window.

The PowerPoint 2013 application opens the file, and a protected view prompt appears. Since downloaded files may contain malware, PowerPoint wants to make sure you trust the source and are willing to leave protected view to edit the file. Notice that the Ribbon is not visible; no editing is permitted.

16　Click **Enable Editing**.

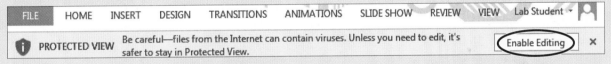

The Ribbon appears, indicating you are ready to edit.

17　Type this subtitle:

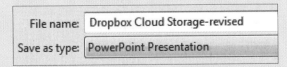

18　Choose **File→Save As→Computer→My Documents**.

19　Add **-revised** to the end of the filename and click **Save**.

20　**Close ☒** PowerPoint.

The Internet Explorer window displaying cloud storage in your Dropbox reappears.

21   Close the preview window.

22   Click the **Upload** button.

Dropbox asks you to select file(s) to upload.

23   Click **Choose Files**.

24   Double-click **Documents**.

25   Double-click the **Dropbox Cloud Storage-revised PowerPoint** file.

Dropbox displays the progress of uploading the file back to cloud storage. The revised PowerPoint file appears in the Cloud Practice folder.

Share Files

Like other cloud storage services, Dropbox lets you share links to files that don't require a Dropbox account to access.

26   Tap End on the keyboard.

27   To get a link to share, point (don't click) over **Dropbox Intro.pdf** and then slide the mouse pointer to the right and click **Share Link**.

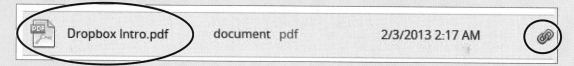

Dropbox displays an online form to share the link.

28 Fill in the form:

A Type `brook@clarity.pro` as the email address of the person you will share the link with.

B Type this message to introduce the shared link.

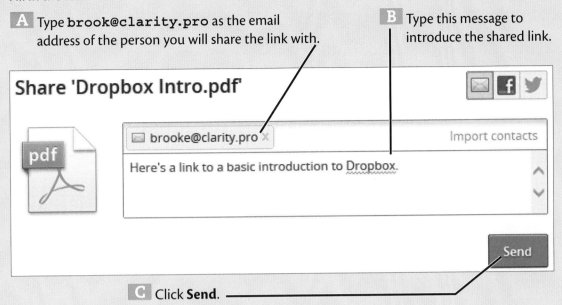

C Click **Send**.

Dropbox indicates that your message is sent and displays a preview of the document.

29 Click **Switch Chairs**.

You are now at Brooke's computer. She's viewing her email. Brooke does not have a Dropbox account yet, but she can still view this shared file.

30 Double-click to open the **Lab Student11 shared...** message, then click **Display Images**.

31 Click the **Click Here to View** link.

A new tab opens in Internet Explorer, and after a pause, the shared file appears. Buttons allow you to share the file with someone else, or to download it to your computer.

32 **Close** ☒ the new Dropbox Intro.pdf tab.

33 Click **Switch Chairs**.

You are back at labstudent11's computer, viewing Dropbox.

Share Folders

This time, you will share a folder with another Dropbox user. In general, folder sharing only works with others who have an account with the same cloud storage service.

34 Click **Sharing**.

Dropbox displays information about shared folders.

35 Click the **New Shared Folder** button at the top-right corner of the window.

36 Share a folder:

A Choose the existing folder option.   **B** Click **Next**.

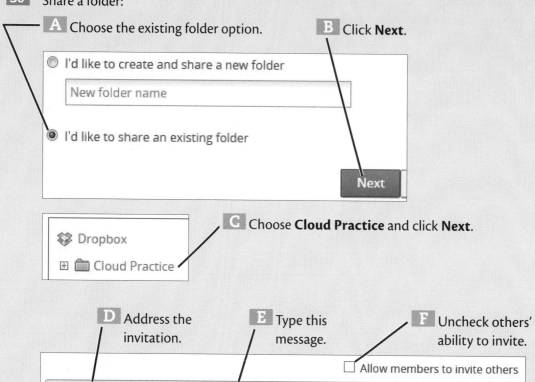

○ I'd like to create and share a new folder

New folder name

◉ I'd like to share an existing folder

Next

Dropbox

⊞ 📁 Cloud Practice

C Choose **Cloud Practice** and click **Next**.

D Address the invitation.   **E** Type this message.   **F** Uncheck others' ability to invite.

☐ Allow members to invite others

owen@clarity.pro   Import contacts

Here's a folder we can share. It's not a link. It will appear in your Dropbox.

Share folder   Cancel

G Click **Share Folder**.

Dropbox emails the invitation. Owen must accept it before the share is complete.

37 Click **Switch Chairs**.
The WebSim displays Owen's computer. Owen has a Dropbox account already.

38 Double-click the **Share Cloud Practice** message, then click **Display Images**.

39 Click **View Folder**.
Dropbox asks Owen to verify his email address. Online services often request this so they can be more certain an account doesn't represent a robot.

40 Click **Send Email**. Then, click the email tab and double-click **Please Verify Your Email Address**.

41 Click the **Verify Your Email** link.
A verification confirmation appears.

42 Click **Done**.
An alert appears beside Sharing in Owen's Dropbox.

43   Click **Sharing**.

44   Click the **New Shared Folder** invitation and then click **Accept**.

Dropbox displays the newly shared folder.

45   Click **Dropbox** (return to the base level).

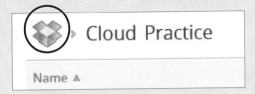

Keep in mind that you are viewing Owen's (not Lab Student's) Dropbox. The shared folder was added to Owen's Dropbox account as if he'd added it himself. An icon marks Cloud Practice as shared.

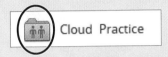

File Compatibility and Conversion

You're still at Owen's computer.

46   Open the **Cloud Practice** folder, click the **Budget-Projection** file, and then click **Download**.

Internet Explorer asks whether Owen wishes to open or save the file.

47   Click the **Open** button near the bottom-right corner of the window.

Excel opens the file. The protected view prompt appears. Notice that the Ribbon does not appear near the top of the window, indicating it's not yet editable.

48   Click the **Enable Editing** button.

49   Choose **File→Save As→Computer→Browse**.

50   Click **Dropbox** in Favorites to display its contents, then open the **Cloud Practice** folder.

51   Change the name and file type:

A Add **-converted** to end of filename.

B Choose **Excel 97-2003 Workbook** in the Save as Type box.

C Click **Save**.

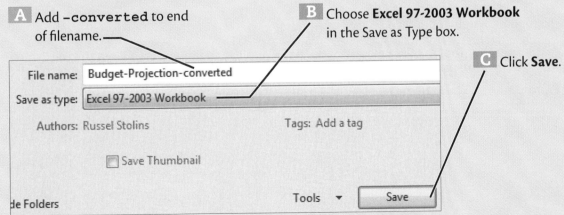

Excel saves the file to the shared (and watched) Cloud Practice folder.

52   **Close** ☒ Excel.

53   Click **Switch Chairs**.

You are back at labstudent11's computer, viewing Dropbox.

54   Open **Cloud Practice**.

The Budget-Projection-converted file appears in the folder, uploaded from Owen's shared Dropbox folder.

55   Close **Internet Explorer**.

---

apply your skills | ecs-0601

Use Cloud Storage

You are a full-time student using cloud storage rather than a USB flash drive. In this exercise, you will use a watched folder on the computer and the web interface to manage your files.

This exercise has some requirements that not all computer labs may be set up for. Your instructor will give you details on which items you'll need to complete and which cloud storage to use. These services and configurations are required.

- **Cloud Storage Account:** OneDrive, Google Drive, or Dropbox
- **Cloud Sync Application:** Installed on the computer
- **Email Address:** With webmail or Outlook access

Store Files Online

1   Create a folder named `AYS 6-1` in your cloud storage drive via a watched folder or the web.

2   Use the **Snipping Tool** to take a picture of the AYS 6-1 folder in the File Explorer or Internet Explorer. Save the snip to your file storage location as `ECS06-A01a-CloudFolder-[FirstInitialLastName]`.

Synchronize Storage

3   Copy these files to the **AYS 6-1** folder in your cloud storage using a watched folder or via the web:

- Backing Up a Flash Drive
- Budget-Projection
- Computer System Mind Map

4   Use the **Snipping Tool** to take a picture of the AYS 6-1 folder containing the files in the File Explorer or Internet Explorer. Save the snip to your file storage location as `ECS06-A01b-CloudFiles-[FirstInitialLastName]`.

Save to a Watched Folder

Skip steps 5–8 if your computer doesn't have a watched folder for cloud storage.

5 Navigate to your **ecs-L06** folder and open the **Broadband** document in **Word 2013**.

6 Save the document directly from the application to the AYS 6-1 folder.

7 Use the **Snipping Tool** to take a picture of the AYS 6-1 folder with the saved file in the File Explorer or Internet Explorer. Save the snip to your file storage location as `ECS06-A01c-WatchedSave-[FirstInitialLastName]`.

8 **Close** ☒ Word.

Web Access to Cloud Storage

9 Start **Internet Explorer** and log in to your cloud storage.

10 Navigate to the **AYS 6-1** folder.

11 Use the **Snipping Tool** to take a picture of the **AYS 6-1** folder contents in Internet Explorer. Save the snip to your file storage location as `ECS06-A01d-CloudWeb-[FirstInitialLastName]`.

Download and Upload

12 Upload the **File Conversion** document to **AYS 6-1** via the web (not a watched folder).

13 Use the **Snipping Tool** to take a picture of the **AYS 6-1** contents in Internet Explorer. Save the snip to your file storage location as `ECS06-A01e-CloudUpload-[FirstInitialLastName]`.

Online Applications

Skip steps 14–16 if you are not using OneDrive or Google Drive for this exercise.

14 Open **File Conversion** in AYS 6-1 for editing with the **Word Web App** (OneDrive) or **Google Docs** (Google Drive).

15 Use the **Snipping Tool** to take a picture of document being edited. Save the snip to your file storage location as `ECS06-A01f-CloudApp-[FirstInitialLastName]`.

16 **Close** ☒ the File Explorer and Internet Explorer windows.

17 Submit your screen snips based on the guidelines provided by your instructor.

apply your skills | ecs-0602

Share Files/Folders

You are a full-time student working on a group project. In this exercise, you will use your cloud storage and sharing capabilities to distribute files to classmates.

This exercise has some requirements that not all computer labs may be set up for. Your instructor will give you details on which items you'll need to complete and which cloud-storage or other service to use. The following services and configuration are required.

- **Cloud Storage Account:** OneDrive, Google Drive, or Dropbox
- **Email Address:** With webmail or Outlook access

Share Files

1. Create a folder named **AYS 6-2** in your cloud storage drive via a watched folder or the web.

2. Copy these files from your ecs-L06 folder into the **AYS 6-2** folder via the watched folder or the web:

   - Broadband
   - Carbon Footprint Recommendations
   - Conversion Test

3. Send a link to **Carbon Footprint Recommendations** in the AYS 6-2 folder via an email message to your instructor with the subject line **AYS 6-2a**.

Share Folders

4. Share the **AYS 6-2** folder via an email message to your instructor with the subject line **AYS 6-2b**.

File Compatibility and Conversion

5. Download **Conversion Test** from AYS 6-2 to your file storage location.

6. Convert the document file to **Word 97-2003** format.

7. Send Conversion Test to your instructor as an attachment to email with the subject line **AYS 6-2c**.

apply your skills | ecs-0603

Do It All

You are a full-time student using cloud storage rather than a USB flash drive. In this exercise, you will use your cloud storage and sharing capabilities to distribute files to classmates and to get access to your coursework from various locations.

This exercise has some requirements that not all computer labs may be set up for. Your instructor will give you details on which items you'll need to complete and which cloud-storage to use. The following services and configurations are required.

- **Cloud Storage Account:** OneDrive, Google Drive, or Dropbox
- **Cloud Sync Application:** Installed on the computer
- **Email Address:** With webmail or Outlook access

Store Files Online

1 Create a folder named `AYS 6-3` in your cloud storage drive via a watched folder or the web.

2 Use the **Snipping Tool** to take a picture of the AYS 6-3 folder in the File Explorer or Internet Explorer. Save the snip to your file storage location as `ECS06-A03a-CloudFolder-[FirstInitialLastName]`.

Synchronize Storage

3 Copy these files to the **AYS 6-3** folder in your cloud storage using a watched folder or via the web:

- Dropbox Intro (PDF document)
- Broadband Internet (picture)
- Cloud Upload & Download (picture)
- Cloud Computing (Word document)

4 Use the **Snipping Tool** to take a picture of the **AYS 6-3** folder with copied files in the **File Explorer** or Internet Explorer. Save the snip to your file storage location as `ECS06-A03b-CloudFiles-[FirstInitialLastName]`.

Save to a Watched Folder

 Skip steps 5–8 if your computer doesn't have a watched folder for cloud storage.

5 Navigate to **ecs-L06** and open the **File Conversion** document in **Word 2013**.

6 Save the file directly from the application to the **AYS 6-3** folder.

7 Use the **Snipping Tool** to take a picture of the **AYS 6-3** folder with the saved file in the **File Explorer** or Internet Explorer. Save the snip to your file storage location as `ECS06-A03c-WatchedSave-[FirstInitialLastName]`.

8 **Close** ☒ Word.

Web Access to Cloud Storage

9 Start **Internet Explorer** and login to your cloud storage.

10 Navigate to the **AYS 6-3** folder.

11 Use the **Snipping Tool** to take a picture of the **AYS 6-3** folder contents in Internet Explorer. Save the snip to your file storage location as `ECS06-A03d-CloudWeb-[FirstInitialLastName]`.

Downloading and Uploading

12 Upload the **Computer System Mind Map** to **AYS 6-3** via the web (not a watched folder).

13 Use the **Snipping Tool** to take a picture of the **AYS 6-3** folder contents in Internet Explorer. Save the snip to your file storage location as `ECS06-A03e-CloudUpload-[FirstInitialLastName]`.

Online Applications

 Skip steps 14–15 if you do not use OneDrive or Google Drive.

14 Open **Cloud Computing** in AYS 6-3 for editing with the **Word Online App** (OneDrive) or **Google Docs** (Google Drive).

15 Use the **Snipping Tool** to take a picture of document being edited. Save the snip to your file storage location as `ECS06-A03f-CloudApp-[FirstInitialLastName]`.

Sharing Files

16 Send a link to **Dropbox Intro** in the AYS 6-3 folder via an email message to your instructor with the subject line `AYS 6-3g`.

Sharing Folders

17 Share the **AYS 6-3** folder via an email message to your instructor with the subject line `AYS 6-3h`.

File Compatibility and Conversion

18 Download **Cloud Computing** from AYS 6-3 to your file storage location.

19 Convert the document file to **Rich Text Format**.

20 Send the file to your instructor as an attachment to email with the subject line `AYS 6-3i`.

21 Submit your screen snips based on the guidelines provided by your instructor.

Edit a Shared Document Collaboratively

In this exercise, you will perform collaborative editing on a shared document.

- Use a service that supports online applications such as OneDrive, Google Drive, Zoho Writer, or some other online collaboration service. To do this, you may need to create a new account with the service, or you can use an account you already have.

- Create a document about a topic of your choice. Type about a half page about the topic.

- Send sharing invitations for the document to two classmates. Explain in an email message what you want added or revised in your initial draft.

- Accept sharing invitations from one or more classmates participating in this assignment. Follow their requests to add more details to the documents.

- Print the final draft of your document after you and your classmates have made revisions to it.

Submit your printed document based on the guidelines provided by your instructor.

Share a Project Folder

In this exercise, you set up a shared folder for a group project, then send invitations to group members and invite them to upload files to the folder.

- If necessary, create an account on a cloud storage service. It could be a service covered in this lesson, or some other service. It may or may not support synchronized (watched) folders on the computers in your computer lab.

- Create a new project folder, then create additional folders within it. You can make up a project and folder names, or you can use the suggestions below.

- Project [Make up your own name]

  - ◆ Budget
  - ◆ Presentations
  - ◆ Reporting
  - ◆ Research

- Upload files from the Lesson 6 folder to your new project. For example, upload spreadsheet (Excel) files to a budget folder. Upload Word documents to a reporting folder. Upload PowerPoint files to a presentation folder.

- Share the folder with two classmates and your instructor via one or more email messages. Your classmates and instructor may have to create new accounts with the cloud storage service you choose. If this is the case, be sure to explain this.

Outlook

7 Email and Attachments

Skills YOU Will Learn

- Navigate to various Outlook 2013 functions
- Reliably locate commands on the Ribbon of an Office 2013 application
- Create and send an email message using Outlook 2013
- Attach a file to an email message using Outlook 2013

in this lesson

Outlook 2013 is the personal information component of the Microsoft Office suite. Many businesses use Outlook for their email services. In addition to email functions, Outlook has calendar and contact management features. In this lesson, you will learn how to navigate in Outlook, how to use its email-related features, and how to send and receive email attachments.

Sending and Receiving Photos

You are organizing a road trip with a friend. Once you find a good place to visit, you save photos from web pages to your USB flash drive. You attach a photo to an email message about the destination.

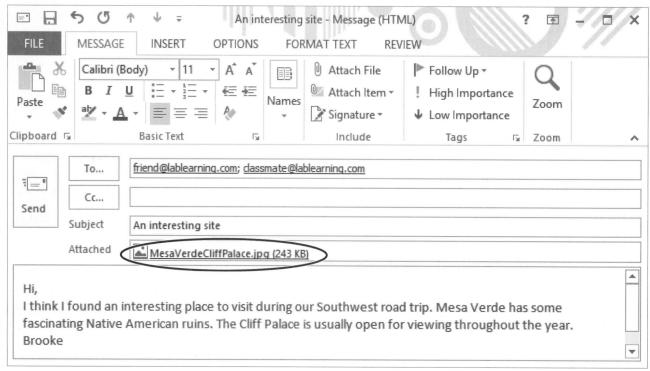

You attach a photo to an email message.

When your friend writes back with another destination suggestion, you save the attached photo from the message to your flash drive. That way the photo is available even when you're not accessing your email.

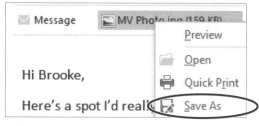

You save a photo from an email message.

What Is Email?

 Video   *Electronic mail (email)* is a service that lets you send electronic messages to specific addresses on the Internet. Most email services also allow you to send files (attachments) with a message.

History

The first email systems were created in the 1960s. Some of the earliest email systems required both users to be online at the same time, much like early instant messaging systems. Internet-based email became popular in the 1970s via ARPANET (the prototype for today's Internet), but was only available to academic and government/military users. When Internet use became available to the general public in the 1990s, email was a primary driver of its popularity. Today, it is estimated that most email messages are actually spam (junk email).

Webmail

Free webmail services are by far the most popular way to access email. They offer easy access from any computer with an Internet connection. Free webmail services support themselves with online ads and the tracking of user messages to create profiles for targeted ads.

Email Clients

An *email client* is an application optimized to work with email. Outlook 2013 is a popular email client application. Email clients often enable advanced formatting and other features that most webmail services don't support, such as setting up group meetings, assigning tasks, and maintenance of corporate email address groups.

Most skills you have with webmail will work smoothly with an email client.

Using Outlook 2013

 Video

Outlook 2013 is the latest version of Microsoft's email and personal information program. Outlook comes with many (but not all) versions of Office 2013. These exercises are about email, but Outlook can help you manage other tasks, too.

The Outlook Program Window

Outlook can handle many functions, and has a navigation scheme to match. It has a dynamic Ribbon that changes with each function you use.

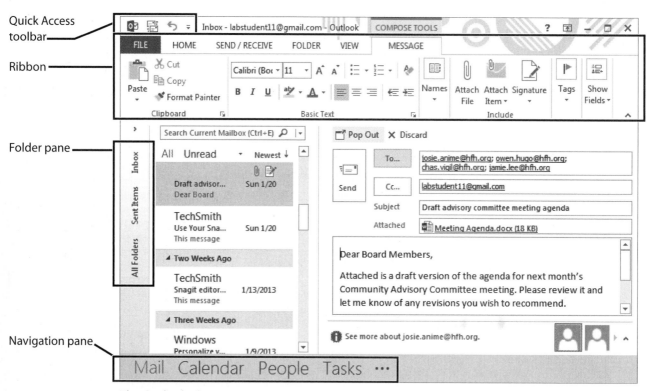

The Outlook 2013 program window

Outlook Task Features

Outlook 2013 comes equipped to help you work with tasks such as:

- **Email:** Outlook is a full email program.

- **RSS Feeds:** Outlook can receive RSS (Really Simple Syndication) feeds. These send website changes directly to Outlook. For example, changes on your favorite news website.

- **Calendar:** Outlook helps you keep track of appointments and events.

- **Contacts:** Outlook stores contact details.

- **Tasks:** Outlook helps you keep track of tasks. You can also assign and track tasks to others.

- **Notes:** Notes store miscellaneous information.

Start Outlook

Guide Me   In this exercise, you will start the Outlook 2013 program.

1 Follow the step(s) for your version of Windows to start Outlook:

Windows 7

■ Choose **Start→All Programs→Microsoft Office 2013→ Outlook 2013**.

Windows 8.1

A Move the mouse toward the **bottom-left** corner of the screen.

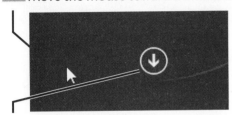

B Click the **Apps** button.

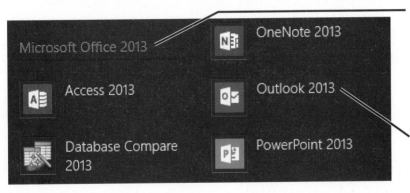

C Scroll to the **Microsoft Office 2013** group. (Try using the scroll wheel on the top of your mouse.)

D Choose **Outlook 2013**. It may be in a different column of the apps menu.

Outlook 2013 appears. Depending on how it is configured, you may see a Welcome window.

Welcome to Outlook 2013

2 Skip the rest of this exercise if the Welcome window did not appear. Continue to the next step if it did appear.

3 **Windows 8.1 Only:** Click **Next** then choose **No** to skip setting up email.

4 Click **Next**.

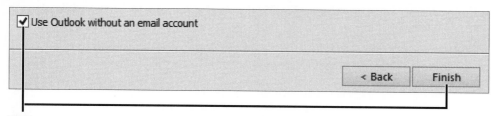

5 Place a checkmark here and then click **Finish**.

The Outlook Program window appears.

---

a closer look

Outlook Compared to Webmail

Outlook shares many similarities with the webmail services most people use for email. Outlook also has additional capabilities most webmail services lack.

- **Email Management:** Like webmail, Outlook manages incoming and outgoing messages, lets you manage contacts, and lets you send and receive email attachments.

- **Hard-drive Based:** Outlook is a traditional application program stored on the computer's hard drive rather than a web-based service like webmail. Unlike webmail, you have to access your Outlook email from the same computer all the time. (Exception, some email services you use with Outlook also support a webmail interface.)

Many webmail services offer a premium (paid) subscription that allows you to access your webmail from an email program such as Outlook.

Introducing the Ribbon

 Video

The *Ribbon* is the bar along the top of Office Suite program windows. If you use Windows 8.1, you've already seen the Ribbon in file-management exercises. The Ribbon contains commands similar to menu bars. Outlook's Ribbon can change significantly depending on your current activity.

Finding Commands on the Ribbon

Some users find the Ribbon interface difficult at first. They look all over each tab, trying to locate commands. Here's a systematic method that works well.

1. **Tab:** Look at the names of the Ribbon tabs and find the one for what you want to do.
2. **Command Group:** Find the command group related to what you want to do.
3. **Command:** When you think you've found the right command group, look at its buttons for the command you need.

Example: Let's say you want to create a new folder. How can you find the New Folder command? It's not on the Home tab.

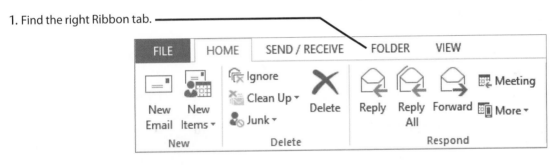

1. Find the right Ribbon tab.

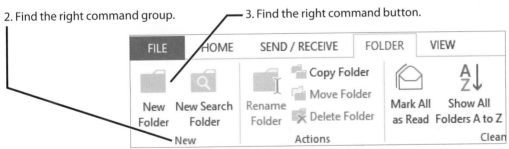

2. Find the right command group.   3. Find the right command button.

Repeat this mantra whenever you use the Ribbon:
Tab→Command Group→Command.

Work with the Ribbon

Guide Me   In this exercise, you will navigate to various functions in Outlook and give some commands via the Ribbon.

1 Notice the commands on the **Home** tab of the Ribbon as you view each Outlook function in the next step.

Outlook has a very dynamic Home tab.

2 If the navigation menu displays words, skip to step 4.

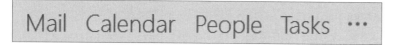

3 Switch off the Compact Navigation option:

A Click the **More** button.

B Click **Navigation Options**.

C Uncheck **Compact Navigation** and click **OK**.

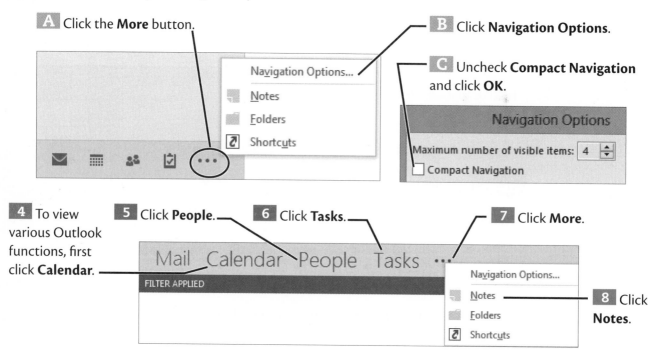

4 To view various Outlook functions, first click **Calendar**.

5 Click **People**.

6 Click **Tasks**.

7 Click **More**.

8 Click **Notes**.

9 Display the **Calendar**.

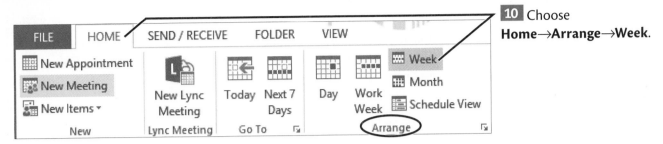

10 Choose **Home→Arrange→Week**.

11 Choose **Home→Arrange→Month** from the Ribbon.
The entire month's dates are displayed.

12 Choose **Home→Arrange→Day**.

13 Click **View** on the Ribbon.

This tab contains a few view commands used on the Home tab and adds new ones.

14 Choose **View→Arrangement→Work Week**.

15 Change the color scheme:

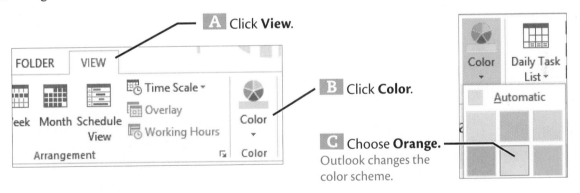

A Click **View**.

B Click **Color**.

C Choose **Orange.**
Outlook changes the
color scheme.

16 Choose **View→Color→Color→Automatic**.
Outlook resets the calendar color.

17 **Close** ☒ the Outlook program window.

Working with Email

Video

If you're like most students studying with this book, sending and receiving email messages are already familiar to you. This beginner's section contains brief coverage of the basics and details about Outlook's email features.

Composing a Message

Composing and sending a message with Outlook 2013 is quite similar to working with other email programs or webmail services. Sent and received messages are usually stored on a drive in your computer rather than online. Outlook's message composition tools are generally more powerful and flexible than webmail. For example, you can insert pictures into the message body.

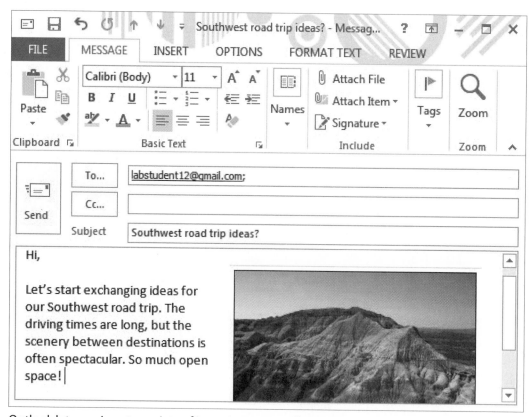

Outlook lets you insert a variety of items into an email message.

Multiple Addressees

You can address email messages to more than one addressee. Simply add a semicolon (;) between each address to separate them.

Email Addresses

All email addresses use the convention shown below. For example, all email addresses always use the "at" (@) symbol to separate the email account name from the domain name.

astudent@lablearning.com

Account Name   Separator   Domain name

---

develop your skills | ecs-0703

Compose an Email Message

 Guide Me In this exercise, you will compose and send a new email message.

 Use the Guide Me to work through this exercise. Go to the Student Resource Center (URL on inside front cover) or your eLab course and click the Guide Me link for this exercise. If you are using an eBook, just click the Guide Me icon under the exercise title.

1 To start an email, display **Mail**.

2 Choose **Home→New→New Email**.

A message window appears.

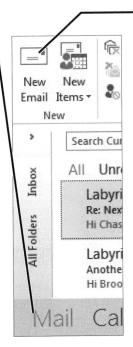

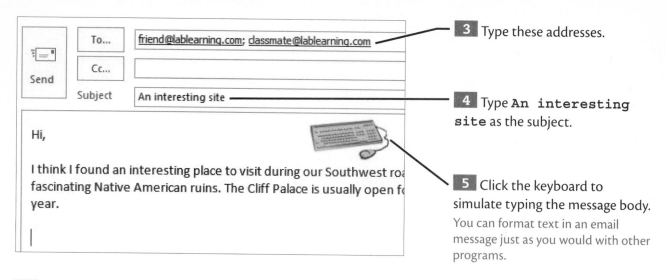

3 Type these addresses.

4 Type `An interesting site` as the subject.

5 Click the keyboard to simulate typing the message body.

You can format text in an email message just as you would with other programs.

6 Format the message text:

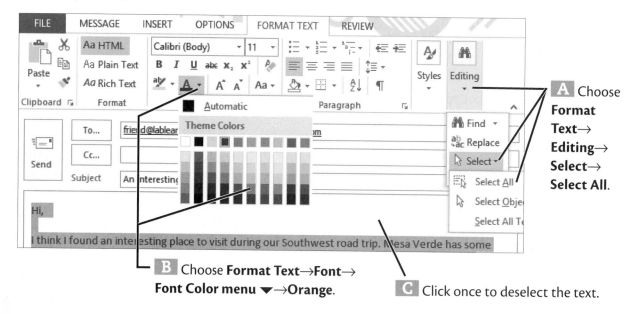

A Choose **Format Text→ Editing→ Select→ Select All**.

B Choose **Format Text→Font→ Font Color menu ▼→Orange**.

C Click once to deselect the text.

7 Save the message.

You will return to the message shortly. Saving your work periodically is a good habit.

Working with Email Attachments

 Video

An *attachment* is a file sent with an email message. Attachments are useful for sending photos, documents, spreadsheets, and other files. An attachment is usually much more convenient and better formatted than retyping material or copying and pasting it into the body of a message.

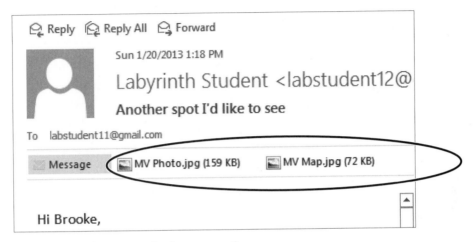

A photo and map attached to an email message.

Sending Attachments

You can attach most types of files to messages. Messages can contain more than one attachment. However, most email services have a maximum attachment file size. So if you attach several full-size digital photos, the message might not go through.

 There are online services that can send files of almost any size, such as http://sharefile.com. These overcome the maximum attachment size limitations of your email service.

a closer look

Avoiding Security Risks

Email attachments and links in messages can be a source of computer viruses. Most antimalware software automatically scans email messages and any attachments for viruses. Outlook warns you if you attach a file that *might* contain a virus. In fact, Outlook refuses to open or access some types of files that might contain viruses. For example, Outlook won't let you open any program file (filenames that end with .exe).

Never open or view an email attachment or click a link from someone you don't know! There is a high risk the attachment file could contain a virus or a link point to an infected website.

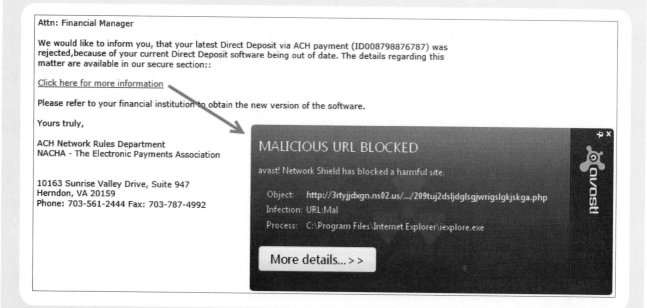

Clicking a message link leads to a malicious website. Fortunately, antimalware software blocked any harmful activity.

Attach a File to a Message

Guide Me   In this exercise, you will attach a photo to an email message.

Use the Guide Me to work through this exercise.

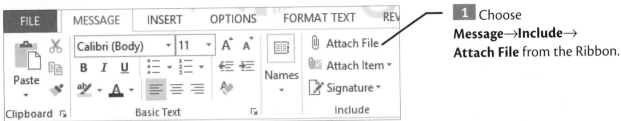

1 Choose **Message→Include→ Attach File** from the Ribbon.

2 Choose **Pictures**.

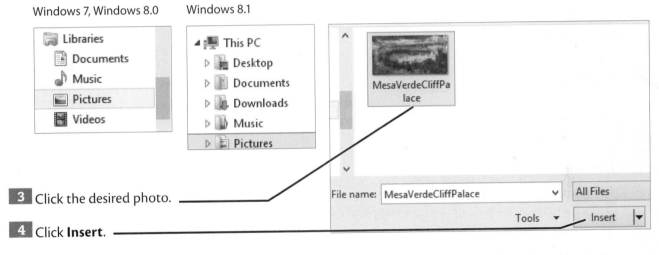

3 Click the desired photo.

4 Click **Insert**.

5 Notice the photo file in the Attached box.

You could attach additional files now, but this one will do.

Subject: An interesting site
Attached: MesaVerdeCliffPalace.jpg (243 KB)

6 Click **Send**.

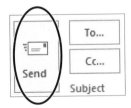

Outlook places the message into the Outbox.

Saving Attachments

 Video

Attachments remain embedded in email messages until you save them. Although you can open an attachment when you view a message, this can be inconvenient. Saving an attachment to a storage drive allows you to work with it normally.

Attachment Security Risks

Opening an attachment can put your computer at risk. It's rare, but any attachment can contain *malware*. Internet Security programs typically scan incoming email and all attachments for malware.

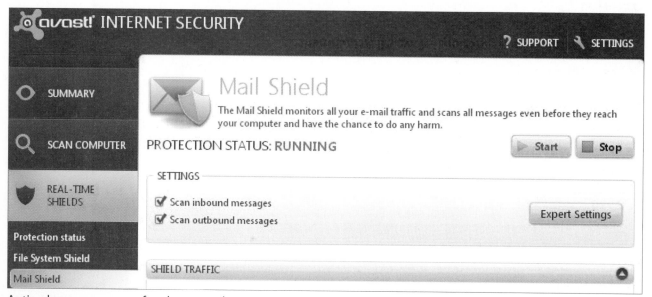

Antimalware programs often have email-scanning capabilities.

Example
You receive a message that appears to be from a friend. It tells you to check out the cool message or program attached. You open the attachment and nothing seems to happen. In reality, the attachment might be invisibly infecting your computer.

 Never open an attachment from someone you don't know. Be careful opening attachments from people you *do* know.

develop your skills | ecs-0705

Save an Attachment

 Guide Me   In this exercise, you will save an attachment to an email message you've received.

Use the Guide Me to work through this exercise.

1 Double-click to open the **Visiting the Blue Mesa** message.

2 Click once to display the **Earthlights** attachment.

The Attachments contextual tab appears.

3 Choose **Attachments→Actions→Save All Attachments**.

A Save All Attachments window lists the attachments to be saved.

4 Click **OK**.

A new window appears displaying the Documents folder, the default location Outlook assumes you'll want to use. However, you can change this destination folder before completing the Save All Attachments command.

5 If necessary, scroll down to **Libraries** or **This PC**, and then choose **Pictures** and click **OK**.

Windows 7, Windows 8.0   Windows 8.1

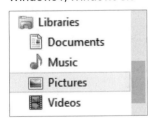   

Outlook copies the attachments into your Pictures folder.

6 Display the **Folder Explorer** and then display the **Pictures Library**.

The files you just saved appear in the folder.

To check your knowledge of the key concepts introduced in this lesson, complete the Concepts Review quiz by choosing the appropriate access option below.

If you are...	Then access the quiz by...
Using eLab	Logging in, choosing Content, and navigating to the Concepts Review quiz for this lesson
Not using eLab	Going to the Student Resource Center (see the inside front cover)

---

reinforce your skills | ecs-0701

Use Outlook 2013 to Send Email

Guide Me   In this exercise, you will compose an email message using Outlook 2013.

Use the Guide Me to work through this exercise.

Use Outlook

1   Start Outlook 2013:

Windows 7

A Click **Start**.

B Choose **All Programs→Microsoft Office 2013→Outlook 2013**.

Windows 8.1

A Display the **Start screen**.

B Click **All Apps**, then scroll to **Office 2013** and click **Outlook 2013**.

2   Click the **More** button on the Navigation panel and choose **Navigation Options**. Make sure **Compact Navigation** is unchecked, click **OK**.

If it didn't before, the Navigation panel now displays words rather than icons.

3   Click **Calendar** in the Navigation panel.

4 Choose **Home→Arrange→Week** from the Ribbon.

5 Click **People** in the Navigation panel to display the contacts view.

There probably won't be any contacts listed in this view. But notice how the Ribbon has changed to commands for working with contacts.

6 Click **Tasks** in the Navigation panel.

There probably won't be any tasks listed in this view. Now the Ribbon features commands for working with tasks.

7 Click **Mail**.

Send an Email Message

8 Choose **Home→New→New E-mail**.

9 Type the following items:

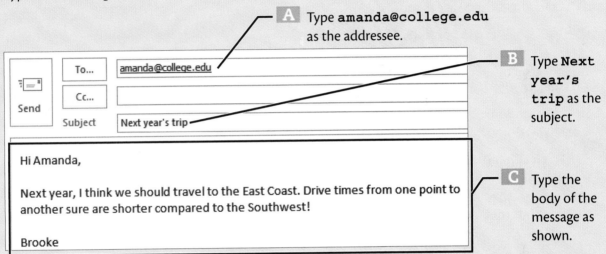

A Type **amanda@college.edu** as the addressee.

B Type **Next year's trip** as the subject.

C Type the body of the message as shown.

10 Click **Send**.

Outlook sends the message.

11 Click **Sent Items** in the left panel, below Outlook Data File.

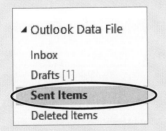

Your just-sent message appears at the top of the list.

Work with Attachments

Guide Me   In this exercise, you will send and receive attachments using Outlook 2013.

Use the Guide Me to work through this exercise.

Send an Attachment

1   Click **Mail** on the Navigation panel.

2   Choose **Home→New→New Email**.

3   Compose the message as shown:

To:	brooke@clarity.pro
CC:	labstudent11@gmail.com
Subject:	The next road trip

Message Body:

Hi,

I think our next road trip should explore an urban landscape.

Sean

4   Start **Internet Explorer** and perform an image search on New York skyline.

5   Click one image found by your search to display it.

6   Use **right-click→Save Picture As** to save the image to your file storage location.

7   Press Alt + Tab on the keyboard to make the email message window active.

8   Choose **Message →Include→Attach File**.

9   Navigate to the picture you saved and attach it to the message.
The attachment file appears below the subject line.

10   Choose **File→Save As** and save the message to your file storage location as RYS 7-2 Next Road Trip.

11   Choose **Send**.

Save an Attachment

12 Choose **Home→Include→Send/Receive All Folders**.

There is a pause as Outlook checks for new messages. A reply to your previous message appears in the Inbox.

13 Click once to display the new reply to your message.

14 Double-click the attachment.

Windows opens the picture in an image-viewer window.

15 Close the photo window:

- **Windows 7: Close** ☒ the photo window.

- **Windows 8.1:** Use Alt + Tab to return to the message window.

16 Right-click the photo attachment, choose **Save As**, and save the attachment to the **Pictures** folder.

17 Open a **File Explorer** window.

18 Click **Pictures** under Libraries.

The photo you just saved is visible.

apply your skills | ecs-0701

Send Email

You've used webmail for years, but your new job requires the use of Outlook 2013. In this exercise, you will send an email message in Outlook.

 You can perform the exercise in any Outlook application, even one that is not set up for email.

Use Outlook 2013

1. Start **Outlook 2013**.

2. Choose to run Outlook without an email account if the **Welcome** window appears.

3. Display the **Calendar** view.

4. Display the Calendar as a **Work Week**.

5. Use the **Snipping Tool** to take a picture of the Calendar view. Save the snip to your file storage location as `ECS07-A01a-Outlook-[FirstInitialLastName]`.

Send an Email Message

6. Compose a new message with these details:

   To: [Your instructor's email address]

   CC: [Your own email address]

   Subject: `AYS 7-1 message`

   Message Body:
   `Hi Personnel Department,`

   `Can you send me an electronic copy of the forms I signed online during this morning's new employee orientation session?`

   `[Your Name]`

7. Use the **Snipping Tool** to take a picture of the message. Save the snip to your file storage location as `ECS07-A01b-Message-[FirstInitialLastName]`.

8. Submit your snipped screens based on the guidelines provided by your instructor.

apply your skills | ecs-0702

Work with Attachments

Your new job requires the sending and receiving of attachments to distribute reports and meeting notes you record for a special project committee. In this exercise, you will send and receive an attachment.

 You can perform the exercise in any Outlook application, even one that is not set up for email.

Send an Attachment

1 Start **Outlook 2013**.

2 Choose to run Outlook without an email account if the **Welcome** window appears.

3 Start a new email message.

To:	[Your instructor's email address]
CC:	[Your own email address]
Subject:	Lesson 7 Message

Message Body:

Hi [Instructor Name],

Thanks. Here are notes I recorded from yesterday's committee meeting.

[Your Name]

4 Attach the **Meeting Notes** document from the **ecs-L07** folder in your file storage location.

5 Use the **Snipping Tool** to take a picture of the message with attachment. Save the snip to your file storage location as `ECS07-A02a-Attachment-[FirstInitialLastName]`.

6 **Close** ☒ the message. Do not save it.

Save an Attachment

Since most computer labs don't have Outlook 2013 set up with an email account, you will open a message exercise file rather than look for it in Outlook's inbox.

7 Minimize ➖ Outlook.

8 Open a **File Explorer** window and then open your **ecs-L07** folder.

9 Double-click to open the **I Vote We Drive Here** message.

10 Save the attached photo to your file storage location as `ECS07-A02b-PhotoSaved-[FirstInitialLastName]`.

11 **Close** ☒ the message.

12 **Close** ☒ the File Explorer window.

13 Submit your snipped screens based on the guidelines provided by your instructor.

apply your skills | ecs-0703

Do It All

You've used webmail for years, but your new job requires the use of Outlook. In this exercise, you will send an email message in Outlook. Since the sending and receiving of attachments is a job requirement as well, you'll also practice those skills.

 You can perform the exercise in any Outlook application, even one that is not set up for email.

Use Outlook

1 Start **Outlook 2013**.

2 Choose to run Outlook without an email account if the **Welcome** window appears.

3 Display the **Calendar** view.

4 Display the Calendar as a **Month**.

5 Use the **Snipping Tool** to take a picture of the Calendar view. Save the snip to your file storage location as `ECS07-A03a-Outlook-[FirstInitialLastName]`.

Send an Email Message

6 Compose a new message with these details:

To:	[Your instructor's email address]
CC:	[Your own email address]
Subject:	`Lesson 7 Assessment`

Message Body:
`Hi [Instructor Name],`

`Here's a message with an attachment.`

`[Your Name]`

7 Use the **Snipping Tool** to take a picture of the message. Save the snip to your file storage location as `ECS07-A03b-Message-[FirstInitialLastName]`.

Send an Attachment

8 Attach the **Meeting Notes** document from the **ecs-L07** folder in your file storage location.

9 Use the **Snipping Tool** to take a picture of the message with attachment. Save the snip to your file storage location as `ECS07-A03c-Attachment-[FirstInitialLastName]`.

10 **Close** ⊠ the message. Do not save it.

Save an Attachment

11 Open the **Map to Mesa Verde** message from the **ecs-L07** folder.

12 Save the **Mesa Verde Route** attachment to your file storage location.

13 Use the **Snipping Tool** to take a picture of your file storage location. Save the snip to your file storage location as `ECS07-A03d-MapSaved-[FirstInitialLastName]`.

14 Submit your snipped screens based on the guidelines provided by your instructor.

learning projects | ecs-0701

Share a Travel Destination

In this exercise, you will search for images, save them, and then send an email message with the images attached.

You do not need Outlook 2013 to complete this exercise. You can use your student email account via webmail if desired.

- Use your favorite search engine to find images of a travel destination anywhere in the world you'd like to visit, a local attraction you'd want to recommend to a visitor, or some other place or event of personal interest.
- Save three to five images you've found to your file storage location. Particularly for web-based images, their size doesn't really matter.
- Send an email message to a friend about the place or event you found photos for. Attach at least three of the photos to the message.

Submit the message with attachments according to the guidelines provided by your instructor.

learning projects | ecs-0702

Get Set Up for a New Project

In this exercise, you will receive attachments for a project from a coworker. You'll create a new project folder for the attachments, then save them to it.

- Open the **LP-7-2** email message in the **ecs-L07** folder. (There is no need to start Outlook first.) Choose to run Outlook without an email account if a Welcome prompt appears. Read the message and notice the files attached to it.
- In your file storage location (optional: or in your cloud storage), create new folders for the project mentioned in the message. The folders should make it easy to store files related to the project budget and promotion.
- Save the message attachments and store them in folders where they make the most sense. (If you are using cloud storage, share the project folder with your instructor.)

You can save all the attachments to one folder, then move them to the new folders. Or, you might save the attachments one at a time to the new folders.

- Take screen snips showing the contents of each new project folder you've set up.

Submit your snipped screens according to the guidelines provided by your instructor.

Quick Reference Guide

This appendix includes a Quick Reference Guide, steps for performing key tasks you have read about and/or practiced in this book. Tasks are organized by subject matter. And, page references are included so you can easily refer to a lesson's discussion as necessary.

File Management

Browsing the Web

Deleting and Restoring Files (see ecs03.22–26 and ecs04.21–24)

Delete a file or folder

- Select the desired file(s) and/or folder(s) and tap Delete. Or, right-click any file or folder and choose Delete.

Restore an item from the Recycle Bin

- Double-click the Recycle Bin on the Desktop.
- Select the file(s) and/or folder(s) to restore.
- Click Restore the Selected Items from the left panel of the Recycle Bin folder window.

Empty the Recycle Bin

- Right-click the Recycle Bin icon and choose Empty Recycle Bin from the context menu. (Remember, this "permanently" deletes the contents of the Recycle Bin.)

Selecting Multiple Files for Commands (see ecs03.16–19 and ecs04.15–18)

Select adjacent files

- Click the first file you wish to select.
- Press and hold Shift while clicking the last file in the desired group; release Shift.

Select nonadjacent files

- Click the first file you wish to select.
- Press and hold Ctrl while clicking any other desired files; release Ctrl.

Deselect a selected file

- Press and hold Ctrl while clicking the file to deselect.

Moving and Copying Files with Cut, Copy, and Paste (see ecs03.16–19 and ecs04.15–18)

Copy files with Copy and Paste

- Select the files to be copied.
- Choose Organize→Copy (Windows 7) or Edit→Copy (Windows 8.0/8.1).
- Navigate to where the files are to be copied.
- Choose Organize→Paste (Windows 7) or Edit→Paste (Windows 8.0/8.1).

Move files with Cut and Paste

- Select the files to be moved.
- Choose Organize→Cut (Windows 7) or Edit→Cut (Windows 8.0/8.1).
- Navigate to where the files are to be moved.
- Choose Organize→Paste (Windows 7) or Edit→Paste (Windows 8.0/8.1).

Renaming Files and Folders (see ecs03.19–21 and ecs04.18–20)

Rename with a right-click

- Right-click the file or folder icon and choose Rename.
- Type the new name and tap Enter.

Rename with click-pause

- Click once on the filename under the icon.
- Pause about one second, then click the filename again.
- Type the new name and tap Enter.

Rename from within a program

- Choose File→Save As.
- Give the file a new name and click Save.

Converting the File Format (see ecs06.25–26)

Convert a file to a different file format

- Open the desired file and choose File→Save As.
- Click Save as Type and choose a new file format.
- (Optional) Change the filename.
- Click Save.

Folders

Searching for Files (see ecs03.10–12 and ecs04.9–11)

Search for a file

- Display the File Explorer window and type the search word(s) in the Search box.

Creating Favorites (see ecs03.8–9)

Create a favorite

- Display the folder/file to add to Favorites.
- Drag the item to the desired location in the Favorites list.

Remove a favorite

- Right-click the item in the Favorites list and choose Remove.

Creating Folders (see ecs03.13–15 and ecs04.11–14)

Create a folder

- Open a Computer or Folder window.
- Display the location in which to create the new folder.
- Click New Folder (Windows 7) or choose Home→New→New Folder (Windows 8.0/8.1).
- Type a name for the new folder and Enter.

Flash Drives

Backing Up Flash Drive Files (see ecs03.27–29 and ecs04.25–28)

Back up files from a flash drive to the hard drive

- Insert your flash drive into a USB port, open a Computer window, and open your flash drive.
- Press Ctrl+A to select all files and folders.
- Press Ctrl+C to copy the selection.
- Display the desired folder to hold your backed-up files.
- Press Ctrl+V to paste the copied selection. (If you've previously made a backup, Windows asks if you wish to overwrite the previous backup.)
- Confirm replacement of existing files:
  - **Windows 7:** Place a checkmark in the Do This for All Current Items checkbox and choose Yes. Or, place a checkmark in the Do This for The Next... checkbox and choose Copy and Replace.
  - **Windows 8.0/8.1:** Choose Yes to All.

Removing Hardware Safely
(see ecs03.30 and ecs04.28–29)

Safely remove a device

- Click Show Hidden Icons in the Notification area.
- Click the Safely Remove Hardware icon.
- Choose the device to eject.
- Look for the Safe to Remove Hardware prompt.

Program Windows

Switching Programs (see ecs02.22–24)

Switch programs using the keyboard

- Press Alt+Tab.
- Tap Tab until the desired program is chosen.
- Release Alt.

Use Aero Flip 3D (Windows 7) / Switch Desktops (Windows 8.0/8.1)

Using Aero Window Commands (see ecs02.25–26)

Use Aero Snap

- *Fill half the screen:* Drag the window's title bar until the mouse pointer touches the right or left side of the screen.
- *Snap vertically:* Drag the bottom of a program window until it reaches the top of the taskbar to snap the rest of the window to the top of the screen.
- *Maximize a window:* Drag the window's title bar to the top of the screen.
- *Restore a window:* Drag the title bar of a maximized window away from the top of the screen.

Use Aero Peek

- *Make all windows transparent:* Point at (don't click) the Show Desktop button.

Use Aero Shake

- *Minimize all but one window:* Point at the title bar of the program to keep on the screen, then hold down the mouse button while moving the mouse back and forth.

Use Aero Flip 3D (Windows 7)

- *Switch windows:* Hold down the Windows key and tap Tab. Release Tab when the desired window shows.

Running Programs

Pinning and Searching for Programs (see ecs02.12–15)

Pin a program button to the taskbar

- Right-click the desired application button on the taskbar and choose Pin This Program to Taskbar.

Pin a program button to the Start menu or screen

- Right-click the program in the Start menu or screen and choose Pin to Start Menu (Windows 7) or Pin to Start (Windows 8.0/8.1).

Search for a program

- **Windows 7:** Click Start and then type a program name in the Search box.
- **Windows 8.0/8.1:** Choose the Search charm and click Apps. Then, type a program name in the Search box.

Switching Programs (see ecs02.22–24)

Switch programs using the keyboard

- Press ⎡Alt⎤+⎡Tab⎤.
- Tap ⎡Tab⎤ until the desired program is chosen.
- Release ⎡Alt⎤.

Use Aero Flip 3D (Windows 7) / Switch Desktops (Windows 8.0/8.1)

Computer

Checking Computer Specs (see ecs01.22–25)

Check the system properties

- **Windows 7:** Click Start. Then, right-click Computer and choose Properties.
- **Windows 8.0/8.1:** Display the Start screen. Point at the bottom-left corner until the Windows Start icon appears, then right-click and choose System.

Display the screen resolution

- **Windows 7:** Right-click a clear area of the Desktop and choose Screen Resolution.
- **Windows 8.0/8.1:** Display the Desktop, then right-click a clear area of it and choose Screen Resolution.

Sleep, Lock, Switch User (see ecs02.27–30)

Switch modes

- **Windows 7:** Choose Start→Shut Down ▶ menu button and choose the desired mode.
- **Windows 8.0/8.1:** Display the charms, choose Power, and choose the desired mode. Or, display the Start screen, click your account name, and choose the desired mode.

Browsing the Web

Using Tabbed Browsing Features (see ecs05.11–13)

Create a new tab

- Click the New Tab button on the tab bar. Or, right-click a link and choose Open Link in New Tab. Or, press ⎡Ctrl⎤+⎡T⎤.

Navigate tabs

- Click the desired tab with the mouse. Or, press ⎡Ctrl⎤+⎡Tab⎤ to move forward and ⎡Ctrl⎤+⎡Shift⎤+⎡Tab⎤ to move backward.

Close tabs

- Click the Close button on the tab. Or, press ⎡Ctrl⎤+⎡W⎤.

Close all but one tab

- Right-click the tab to be kept open and choose Close Other Tabs.

Searching the Web (see ecs05.6–8)

Perform an instant search

- Type the desired keyword(s) in the address bar and tap ⎡Enter⎤.

Working with Search Providers (see ecs05.8–11)

Change the default search provider

- Click the Tools button and choose Manage Add Ons.
- Choose Search Providers in the left panel.
- Right-click the desired search provider and choose Set as Default.
- Click Close.

Add a new search provider

- Click the address bar search menu button and choose Add.

Email

Composing Email Messages (see ecs07.10–12)

Create a new message

- Choose Email in the Navigation pane.
- Choose Home→New→New Email.

Send a message to multiple addresses

- Place a semicolon between each email address.

Sending and Receiving Attachments (see ecs07.13–17)

Send an attachment file

- Create the new email message.
- Choose Message→Include→Attach File.
- Navigate to the attachment file, select it, and click Insert.

Save an attachment file

- Click once on the attachment in the message.
- Choose Attachments→Actions→Save As.

Save all attachment files

Glossary

Aero interface The 3D look of some versions of Windows

antivirus program Software designed to stop computer viruses from infecting files on the computer

application program Software designed to help you get work done

attachment A file embedded in and sent with an email message

back up To create a copy of files in a second location, such as an external storage drive or the cloud

Blog An online journal; short for *web log*

cable modem Device designed to send and receive digital data over a television cable system

Charms In Windows, a set of basic commands that appears when you point at the upper-right corner of the screen

Click A tap and release of the mouse button; used to select objects and commands

cloud Services and storage with an unknown physical location

Cloud storage Files stored in the cloud rather than on a local physical drive

Desktop Place where one or more traditional computer applications run simultaneously; Windows also runs limited applications (apps) on its tablet Desktop

domain name The base electronic address of a location on the Internet

Double-click To click twice in quick succession; usually used as a shortcut to a commonly used command, such as Open

downloading Act of transferring a file from a remote computer or storage service to your local computer or tablet

Drag Mouse motion with the mouse button held down as you move an object with the mouse

drive letter Alphabetical designation assigned to storage devices

Electronic mail (email) Email messages travel around the world in seconds via the Internet

email client Application that helps you send, receive, and store email; runs on your local computer or tablet

ergonomics Science of creating work environments and furnishings well-tuned to the shape and function of the human body

Favorites Bookmarks that make it easy to return to a specific web page

Files Group of computer data with a common purpose

file conversion Saving a file in a different format

file sharing To give access to a file in the cloud or network storage to other users

folder Electronic location in which you store groups of related files

folder sharing To give access to an entire folder in the cloud or network storage to other users; usually requires that the other users subscribe to the same cloud storage service

gigabytes Used to measure file size; approximately one billion bytes of data (about 3,000 books)

gigahertz (GHz) One billion pulses of electricity in an electrical circuit in a single second; the speed of most processors sold today is measured in gigahertz

Hardware Physical components of a computer system

insertion point Blinking indicator where text will appear on the screen when typing; also called the *cursor*

Internet The world's largest computer network, used by billions of individuals daily

Libraries Part of the Windows file storage hierarchy; can contain folders and files from more than one storage drive

malware Generic term for malicious software viruses that can damage a computer system

modem Device that lets a computer communicate digital data to other computers over a non-digital communication line, such as a telephone line

monitor The computer screen on a desktop computer

mouse pointer Indicator that moves on the screen in response to the mouse

MP3 (Moving Picture Experts Group Layer-3 Audio) First popular format for highly compressed music files

multitasking Running more than one program simultaneously so you can switch between them quickly; can only be performed on the normal (not tablet) Desktop

Online conferencing Service that allows multiple persons to meet online to share screens, files, webcam images, and voice communications

operating system Software that manages your system, such as Windows

pin To add a program icon to the taskbar or Start screen for easy access to an application

pixels Single dots of light on a computer or tablet screen

Point Positioning the mouse pointer on an object without clicking

port Place (usually at the back of the computer) to plug in a cable

Processor Single silicon chip containing the complete circuitry of a computer; modern processors can contain two (duo), four (quad), or more processors on a single chip

RAM (Random Access Memory) Computer chip designed to temporarily store data to be processed

resolution Measure of the sharpness of a computer screen or a printout

Ribbon Interface for some Microsoft Office applications; replaces the traditional menu bar and toolbars with one large toolbar

Right-click Click motion using the right (not left) mouse button; usually used to display a pop-up menu of commands

scanner Device built into all-in-one printers that turns photographs and other images into computer files

Sleep Low-power mode from which the computer or tablet wakes when you click or tap

Snap Aero feature that enables a window to be resized by dragging it to the side or top of the Desktop

Software Logical component of a computer system; composed of digital code stored as files; helps you get work done

synchronization (sync) Automatic updating of files on a device with the latest versions of the same files on other devices

Tabbed browsing Capability to open multiple web pages within a browser window in Internet Explorer and many other web browsers

Tablet Desktop In Windows, the place where limited tablet apps run

taskbar Bar at the bottom of the Windows desktop displaying a Start button (Windows 7 only) and icons for pinned and running applications

terabytes Used to measure file size; approximately one trillion bytes of data (about 120 hours of HD video)

Threaded discussion Sequence of posts and replies as part of an online communication among multiple participants

uploading The act of transmitting a local file to a remote computer or storage service

URL (Uniform Resource Locator) Electronic address of a website

USB (Universal Serial Bus) flash drive Small file storage device that plugs into a computer's USB port

USB (Universal Serial Bus) port Used to connect devices such as cameras, MP3 players, and external hard drives

viruses Programs that invisibly infects files and disrupts operation of a computer in some way; spread largely via the Internet

watched folder Folder that automatically synchronizes its content with a cloud storage service

web (Word Wide Web) Collection of billions of pages accessible via the Internet

Web 2.0 New generation of web creations that focus on interactivity and social networking

web access Ability to view and work with files stored on the cloud via a web browser rather than the service's application program or phone/tablet app

web browser Application optimized for viewing web pages

website Collection of web pages owned by a specific organization or individual

Index